Healthcare and Human Dignity

Critical Issues in Health and Medicine

Edited by Rima D. Apple, University of Wisconsin–Madison, and
Janet Golden, Rutgers University–Camden

Growing criticism of the U.S. healthcare system is coming from consumers, politicians, the media, activists, and healthcare professionals. Critical Issues in Health and Medicine is a collection of books that explores these contemporary dilemmas from a variety of perspectives, among them political, legal, historical, sociological, and comparative, and with attention to crucial dimensions such as race, gender, ethnicity, sexuality, and culture.

For a list of titles in the series, see the last page of the book.

Healthcare and Human Dignity

Law Matters

Frank M. McClellan

Rutgers University Press

New Brunswick, Camden, and Newark, New Jersey, and London

Library of Congress Cataloging-in-Publication Data

Names: McClellan, Frank M., author.
Title: Healthcare and human dignity: law matters / Frank McClellan.
Description: New Brunswick, New Jersey: Rutgers University Press, [2019] |
    Includes bibliographical references and index.
Identifiers: LCCN 2019012448 | ISBN 9781978802957 (pbk.) | ISBN 9781978802964 |
    ISBN 9781978802971 | ISBN 9781978802988
Subjects: | MESH: Healthcare Disparities—legislation & jurisprudence | Health Services
    Accessibility—legislation & jurisprudence | Respect | Socioeconomic Factors | United
    States
Classification: LCC RA563.M56 | NLM W 33 AA1 | DDC 362.1089—dc23
LC record available at https://lccn.loc.gov/2019012448

A British Cataloging-in-Publication record for this book is available from the British Library.

♻ The paper used in this publication meets the requirements of the American National
Standard for Information Sciences—Permanence of Paper for Printed Library Materials,
ANSI Z39.48-1992.

www.rutgersuniversitypress.org

Manufactured in the United States of America

In memory of my parents, Gradie and Lucinda McClellan.

Contents

Healthcare and Human Dignity

Part 1

Fighting for Access to Care

Human Dignity as a Lived Experience

We take human dignity for granted until it is snatched away. "Imagine feeling like you have no power and no voice."[1] These words were spoken by Aly Raisman, a two-time Olympic gold medal winner, in her testimony at the sentencing hearing of Lawrence G. Nassar, a doctor specializing in gynecology who had been abusing his young patients for years. He had been entrusted to provide medical care to the girls, many of whom were training for sports as college and Olympic athletes. The doctor was convicted in federal court on charges of child pornography and faced criminal charges in state court for multiple counts of sexual assault on minors. He was sentenced to sixty years in prison on the federal charge. At his state sentencing hearing, 140 women and girls filed victim impact statements, and many of the patients testified to the specific acts of abuse and how they had been emotionally traumatized. The Michigan state trial judge sentenced Nassar to 40 to 175 years in prison.[2]

Ms. Raisman's description captures the feeling of agony and helplessness of a person who suffered a violation of her human dignity by a person with superior power: the women and girls testified that, under the guise of conducting pelvic exams, Nassar would tell them to lie on a table while he probed their vaginas.[3] The violations of their bodies did not cause serious physical harm. However, the testimony of the victims clearly established that they had sustained severe emotional harm. Some contemplated suicide.[4] Their human dignity had been violated, and they felt powerless to seek redress. Ms. Raisman testified further about the restorative feeling of regaining her dignity now that she could publicly confront the person who assaulted her.[5]

In addition to the criminal penalties imposed on Dr. Nassar, Michigan State University settled a civil lawsuit against the university based on allegations that the university either deliberately ignored the conduct of Dr. Nassar or failed to exercise reasonable care to protect the women and girls from the harm he inflicted on them. The university agreed to a settlement of $500 million to be paid to 331 women and girls who joined the lawsuit alleging that Dr. Nassar sexually molested them.[6]

Assaults on human dignity usually reflect an abuse or misuse of power that attacks a person's sense of worth. The assault goes beyond a mere insult and demonstrates a total disrespect of the person. Insults from a person on an equal level can be rebuffed, but if the words or actions come from someone with power over the person being insulted, there is a good chance that the latter's sense of worth will be undermined. It is remarkable how often victims' stories of feeling indignant involve a use of power that is driven by animus against a person's race, gender, religion, or sexual orientation.

Healthcare offers an environment that is ripe for violations of human dignity. There is a vast imbalance of power between the healthcare professional and a patient. The superior knowledge and skill possessed by healthcare professionals and their control over access to diagnosis and treatment compel patients to trust them. In addition, the personal nature of medical care necessitates an intimacy in the interactions that shields the perpetrator's conduct and decision making from criticism. Most medical treatment occurs in private, where the only witnesses to the interaction are the patient and her doctor and/or nurse and other allied healthcare professionals. After the care is rendered, the healthcare provider will enter a written or electronic record of what was done, but this record is kept confidential to protect the privacy of the patient in accordance with federal and state laws, as well as the fiduciary duties of healthcare providers. The private nature of the doctor-patient interaction combines with the imbalance of power to shield misconduct by healthcare professionals for long periods of time. In 2018 the University of Southern California (USC) acknowledged a deplorable example of long-standing abuse when it paid $215 million to settle claims of female students that they were sexually abused by a gynecologist employed by the university.[7] The gynecologist involved, Dr. George Tyndall, practiced at USC for nearly thirty years until he was suspended in 2016 after a complaint by a healthcare worker who alleged that Dr. Tyndall made sexually inappropriate comments to patients. The settlement funds were made available to thousands of women Dr. Tyndall treated during his thirty-year tenure at USC, regardless of whether the patients made allegations of abuse against Dr. Tyndall. Doctors and nurses are members of caring professions who take oaths to put the best interests of their patients before their own interests in earning money and gaining prestige. Nevertheless, the healthcare system sometimes fails to provide a shield against inhumane conduct. The history of healthcare in America offers disturbing examples of patients not being treated with the dignity they deserve as human beings.[8] Examples include racial, gender, sexual orientation, class, and other group-based discrimination. I think all of these examples represent an invasion of human dignity, and we gain new insight as to the common motivations and resulting injuries when we view this conduct and evaluate it in the light of human dignity as a predominant value that should govern relationships among all human beings.

The Tuskegee Syphilis Study ranks as one of the cruelest examples in medicine of the abuse of human beings. The goal of the study, conducted by the U.S. Public Health Service, was to assess the impact of untreated syphilis on the human body. The methodology required the researchers to systematically ensure that the 399 men enrolled in the study never got treatment for the disease.[9] The researchers ensured that the participants did not receive treatment, deceived them into believing that they were being treated for "bad blood," allowed them to unwittingly spread the disease to their sexual partners, precluded them from enrolling in the armed forces, where they would be examined and treated, and blocked them from getting treatment from anywhere else—even after penicillin was proved to be effective and was adopted as a standard of care in the country.

The cruelty and disrespect for an entire community continued even after the barbaric conduct of the Nazis was exposed and condemned during the Nuremberg trials and the subsequent adoption of international declarations of rights to human dignity. The researchers employed by the U.S. Health Service failed to grasp any connection between what they were doing to the African American men in the Tuskegee Syphilis Study and what the Nazis were doing when they subjected Jews held in concentration camps to cruel medical experiments. Among the most cruel and notorious medical studies conducted by the Nazis were "fatal experiments on low pressure, exposure to freezing temperatures, and infectious diseases when research could be taken to the point of death." Moreover, "racial priorities came increasingly to the fore, as exemplified by Schumann's X-ray sterilization experiments on Jews in Auschwitz."[10] The results of the studies revealed that the Nazis had completely obliterated any sense of common humanity:

> Nearly a quarter of confirmed victims were either killed to obtain their
> organs for research, or died as a result of experiments taking the research

subject to the point of death (notoriously, the experiments on freezing and low pressure at Dachau). The euthanasia killings and executions were sources of bodies for research, and the extent that this happened and research conducted before and after the end of the war is still being documented. Of the fully documented victims 781 died before the end of the war as a result of the experiments: research subjects were weakened by the strain of the experiment such as a deliberate infection or severe cold, or they were deliberately killed because it was feared that they would testify against the perpetrators.[11]

Nevertheless, Dr. John R. Heller, who served as a chief medical officer for the Tuskegee Syphilis Study, offered a vigorous defense of the morality of the experiment and expressed anger and frustration that anyone could not see the difference between the Nazi experiments and the Tuskegee Syphilis Study. He responded emphatically that the difference was that there was "no similarity at all between them."[12]

Egregious violations of dignity are often fueled by a conscious or unconscious bias against a specific group of people. Yet, to recognize the deprivation of human dignity when it occurs, one has to first recognize another person as a human being. Dr. Heller's failure to see a similarity between the Nazi experiments and the Tuskegee Syphilis Study he was overseeing reflects an ability to blot out a vision of common humanity. At the same time as Dr. Heller defended the morality of the Tuskegee Syphilis Study, he saw clearly the horrendous nature of the experiments done by Nazi scientists: "I, like most everybody else, was horrified at the things that were practiced upon the Jewish people, such as doing experiments while the patients were not only alive but doing such things as would cause their deaths."[13]

The inhumane treatment of people with HIV or AIDS when the HIV virus was first discovered should sensitize us to how easily healthcare can be distorted to reflect social biases. Unfortunately, the public has an extremely short memory about violations of human dignity and needs to be constantly reminded. I have taught healthcare law for forty years. Each year, I ask the students in my class how many have heard of the Tuskegee Syphilis Study, and each year fewer than 20 percent of them indicate that they have any familiarity with the study. I believe that if we take the time to reflect on these events, looking at historical and current-day cases, we will recognize the need to remain vigilant in identifying and deterring violations of human dignity in medical research and practice.

We should not wait until violations of human dignity occur on a mass basis before we become concerned. There are times when injuries are caused by interactions with the healthcare system that result from conscious abuse or misuse of power or reckless disregard of the interests of others. In those cases, the results are intended, or the risks of their occurrence are consciously disregarded, because the person in power is primarily seeking to achieve a goal that he regards as more important than the potential harm to the victim. It is this type of case that is the subject of this book.

A better understanding of the importance of human dignity in healthcare can help patients, providers, third-party payers, and policy makers develop more effective strategies to protect against abuses and misuses of power. The strategies I advocate flow from the importance of people in power acting with humility. Healthcare professionals, like all other members of the human community who are entrusted with making life-and-death decisions, should consciously acknowledge the importance of respecting the values of vulnerable people who must live with the consequences of the decisions made about their health in terms of both practices and policies. To make respect for others meaningful requires that the person in power pause before acting on any important decision and try to see the world through the eyes of the person who has the most at stake in the encounter. The purpose of the pause is to listen and empathize. In that way the human dignity of another person is respected and affirmed through a shared decision-making process in which the patient holds the trump card.

The meaning and complexity of human dignity in healthcare from a legal perspective will be discussed in detail in chapter 2 and throughout this book. A definition of the essential assets of human dignity from a historical and philosophical perspective as set forth by George Kateb in *Human Dignity* offers a useful compass: "The core idea of human dignity is that on earth, humanity is the greatest type of beings [*sic*] . . . and that every member deserves to be treated in a manner consonant with the high worth of the species."[14]

In the past two decades, a multitude of studies have unveiled persistent inequalities in health and healthcare in America based on race, gender, and ethnicity. In this book, I dive under the statistics and present some stories that show the impact of disparate care on the human dignity of individuals who trusted the healthcare system. My goal in the selection and telling of these stories is not to produce anger or despair, but rather to make apparent some of the forces that must be addressed if we are to maximize protection of vulnerable populations who depend on the healthcare system. The problems of conscious bias, unconscious bias, income inequality, and institutional biases must all be addressed. Recognizing human dignity as a value that warrants the highest consideration and protection can provide critical assistance in making policy decisions.

The stories that introduce each chapter relate the experience of an individual or a family who sought care from a healthcare provider or insurer and encountered a response that assaulted their human dignity. Biases based on gender, sexual orientation, race, and class flow through many of the stories. Each story reflects a true event, although I have not identified the source of the story in every case, primarily to protect the privacy of the individuals involved. Many of the stories are based on published cases that are available to the public, and for those stories I have provided citations. However, some of the events involved cases where I served as counsel to one of the parties; where these cases have settled pursuant to confidentiality agreements, I have changed the names of the parties. While these types of cases represent a small percentage of experiences in the American healthcare system, the mounting books, studies, and literature documenting health disparities among various groups in America suggest that these cases require attention. It is one thing for a person to suffer a physical or emotional injury because of a medical error; it is quite another to suffer a personal injury because of policy, practice, or individual bias that treats a person as though one's life does not matter, or that, because of some group-based prejudice, one does not matter as much as members of another group. The better we understand the forces in operation in these situations, the more likely it is we can identify effective strategies to address the individual and structural forces that contribute to assaults on human dignity in healthcare.

In this book, I argue that law has a critical role to play in protecting the human dignity of individuals who seek healthcare, and that to perform their roles effectively, lawmakers and policy makers must be willing to face bigotry and biases directly. They must also acknowledge and seek remedies when evidence shows that practices and policies produce a disparate impact on identifiable groups of people. The negative impact on human dignity occurs whether the unequal treatment flows from conscious or unconscious bias. Disparate impact reflects serious harm, regardless of whether the policy or practice is implemented consciously or unconsciously to produce the impact. Law cannot by itself solve the problems. However, many of the problems cannot be solved without enacting and enforcing laws tailored to encourage and govern conduct that is respectful of other members of the community.

The law in the United States has not settled on a single definition of dignity. However, important constitutional provisions, statutes, and court decisions rest on the importance that our society places on affording human dignity to each member of the community. I will argue that the goal of promoting and protecting human dignity serves as the predominant rationale for federal statutes that have been passed by Congress since the 1960s aimed at protecting people who find themselves in vulnerable situations. Legislation and court decisions prohibiting discrimination based on race, gender, sexual orientation, and disability, to name a few, rest on a foundation of people's individual right to human dignity. With the exception of those who suffer an instantaneous death, everyone will need healthcare at some point in his life and will have to depend on professionals who provide medical care. Some will feel more vulnerable than others, but all will expect and should demand treatment with dignity. I have selected stories for this book that illustrate the importance of protecting human dignity in healthcare and the role that the law can play in encouraging practices and policy that treat human dignity as a predominant value.

Chapter 1

Healthcare and Law

Appreciating the Need to Protect Human Dignity

Demanding Respect

George Hicks and Allen Carter lived as a couple for fifteen years. They were not legally married because the state did not recognize same-sex marriages; however, all of their friends and neighbors viewed them as a couple and respected their vows to spend their lives together as a couple. One day George, who was HIV positive, became very ill and was transported to the hospital suffering from shortness of breath. He was diagnosed with AIDS. When Allen visited George in the hospital, George's hospital roommate heard them discussing the fact that George had AIDS and was expected to survive only for a few more days. After Allen left the room, George's roommate called the nurse on duty and demanded that either he or George be moved to another room. In response to this demand, the hospital agreed to move George to a private room, notwithstanding George's irate objections to being moved. Allen returned to see George the next day but was told that because George was terminally ill, hospital policy limited visitors to blood relatives and spouses. Allen protested and threatened to sue the hospital if he was not allowed to see George that moment. The nurses responded by calling the security guards, who escorted Allen out of the hospital. Allen spent the rest of the day frantically calling lawyers, hoping to find someone to represent him and get a court order allowing visitation. Allen was not able to secure legal assistance that day, and George died that night.

I served for a decade on the board of directors of Philadelphia Fight, a nonprofit organization dedicated to improving both access to care and quality of care available to people who contracted HIV. For more than two decades I also served on the board of directors of the AIDS Law Project of Pennsylvania, one of the few organizations devoted to representing people with HIV and AIDS and their loved ones. The story that opens this chapter highlights the dignity and legal issues that were presented to both organizations repeatedly, continuing to the present day. I have not used the real names of the clients and patients to protect their privacy. However, the same story, with minor factual variations, has unfolded many times in the past two decades in the context of healthcare, housing, employment, education, and recreation.

Most of the debate about healthcare in recent years has centered on the economic challenges of establishing a financially sustainable system. Healthcare costs continue to rise so fast that experts agree that we must employ payment and cost containment strategies for healthcare delivery that will support a sustainable system.[1] However, for a system to be sustainable, it must also be equitable and humane. An economically sustainable system that provides excellent care and access to the wealthy and the upper middle class but denies care to a large portion of the population based on race, gender, sexual orientation, and low income is not politically or socially sustainable. I argue that respect for individual human dignity should be a critical criterion for a healthcare system relied on by a developed country such as the United States.

Every day millions of people who reside in the United States confront challenges to their dignity when they need healthcare. Gaining access to a doctor, hospital, or pharmacy requires an individual to place both her health and her dignity on the line. From the first contact with the receptionist, where proof of ability to pay serves as the critical qualifying factor for access, to decisions about what tests or treatments are warranted, the patient and her family are made conscious of external assessments of her worth. The assessment of the value of a patient's worth is even more pronounced if things go wrong in the delivery of the medical care. Dignity is on the line for all patients, but members of the populations in America who have historically faced race, class, and other group-based discrimination in gaining access to quality healthcare on an equal basis have learned to be particularly sensitive to signs of disrespect from healthcare providers.

African Americans have long appreciated the emotional and physical harm caused by a denial of equitable access to healthcare. In the twentieth century it took a fifty-year political struggle to end racial discrimination in access to hospitals. In 1965 the United States Congress passed the Medicare statute that provided healthcare financing for seniors and prohibited racial discrimination on the part of hospitals that received federal funding. The Medicare statute was followed by the enactment of Title VI of the Civil Rights Act of 1966, which pro-hibited racial discrimination on a broader basis by any institution receiving federal funding.[2]

The AIDS epidemic ushered in a new group of people who were subjected to discrimination by healthcare providers and many others in the communities in which they worked and lived. Members of the community who contracted HIV were treated as outsiders who were not entitled to equal rights and privi-leges accorded other members of the community. In the 1980s, the first patients diagnosed with HIV/AIDS confronted healthcare decision making that directly assaulted their self-worth.[3] Because the first discovered victims were gay, the disease was viewed as a gay disease, and the victims were often treated as not worthy of medical care. During those early years, many communities disparaged and ostracized same-sex couples. Policy makers acted as though HIV/AIDS did not warrant a significant allocation of healthcare resources to find an effective treatment.[4] Providers were frightened. Institutional policies were slanted accord-ing to social judgments about the worth of the patients. Some commentators argued openly that patients had brought their suffering on themselves and did not deserve equal healthcare treatment.[5] Harvey Milk, widely recognized as the first openly gay politician, ignited a movement to respect and appreciate the character and talents of gay members of the community, challenging the preva-lent view in many communities that being gay was something to conceal and be ashamed of. Tragically, Mr. Milk was assassinated in 1978, cutting short the contributions he would have been able to make to the movement to humanize Americans particularly as to sexual identity and preference.[6] In a moving and illuminating book published in 2016 titled *How to Survive a Plague: The Inside Story of How Citizens and Science Tamed AIDS*, David France offers this sober-ing account of the responses in the United States to initial reports of HIV: "Nobody left those years uncorrupted by what they'd witnessed, not only the mass deaths—100,000 lost in New Your City alone, snatched from tightly drawn social circles—but also the foul truths that a microscopic virus had revealed about American culture: politicians who welcomed the plague as proof of God's will, doctors who refused the victims medical care, clergymen and often even parents themselves who withheld all but a shiver of grief. Such betrayal would be impossible to forget in subsequent years."[7]

America's response to the AIDS epidemic offers disturbing proof that many members of the community remain insensitive to the suffering of other people until they see a person they can identify with as a human being. The ability to empathize is linked to seeing someone who is like the beholder or is a person the beholder already admires. Often the person who evokes the empathy is a celebrity or a public figure. With AIDS, a succession of public figures who acknowledged that they were HIV positive changed the public perception of the disease and the need to enact laws and public policies to help the victims: Rock Hudson, Arthur Ashe, and Ervin "Magic" Johnson were among the most highly recognized public figures to fall victim to HIV. Each made large segments of the American public recognize the need to protect the human dignity of persons they had held in such high regard for most of their lives.

Arthur Ashe, an extraordinarily successful professional tennis player and the first African American male to win the prestigious Wimbledon tournament, wrote about his painful personal experiences after he learned he had contracted HIV. He observed how both the public and close friends struggled with their perceptions of him after the public announcement of his illness. Was he gay or did he use illicit drugs? He answered the inquiries by reporting that he con- tracted the virus through a blood transfusion he underwent following heart surgery. However, in his memoir titled *Days of Grace*, Mr. Ashe acknowledged that he knew that dignity was at stake because of the stigma large portions of the public attached to HIV.

Arthur Ashe personified dignity and could not allow himself to be governed by negative social attitudes, particularly with respect to an individual's sexual orientation. Rather than run from the questions about how he contracted HIV, he decided to confront the question of why people would condemn an individ- ual because of his or her sexual orientation. He began to study and explore the complexities of sexual attitudes and orientation among professional athletes as a way of better understanding and protecting human dignity. He believed that humanity required a willingness to try to better understand and help to the degree possible each human being afflicted with HIV, rather than condemning a person who was different. Moreover, he wanted the public to appreciate what it meant to be struck with this illness, which at that time was regarded as a certain death sentence. He explained: "By 1992, I was taking about thirty pills, including natural vitamins, every day. My annual bill for prescription drugs alone runs to about $18,000. However, the cost fell dramatically after I started getting my drugs from my primary insurance carrier. It pains me to think of the many AIDS patients who must face such expense without adequate insurance."[8]

Each public figure who openly acknowledged that he or she had contracted HIV was preceded and followed by thousands of private persons with similar diagnoses who touched the lives of people who were fortunate enough to know them as individuals. People who contracted HIV came from a wide variety of income and racial groups, and many were highly educated and politically astute.

Working through organized groups who sometimes sharply disagreed on strategies, they managed to change the political, scientific, and medical approach to research and healthcare related to HIV and AIDS.

AIDS activists made substantial gains in power when they secured a seat at the decision-making tables of major scientific research organizations, healthcare providers, insurance companies, and the U.S. Food and Drug Administration (FDA). HIV healthcare advocates also achieved changes in federal and state law. For example, the FDA agreed to adopt a new regulation that allowed victims of HIV to gain early access to promising therapeutic drugs that had not completed the full scientific testing process that was regarded as essential to assessing the true safety and effectiveness of the drugs. The early access to potentially helpful therapeutic drugs was known as a "compassionate use" exception, acknowledging the argument of the HIV community of advocates that people who were dying should be permitted an opportunity to try to extend their lives by gaining access to drugs that were promising but not yet fully tested.[9] Advocates also succeeded in gaining protection of the dignity of HIV positive individuals by invoking federal legislation that protects the rights of the disabled.[10] On the state level, individuals who brought claims relying on tort law received mixed results, but nevertheless publicized examples of wrongful conduct that caused emotional harm to individuals just because they had a disease.[11]

The AIDS epidemic offers many political, ethical, social, economic, and moral lessons about science, healthcare, and the importance of law in promoting social justice. In my view, the most important lesson is that human dignity is a value that should always be paramount when we consider the healthcare demands and needs of individuals and groups, particularly those who have been forced to live outside of the established political, social, and scientific power structure. During the past four decades, individuals suffering from HIV/AIDS and their supporters have highlighted the importance of human dignity in a struggle for access to healthcare.[12] Advocates for equitable care for people who have contracted HIV have also demonstrated the critical role played by law in protecting the dignity of patients by insisting on the proper use and allocation of power between providers and patients.

Despite the political and legal victories, it took two decades of social struggle, public education efforts, and scientific advancements for HIV/AIDS patients to receive access to humane healthcare. Even today, however, those with HIV continue to be stigmatized by some citizens. A stunning example received widespread news coverage on August 25, 2017. Aetna, a healthcare insurance company, had violated the privacy of 12,000 customers by mailing letters with envelopes that clearly exposed that these customers were taking medicine to treat or prevent HIV.[13] One customer complained that he was immediately kicked out of his house because someone saw his HIV status. The AIDS Law Project of Pennsylvania joined with two other law firms to file a class action lawsuit against Aetna. The lawsuit resulted in a monetary settlement of $17 million for the people whose rights were violated, which is believed to be one the largest ever for a company's breach of its duty to maintain and protect the privacy of the personal health data of its customers.

The legal battle over HIV/AIDS epitomizes how issues of race, class, gender, and sexual orientation must be addressed to ensure protection of human dignity in the healthcare context. The Aetna case is just one example of many cases involving human dignity that make the front page of the papers. Much less well known by the public are the decisions courts have made to protect a patient's dignity in the ordinary day-to-day healthcare context. As I continue to relate stories about the experiences of individuals who seek healthcare in America, I will pose the question of whether the person involved in the clinical encounter was treated as a human being who mattered. Often the moral and ethical answer to the question of what to do in healthcare can be answered by asking the following questions: Is this somebody, or nobody? If this is somebody, then what type of healthcare should he get, if any? What role should our aspirations for equality play in answering these questions?

In the prologue to *And the Band Played On: Politics, People, and the AIDS Epidemic* (1987), Randy Shilts warns us that his book presents a detailed recitation of the shameful behavior of many individuals and groups toward the AIDS epidemic: "It is a tale that bears telling, so that it will never happen again, to any people, anywhere."[14]

We should never forget the reactions of many Americans to a disease that resulted in "many victims of the epidemic who fought rejection, fear, isolation and their own deadly prognoses to make people understand and to make people care."[15] But we must also celebrate the success of a community of activists who collaborated with scientists, drug manufacturers, government officials, and healthcare providers for a decade and a half to discover antiviral drugs that would eliminate HIV from a victim's body. In his 2016 book David France describes the miracle that ended the epidemic and its impact on HIV patients: "Within two years, the lasting power of these drugs was undeniable. The hospitals emptied and the ward signs were taken down. The epidemic that had wiped out a generation of gay men and then torn huge holes through African American and Latino families in most major American cities, the plague that burned through Europe, sub-Saharan Africa, Asia, and the Pacific, claiming millions and millions of lives worldwide, had been all but vanquished."[16]

But in truth the inequitable barriers to access to the lifesaving medicine would soon reveal that only people with wealth or health insurance were saved, in America and around the globe. In a 2002 book that viewed AIDS from a global perspective, the authors pleaded with the rich nations of the world to take note of the disparities: "With the development of anti-retroviral therapies (ARTS) the epidemic defines who is saved and who is left to die from the disease and its impacts. In its distribution across the continents and in relation to access to drugs that can save lives, it is a global epidemic that defines the excluded of the world—the wretched of the earth. Above all, HIV/AIDS defines those who can purchase well-being and those who cannot."[17]

HIV and AIDS continue to pose life-threatening challenges to the world that warrant primary concern. However, the discussion and concerns about human dignity and healthcare go beyond relating the lessons of the AID/HIV epidemic to a consideration of the impact of the current American healthcare system on human dignity. As I write this book, the country is already facing another epidemic, called the "opioid crisis."[18] That crisis, caused by widespread drug addiction to pain-killing prescription drugs, has demonstrated once again how stigma and stereotypes operate as barriers to both healthcare and human dignity. The initial reaction to the illness was to characterize the victims as drug addicts who were responsible for inflicting harm on themselves. It was not until large numbers of white and middle-class people acknowledged an addiction to opioids that the problem received a second look that led to recognizing the addiction as an illness that posed a widespread public health crisis. It should not take an epidemic to motivate America to reform the healthcare system to address disparities and provide for humane healthcare for all. If we don't remember the risks and dangers revealed by injecting group-based bias into healthcare laws, policies, and practices, we are destined to make the same mistakes again.

Law Matters: Introduction to the Powers and Limitations of American Law

The healthcare discrimination cases described in this chapter, and throughout this book, reveal the importance of having access to a legal system that protects the dignity of all members of the community. Without legal advocacy, the indignity suffered by the victims of discrimination would go unaddressed. An after-the-fact public relations campaign protest may gain the attention of mainline media or social media, but the publicity is usually too late to help the people who have been injured. It is important to note that while the Americans with Disabilities Act, enacted in 1990, and the Rehabilitation Act of 1973 prohibit discrimination against individuals based on a disability, including HIV/AIDS, these federal statutes do not authorize private persons to bring lawsuits against violators of the statutes. Only federal agencies can sue under these statutes, and the remedies of monetary fines and penalties do not go to the injured parties.[19] The following case illustrates the challenge faced by victims of egregious violations of human dignity who do not suffer physical harm.

Janice Langbehn and Lisa Marie Pond were lifetime committed partners who had lived together for twenty years before Ms. Pond became severely ill and had to be hospitalized. They had jointly adopted four children, and the entire family was on its way to embark on a vacation cruise when Ms. Pond collapsed.[20] They rushed Ms. Pond to Jackson Memorial Hospital in Miami, Florida, where the admitting clerk, who controlled family members' access to hospital patients, denied them access to Ms. Pond for the next eight hours. After the clerk denied the family access to Ms. Pond, the family spoke to a social worker, and according to Ms. Langbehn, he told her they would be provided neither information nor access to Ms. Pond because they were in an "anti-gay city and state."[21]

Ms. Langbehn also alleged that the social worker informed her that she could not do anything about being denied information and access because it was a holiday weekend and she would not be able to find a judge to consider her claim. After the hospital staff received a faxed copy of a power of attorney, which authorized Ms. Langbehn to make medical decisions for Ms. Pond, they continued to deny her information and access.[22] Upon arrival at the hospital, Ms. Pond was semiconscious and responsive; however, her condition quickly deteriorated, and she was first scheduled for surgery; due to her rapid deterioration, however, she was transferred from the trauma area to an intensive care unit. Ms. Langbehn was not informed of the transfer. When Ms. Pond's sister and brother-in-law arrived that night, they were informed of the transfer and given confidential medical records and information about Ms. Pond's condition. At some point Ms. Langbehn and the children were allowed to visit Ms. Pond in the intensive care unit before she died from an aneurysm in her brain.

Ms. Langbehn later brought a lawsuit against the hospital and the treating doctors, seeking compensatory damages, nominal damages, and punitive damages for the emotional and physical harm suffered by her and her children. They argued that the hospital and its staff owed them a duty to provide information and visitation and that the breach of their duty constituted an intentional or negligent infliction of emotional distress. In dismissing the lawsuit, the court expressed sympathy but concluded that it could offer Ms. Langbehn and her children no legal relief. The court explained:

If the plaintiffs' allegations are true . . . the defendants' lack of sensitivity and attention to Ms. Langbehn, Ms. Pond, and their children caused them needless distress during a time of anguish and vulnerability. The defendants' failure to provide Ms. Langbehn and her children frequent updates on Ms. Pond's status, to allow Ms. Langbehn and her children to visit Ms. Pond after emergency medical care ceased, to inform Ms. Langbehn that Ms. Pond had been transferred to the intensive care unit, and to provide Ms. Langbehn Ms. Pond's medical records as she requested, exhibited a lack of compassion and was unbecoming of a renowned trauma center like Ryder. Unfortunately, no relief is available under Florida law for these failures based on the allegations pled in the amended complaint. *Cf. Tanner,* 696 So.2d at 708 ("the law does not provide a remedy for every wrong").[23]

The view that deliberate harm to human dignity does not by itself represent the type of wrongful conduct or produce the kind of harm that warrants legal protection under U.S. law is the central proposition explored and challenged in this book. Admittedly, the court's resolution of the claim Langbehn based on inadequate proof of substantial physical or emotional harm is consistent with tort law precedent in most states. However, I contend that harm to dignity alone in circumstances such as the Langbehn case should be enough to support a claim for nominal and punitive damages.[24]

In the Langbehn case, where a family was denied equitable health care because of homophobia exhibited by the healthcare staff, the law did not provide an effective remedy because the couple needed immediate legal assistance and could not gain access to an attorney or a court in time to protect their rights. This case presents a disturbing reality that timely access to legal advocates and courts often proves critical to the protection of civil and human rights and that healthcare represents an exceptional challenge to achieving social justice. There is no way to replace the moments lost by a dying person and her loved ones at the end of life. In most states, criminal law sanctions would not be available because the hospital and staff did not commit a crime. The remedy available to the family depends upon the state law that governs personal injury claims, and most often that remedy would be an award of monetary damages. The main challenge the family faces is persuading the court that the emotional harm they suffered by itself warrants compensation. Exploring and assessing the law applicable to claims of harm to dignity will be a focus of later chapters in this book.

American courts have struggled with developing a tort doctrine that would allow for compensation for emotional distress and harm to dignity. Courts have been concerned that they will open a floodgate of litigation if these types of personal interests warrant legal adjudication. Two legal doctrines have been invoked by injured parties under state tort law: intentional infliction of emotional distress and negligent infliction of emotional distress. In my view, both legal doctrines as currently defined by the courts provide insufficient protection to personal dignity. Another case that highlights the compelling need for the legal protection of dignity in circumstances similar to the Langbehn case also involved a same-sex couple who were denied visitation rights with each other in the hospital when one was dying and moved into the intensive care ward of the hospital. The couple had the foresight and the means to effectuate legal documents expressing their will in the event that one of them became severely ill. The document, designated as a surrogate power of attorney, provided for visitation not only for medical decision making but also for companionship and comfort. Notwithstanding the execution of the surrogate decision-making legal document, the nurse providing care denied visitation to Sharon Reed, the life partner of the patient, Jo Ann Ritchie. Reed filed a lawsuit after Ritchie died, alleging that the denial was based on bias against her and her partner as a same sex-couple.[25] The nurse denied this claim and asserted that the denial of visitation was because of medical reasons. The nurse asserted that Ms. Reed was upsetting Ms. Ritchie, who was very ill, and Ms. Reed's presence was having a negative effect on her breathing.

The trial court declared that the lawsuit would be meritorious under state law if Ms. Reed could prove that she was denied visitation based on bias reasons and not medical reasons. On the other hand, if she was denied visitation for medical reasons, there would be no reason to grant her relief.[26] The decision affirmed the right of same-sex couples to visitation but did not present an opinion that explained or buttressed the right to affection and companionship on the part of a patient and her loved one who is hospitalized. Neither did the court reach or discuss the challenging issue of what level of emotional distress or physical injury, if any, would be required to validate the lawsuit.

As I continue to recount stories of personal assaults to dignity in this book, I will attempt to clarify the meaning and significance of dignity in healthcare. I will argue that courts and legislators should declare that human dignity represents a distinct social value that requires respect by healthcare providers and legal protection by the courts. Effective protection of human dignity of patients in the healthcare system will require addressing three pernicious forces. First, and most persistent, is the proclivity of healthcare practitioners and policy makers to judge the value of individual patients and their families based on group identification related to sexual orientation, race, gender, and socioeconomic status. Second is the abuse of power to pursue social goals such as power, wealth, and prestige in a manner that marginalizes and harms patients. Third is the devaluing of people based on a stigmatization related to a disease. While these forces that damage individual human dignity are not restricted to healthcare, the harm caused is magnified by the needs of patients and the dependency of patients and their families on providers. I have selected cases and stories to demonstrate the devastating effects that these negative forces have on the human spirit. I then identify people, programs, and strategies that offer effective ways of protecting human dignity.

Chapter 2

Philosophical and Legal Conceptions of Dignity

Trusting Your Doctor

Janet Lucchesi was five months pregnant when she went into premature labor and was taken to Desert Samaritan Hospital. The attending physician examined her and determined that this was a high-risk delivery and that it was in the best interest of Mrs. Lucchesi to transfer her to Good Samaritan Hospital, which had a medical staff that specialized in high-risk deliveries.[1] He contacted Dr. Frederic Stimmell, a specialist in high-risk deliveries at Good Samaritan Hospital who agreed that the child had almost no chance of survival but that the transfer would assure Mrs. Lucchesi that doctors were doing everything they could to help her. Dr. Stimmell was home when he was contacted but said he would be ready when Mrs. Lucchesi arrived. Despite being fewer than twenty-five minutes away from the hospital, Dr. Stimmell decided not to go to the hospital, but instead to allow the residents and interns to perform the delivery. The child presented for birth in a double footing breech position, and the residents, who had never delivered a child under these circumstances, decapitated the child as they tugged to deliver her.[2] When Dr. Stimmell arrived at the hospital a few hours later, he spoke with Mrs. Lucchesi and told her that the delivery was traumatic and that the baby did not survive. However, he did not tell her that he was not present for the delivery and that the child had been decapitated in the delivery process.[3]

A few months later, Mrs. Lucchesi discovered what had happened and brought a lawsuit against Dr. Stimmell and the hospital seeking an award of monetary damages. Her principal claim of harm was that the doctor had caused her to experience severe emotional distress by failing to dignify the birth of her child with his presence and by failing to tell her the complete truth about the physical harm her child suffered during the birthing process.[4]

The court in *Lucchesi* concluded that the facts in this case warranted a jury deciding whether Dr. Stimmell had engaged in conduct outrageous enough to warrant holding him liable to Mrs. Lucchesi for intentional infliction of emotional distress. The court in *Lucchesi* held that, in order for a defendant to be held liable for the tort claim of intentional infliction of emotional distress, "(1) the defendant's conduct must be capable of being characterized as 'extreme and outrageous'; (2) the defendant must either intend to cause emotional distress or recklessly disregard the near certainty that distress will result from his conduct; and (3) the defendant's conduct must have caused severe and emotional distress."[5]

This tort claim is described as intentional infliction of emotional distress or outrage, and its effectiveness as a tool for protecting and addressing a patient's right to dignity in the healthcare context will serve as a central focus of this book. The law concerning the tort of intentional infliction of emotional distress is introduced in the present chapter and discussed in more detail in chapter 4.

I argue that some invasions of individual dignity warrant legal redress in a civil action without a requirement of proof that the victim suffered severe emotional distress. For example, when a doctor uses his professional status to sexually molest his female patients, or when a doctor fails to honor a promise to be present for the delivery of a newborn, courts should allow patients to seek an award of monetary damages. In such cases, the law should declare that the harm to dignity by itself justifies a tort claim. The degree of emotional distress caused by the outrageous conduct should be considered as a part of the assessment of the monetary damage award. In short, I contend that even if the emotional distress is not severe, the conduct may warrant legal redress to deter outrageous conduct and achieve social justice.[6]

Defining Dignity

Dignity is a complex and elusive concept, frequently invoked but rarely defined. The Presidential Commission on Bioethics commissioned scholarly papers on the meaning of dignity within the context of bioethics, and neither the scholars nor the Presidential Commission could reach a consensus.[7] Indeed, one scholar argued that dignity is a vague term that adds nothing to understanding value conflicts that could not be better understood by focusing on other values that are more concrete and capable of being defined.[8]

In contrast, another commentator asserted: "All too often, dignity, like many of the more precious but intangible phenomena of human life, is taken for granted.

Only when it is threatened, demeaned, or wrenched forcibly from us do we understand how inseparable our dignity is from our humanity."[9] Professor Rebecca Dresser describes the importance of dignity in healthcare in a thoughtful article titled "Human Dignity and the Seriously Ill Patient": "For patients, dignity is a precious possession. Serious illness threatens one's place in the human community. Ordinary activities fall by the wayside and relationships are no longer the same. How should the patient, clinicians, loved ones, and others respond to this disruption, this new vulnerability?"[10]

When health concerns are involved, dignity is at stake even if the patient does not have a serious illness. The disparity in knowledge and power between the doctor and the patient by itself creates a sense of vulnerability on the part of the patient. Like many other interactions with healthcare professionals, waiting to learn whether the Pap smear or the PSA exam raises medical concerns about the presence of cancer places a patient in a position of uncertainty and vulnerability. In short, the power imbalance between doctors and patients, combined with the vulnerability and dependency experienced by patients when they are ill, places human dignity at risk.

As noted in the introduction to this book, I think George Kateb offered important guidance in arguing that a core concept of human dignity is that every human being "deserves to be treated in a manner consonant with the high worth of the species."[11] In my mind, that means that we must examine the conditions in which human beings live to make a determination of the minimum values that each person is entitled to possess and enjoy. Dignity derives its meaning from lived experiences that reflect the fundamental needs and entitlements of individuals by virtue of being members of the human species.

Harold Laswell and Myres McDougal, influential scholars from the Political Science Department and the Law School at Yale University, developed a theoretical framework for assessing and appreciating the values that are important to understanding human dignity.[12] They argued that each human being in every community is entitled to minimum access to each of the following values in order to protect and promote human dignity: respect, power, enlightenment, well-being, wealth, skill, affection, and rectitude. They contended that, while culture may have an impact on the minimum of each value a community can provide, each community should set an aspiration of providing and protecting a minimum access to each of these values in order to afford human dignity to each member of the community. In support of their description of the basic values of human dignity, they cited the findings of modern science about the link between simple respect for human dignity and the shaping of all other values. Further evidence of the essential aspects of access to all of these values can be found through empirical observations of the demands of people over time all over the world. They observe: "The important fact is that the peoples of the world, whatever their differences in cultural traditions and styles of justification, are today increasingly demanding the enhanced protection of all those basic rights, commonly characterized in empirical reference as those of human dignity, by the processes of law in all the different communities of which they are members, including especially the international or world community."[13]

Laswell and McDougal argued that the value of respect was "an indispensable component and determinant in all human rights."[14] In addition, the paramount demand relating to power is "for recognition as a human being."[15] This conception of fundamental values essential to maintain human dignity throws light on the rules and principles of law that should govern healthcare and that promote or impair human dignity.

Recognition of someone as being worthy of respect as a human being and deserving equal treatment depends on our ability to empathize with another person. The first chapter of this book offers an opportunity for empathy with victims of HIV/AIDS to encourage a view of the world through the eyes and experiences of a person who has been subordinated or marginalized, particularly based on a disease or an immutable human characteristic such as race, gender, or sexual orientation. Refusing to help a person who is ill or who has suffered an injury reveals a willingness to treat the person as not worthy of being regarded as a valued member of the human community.

Reverend Jesse Jackson, a veteran of the civil rights movement, popularized a poem written in the 1950s by Reverend William Holmes Borders Sr., pastor of Wheat Street Baptist Church in Atlanta, Georgia, titled "I Am Somebody." Reverend Jackson served as a leader of a Chicago organization called Operation PUSH that undertook a mission to motivate and mentor African American youth. He often spoke to groups of youth and other audiences with a call-and-response chant of a free-verse version of the poem. In 1971 Reverend Jackson recited the poem on *Sesame Street*.[16] In 1972 he recited it at the Wattstax concert in the Los Angeles Coliseum.[17]

> I may be poor . . .
> But I am . . .
> Somebody . . .
> I may be on welfare . . .
> But I am . . .
> Somebody . . .
> I may be unskilled . . .

But I am . . .
Somebody . . .

This poem was chanted back by the audience after each phrase with a ring-ing tone of pride that would bring tears to the eyes of the participants and onlookers. People who have been treated as outsiders have no difficulty in understanding and appreciating the importance of dignity when it means being treated with respect.

Rosa Parks understood that her dignity was at stake when she refused to give up her seat on a public bus to a white man who asserted a claim to sit in the seat because of the privilege America afforded white people under a system of formal racial segregation and subordination that replaced slavery.[18] Her demand for the equal right to participate in and share the public transportation resources of the community on an equal basis with other members of the com-munity highlights a critical aspect of human dignity based on the importance of equality.

George Kateb describes human dignity as an existential value that reflects worthiness and equality: "The truth of personal identity is at stake when any individual is treated as if he or she is not a human being like any other, and therefore treated as more or less than human. The truth of identity is also at stake when a person is treated as if he or she is just one more human being in a spe-cies, and not, instead, a unique individual who is irreplaceable and not exchange-able for another."[19]

Law Matters

Human dignity as a predominant value does critical work to support the recog-nition and protection of human rights. The newly established democratic gov-ernment of South Africa adopted a constitution that identified healthcare as a constitutionally protected right.[20] Unlike the U.S. Constitution, which adopted a Bill of Rights that enumerates limitations on government action that interfere with fundamental rights, the South African Constitution enumerates specific affirmative or positive rights, identifying rights that the government is obligated to guarantee to citizens and other members of the nation.[21] Notably, one of the rights the South African Constitution identifies is the right to healthcare.[22]

HIV victims in South Africa who were being deprived of therapeutic drugs sued the government for breach of its duty to provide healthcare to HIV patients. In large part, the government at the time refused healthcare to these patients because its president did not believe that AIDS was caused by a virus. In response to the lawsuit, the South African Supreme Court noted that South Africa's

Constitution declared expressly that the government had a positive duty to its citizens to provide healthcare. The Court's opinion noted that the Constitution expressly recognized healthcare as a human right. In light of this recognition, the court declared that the government had an obligation to use its resources to protect this fundamental right. However, the Court then acknowledged that the right to healthcare was subject to the availability of resources.[23]

The United States has never recognized healthcare as a legal right to which all citizens are entitled.[24] The reluctance to endorse the concept of a legal right to healthcare—even as an aspiration—is driven by both an economic view of the costs and a political view that places more weight on personal responsibility for individual well-being than on a community duty to assure that basic human needs of all of its members are met.

U.S. law has failed to embrace a single definition of dignity, and yet there are many circumstances that have prompted courts to invoke legal protection for the dignity of an individual. Not all violations of dignity warrant legal redress, but some certainly do. Egregious violations of an individual's dignity—even when unaccompanied by severe physical or emotional harm—may warrant protection by courts or healthcare institutions. The challenge to the law is to identify and provide guidance as to when dignity warrants legal protection in the context of healthcare.

In reviewing the use of the term "dignity" by the U.S. Supreme Court, Professor Leslie Meltzer Henry found that it was used to support five different concepts: institutional status, equality, liberty, personal integrity, and collective virtue.[25] For example, she describes how the judicial system recognizes dignity as institutional status through its respect toward judges and courtrooms.[26] Dignity in the form of equality can be seen in Supreme Court decisions beginning in the 1940s and became even more prevalent during the civil rights era with equal rights cases being decided on the basis of human dignity.[27] Professor Henry further discusses that the Supreme Court describes dignity as liberty in cases involving abortion rights and same-sex marriage,[28] and as personal integrity primarily in defamation suits,[29] and that it describes collective virtue as dignity "to stop or limit activities that do not comport with how a decent society should respect the dignity of human life."[30]

Notwithstanding the challenge of defining the meaning of dignity, many statutes and court decisions identify dignity as a paramount value that warrants legal protection.[31] Most often, dignity is tied to, and dependent upon, access to another important human need essential to physical or spiritual survival, such as food, housing, medical care, or religion. The conception of dignity as tied to some other fundamental value is illustrated by the decision of the U.S. Supreme

Court affirming the right of same-sex couples to marry. Justice Kennedy, writing for the majority of the Court in *Obergefell v. Hodges*,[32] explained why states are constitutionally required to recognize same-sex marriages:

> No union is more profound than marriage, for it embodies the highest ideals of love, fidelity, devotion, sacrifice, and family. In forming a marital union, two people become something greater than once they were. As some of the petitioners in these cases demonstrate, marriage embodies a love that may endure even past death. It would misunderstand these men and women to say they disrespect the idea of marriage. Their plea is that they do respect it, respect it so deeply that they seek to find its fulfillment for themselves. Their hope is not to be condemned to live in loneliness, excluded from one of civilization's oldest institutions. They ask for equal dignity in the eyes of the law. The Constitution grants them that right.[33]

One commentator has noted the significance of the Supreme Court endorsing a jurisprudence of dignity as applied to personal sexual preferences, as distinguished from a jurisdiction of stigma. Reporting on her experience as an openly gay person, she declared: "The language of *Obergefell* reflects an acceptance of and respect for gay men and lesbians that—regardless of one's actual desire to marry or attitudes toward the institution of marriage—will profoundly change not only how the law treats LGB individuals, but also how we are treated by others, as well as how we perceive ourselves. I do not mean to assert that *Obergefell* is without its flaws, or that LGB people are without dignity and self-respect absent *Obergefell*; fundamentally, however, the symbolic and genuine power of the Court's dignity-based reasoning is extraordinary."[34]

A recent scholarly article analyzing historic and current treatments of the concept of dignity in tort law concluded that, despite the growing recognition of the importance of protecting human dignity with specific laws, the courts and commentators have not settled on a unified conception of what constitutes a dignitary tort.[35] The authors attribute the lack of uniformity to the peculiar manner in which tort law is made, namely, by examining tort claims to see if they fit into established causes of action and assessing the lawsuits on a case-by-case basis in light of each state's tort law.[36] In other words, most rights and duties recognized as supporting private claims for compensation for personal injuries are decided based on facts and claims in individual cases, rather than from the top down by state or federal legislatures.

In the ordinary day-to-day healthcare context, court decisions made to protect a patient's dignity are not well known by the public. However, courts have found dignity to be an important concept in connection with a variety of personal interests, including bodily integrity, emotional tranquility, and reputation when developing and applying tort law. Several tort claims have been authorized to protect these personal interests, including claims for battery, intentional infliction of emotional distress, and defamation.[37]

In medical malpractice law, critical protection of human dignity comes from the doctrine of "informed consent."[38] The informed consent doctrine endorsed the principle that individual patients have the ultimate authority over what medical care they choose to undergo or reject.[39] It is not widely known that the author of one of the seminal cases that led to nationwide recognition of the informed consent doctrine was Judge Spottswood Robinson, a highly respected judge on the D.C. Circuit who was a veteran civil rights lawyer prior to becoming a judge.[40] In addition to protecting a patient's right to decide what treatment and testing he wants to undergo, the past two decades have generated many highly publicized cases protecting a patient's right to decline proposed medical care, even if the result of declining the care is imminent death.[41] In short, a legal command to respect each patient's dignity has revolutionized the doctor-patient relationship in America.

When healthcare providers infringe on a patient's dignity, the legal system faces a challenge of determining whether the harm to a patient's dignity warrants legal protection and redress. The facts of the *Lucchesi* case that introduced this chapter demonstrate the need for a legal rule protecting dignity as a distinct value. A woman who is ready to deliver her baby is told by her doctors that the situation is dire, but a high-risk specialist has promised that he will be at the delivery to make sure that everything possible is done to save her newborn baby. The specialist decided to stay home and allow inexperienced residents to deliver the child. The court explained that conduct such as this could be reasonably judged to be outrageous, but in reaching its decision, the court relied heavily on the doctor's recognition of the emotional distress the mother was experiencing:

> In the present case, a practicing obstetrician, Dr. Shill, determined that Mrs. Lucchesi's premature delivery constituted a particularly complex medical situation requiring the expertise of a specialist. Dr. Stimmell, a specialist in high-risk deliveries, agreed that if there was any hope of saving the baby, the mother must be transported to a hospital where special facilities were available. The specialist further agreed that transporting the mother would benefit her psychologically by alleviating some of the stress and emotional upset the situation was causing her. Then, after

stating that he would assume responsibility for the mother's care, Dr. Stimmell made no effort to meet the mother at the hospital. Instead, Mrs. Lucchesi was left to be attended during a traumatic delivery by a first-year intern and a third-year resident—neither of whom had any experience with the type of breech delivery taking place (and who, presumably, had less experience than the obstetrician who originally indicated that the situation was too complex for his medical skills). The delivery was finally accomplished when the resident, tugging on the baby in an effort to extricate it from the birth canal, decapitated the child.[42]

In my view, even if the mother did not suffer severe emotional distress, she was entitled to bring a tort claim against Dr. Stimmell. Viewed in the context of lived experiences, human dignity is more than an abstract social value; it is an existential value that guides life-and-death decisions. While Dr. Stimmell likely could not have saved the life of the premature newborn, his decision to not dignify Mrs. Lucchesi's need for professional care sent a clear message that he did not value her as a human being who needed his professional help. Viewing human dignity as an existential value that protects individuals both as members of the human species and as unique individuals worthy of respect allows a better appreciation of why legal rules and cultural norms should be developed and reinforced using the protection of individual dignity as a predominant value. An egregious wrong occurred independent of whether the mother suffered severe emotional distress.

This book recounts stories that demonstrate the need to identify laws, policies, and practices that promote or undermine human dignity in healthcare. I acknowledge at the outset that thinking about human dignity does not always supply easy or clear answers to healthcare decision making. On the other hand, adopting or allowing practices and policies based on concerns about financial costs and economic efficiency, while failing to consider the impact on human dignity, threatens to undermine central founding principles for the United States embodied in concepts of freedom and equality.

Chapter 3

Emergency Care in America

Law, Morality, and Ethics

"I'm nobody. Who are you?
Are you nobody too?"

—Emily Dickinson

Economic vs. Moral Decision Making

If a coal mine caves in, trapping workers and threatening their lives, the public demands that governments and private businesses spend whatever it takes to save the miners. We feel morally bound to try to save all human life. On the other hand, if we are asked to put in safety features that will avoid the mine from caving, we argue about budgets, and debate whether the safety measures are worth the cost. Guido Calabresi,[1] a prominent and influential law professor emeritus at Yale University, offers a helpful explanation for why we treat prevention differently from rescue. He contends that an overlooked feature of a free market system governing the distribution of goods and services is that the market allows the average citizen to avoid making moral judgments and taking responsibility for harm suffered by individuals.[2] The marketplace hides the moral issue underlying a decision to save or take human life, and no one feels personally responsible to respond.

Decisions about healthcare reflect that same proclivity to ignore moral issues. A healthcare emergency that threatens to take the life of a specific person compels us to confront the fact that the marketplace often resolves healthcare issues in a manner that clashes with our moral values. This chapter describes some disturbing cases related to this conflict that required resolution by courts, exposing the moral or immoral decisions that were made. The cases illustrate the legal approach taken before and after the adoption of a federal statute defining the legal duty of hospitals to treat emergency patients. The court decisions demonstrate that current U.S. law attempts to acknowledge our asserted moral value that human life is priceless. However, the law limits its application to the time of the emergency. When the individual leaves the hospital, healthcare providers and society are legally permitted to close their eyes to the probability that the source of danger that caused the emergency will cause harm to the person who has been temporarily spared the threat of serious harm or death. The cases discussed below show how the law applicable to emergencies has been interpreted and applied.

Seeking Help from Strangers

A Pregnant Woman

Rosa Rivera was nine months pregnant and ready to deliver her baby. She rushed to a hospital emergency room. The doctor who was responsible for attending to emergency room patients refused to treat her. The court opinion summarized the facts as follows:

> Mrs. Rosa Rivera arrived in the emergency room of DeTar Hospital in Victoria, Texas at approximately 4:00 P.M. on December 5, 1986. At or near term with her sixth child, she was experiencing one-minute, moderate contractions every three minutes and her membranes had ruptured. Two obstetrical nurses, Tammy Kotsur and Donna Keining, examined her and found indicia of labor and dangerously high blood pressure. Because Rivera had received no prenatal care, and had neither a regular doctor nor means of payment, Kotsur telephoned Burditt, who was next on DeTar's rotating call-list of physicians responsible for such "unaligned" obstetrics patients. Upon hearing Rivera's history and condition, Burditt told Kotsur that he "didn't want to take care of this lady" and asked her to prepare Rivera for transfer to John Sealy Hospital in Galveston, Texas, 170 miles away. Burditt agreed to call back in five to ten minutes.[3]

When the nurses responded that under federal law and hospital policy the physician was required to examine and stabilize her, Dr. Michael L. Burditt replied, "Until De Tar [sic] Hospital pays my malpractice insurance, I will pick and choose those patients that I want to treat."[4]

Ms. Rivera was transported by an ambulance headed toward the other hospital, but never made it in time for the birth. The nurse accompanying her in the ambulance delivered the baby, and the ambulance turned around and took them back to the hospital where the doctor had rejected them.[5] Fortunately, the mother and her newborn baby, weighing 6 pounds, survived the birthing process without immediately recognizable injuries.[6]

Ms. Rivera filed a lawsuit against the hospital and Dr. Burditt alleging a violation of the federal Emergency Medical Treatment and Active Labor Act (EMTALA).[7] She succeeded in winning a judgment against the doctor and the hospital. Dr. Burditt was fined $20,000.[8]

The ethical and moral questions that arise from the medical decision making that risked Ms. Rivera's life and dignity, and potentially the life of her baby, cannot be fully answered based on the facts presented in the court opinion. To fairly assess the moral and ethical issues, we need more information that enables us to see the world through the eyes of Dr. Burditt. Was he burned out by the healthcare system? Had the medical malpractice system of resolving disputes taken such a toll on him that he was unwilling to fulfill his legal and ethical duty to heal and do no harm?[9] Was he just having a bad day? Answers to questions such as these are not likely to change our moral judgment about his conduct on that day, but they may lead us to adopt effective solutions to the moral and ethical dilemmas raised by our conflicting legal, ethical, and moral standards for granting or withholding access to healthcare.

Reflections on Law, Morality and Ethics

First-year law students are surprised when they study tort law and read cases where courts endorse a legal rule stating that a moral duty is distinguishable from a legal duty, and therefore a private citizen has no duty to come to the aid of another in danger so long as he or she did not create the danger. Medical malpractice law falls within the rubric of tort law. Historically, courts held that doctors and hospitals had no duty to provide medical care to people who did not have preexisting and ongoing relationships with the healthcare provider. The "no duty rule" applied even when people needed emergency medical care to save their lives. The medical profession, like the legal profession and other professional associations, is empowered by law to set its own ethical standards for acceptable professional behavior. Those standards are held by the courts as separate and distinct from a legally enforceable duty owed to a patient who asserts a personal injury claim.

In this book, I consider a moral issue as a personal and/or community assessment of right and wrong. I use the term "ethical issue" to refer to the judgments of a profession about right and wrong conduct. The legal issue will then be considered in terms of whether the community is prepared to use the power of the law to command conformity with an established standard of conduct.

A medical malpractice action most often involves a claim that a healthcare provider has negligently breached a duty owed to a patient and that the breach of duty has caused physical or emotional harm to the patient that warrants monetary compensation. There are four elements of proof required by the common law adopted in all states for a tort action based on negligence: duty, breach of duty, proximate cause, and damages. The failure to prove any one of the elements of a negligence claim will result in the patient's lawsuit being dismissed. It is the "no duty rule" that prompts the dismissal of emergency care medical malpractice cases under the tort law applied in most states.

Federal law may also be invoked as an alternative or additional basis of claiming a legal duty to provide healthcare. The source of the duty claim may be a federal statute or the Constitution of the United States. EMTALA represents a mandatory approach to emergency healthcare directed by a federal statute. The Affordable Care Act, popularly known as Obamacare, reflects a congressional determination of the rules that govern access to health insurance. Political controversy over Obamacare evoked lawsuits asserting claims of a clash between federal law, U.S. constitutional provisions protecting individual liberty, and states' rights. The federalism issues are addressed in chapter 11. The present chapter concentrates on state and federal law applicable to requests for emergency medical care.

Children from Another Country

Two children suffered serious burns when a stove exploded in their home. They were rushed to a hospital emergency room for treatment. The challenge they confronted when they sought emergency medical care arose from the fact that the children lived in Mexico, where the accident occurred, and were brought across the border seeking care in a private hospital in Arizona. When the children arrived at the hospital, they were denied care because the hospital asserted it did not have a legal duty to treat them.[10]

The Guerreros, the family that sought treatment for their children burned in the fire, sued the hospital, asserting that the hospital breached its legal duty and should be held liable for the harm the children suffered, which would have been prevented by emergency medical care.[11] The issue before the court was whether the hospital had a duty to treat the children. After first acknowledging the established rule of American law that a hospital generally has a right to decide who it will accept as a patient,[12] the court emphasized that Arizona had passed legislation that expressed a new public policy that required licensed hospitals with emergency rooms to provide emergency care to all persons who come to the emergency room evidencing an unmistakable emergency.[13] The duty imposed by state law did not exclude immigrants living outside of the state at the time that they sought the care.

The decision of the Arizona Supreme Court started a trend that was subsequently followed in other states whereby the courts scrutinize the statutes and regulations governing hospitals in the state, as well as the customs established by a hospital in offering emergency room care, to determine whether a hospital has a duty to provide emergency healthcare to a patient.[14]

The Wallet Biopsy

Denial of emergency care is by no means limited to immigrants and citizens of other countries who visit the United States Private hospitals, whether profit or nonprofit, must generate enough revenue to sustain their existence. Consequently, most seek to avoid caring for patients who will generate little or no payment for healthcare services. At a minimum, most hospitals seek to limit the number of nonpaying or low-paying patients they treat. The following case reveals the experience of too many American citizens who seek emergency medical care from a hospital.

In *Thompson v. Sun City Community Hospital, Inc.*,[15] a thirteen-year-old boy who had suffered serious injuries in an accident was rushed to the hospital by ambulance. The emergency room physician examined him, administered fluids, and ordered blood. He then summoned an orthopedic surgeon, who determined that the boy had injured an artery in his left leg and needed immediate surgery. The orthopedic surgeon consulted a vascular surgeon by phone. A little over an hour later, the boy was transferred to a county hospital to have the surgery pursuant to a hospital policy that emergency charity patients are transferred to a county hospital whenever a physician determines that they are "medically transferable."[16] After being sued by the boy and his mother, the hospital admitted that the policy of transferring charity patients to a county hospital was based on financial considerations, and that was the reason the boy was transferred. The civil lawsuit brought against the hospital alleged that by transferring the boy in these circumstances the hospital breached its duty to exercise reasonable care to treat him.

The Arizona Supreme Court decided that Thompson had asserted a valid tort claim and that the hospital could be held liable to him for compensatory damages. The court noted that Arizona statutes and regulations placed a general duty on hospitals, private and public, to provide medical care to all patients who come to the hospital with an emergency medical condition. The court further explained: "The patient may not be transferred until all medically indicated emergency care has been completed."[17]

In the absence of a state statute, a patient suing under state tort law has a much more difficult challenge of persuading a court that the state's public policy mandates a private hospital to treat all emergency patients without considering the patient's ability to pay. However, in some states, the courts have found a duty to treat all patients if the hospital has established a custom that the patient relied on in coming to the hospital.[18]

It is significant to underscore that while the court in Thompson validated the lawsuit brought in behalf of the Thompson boy, it refused to find merit in his mother's claim that she was entitled to recover from the hospital for the emotional distress she suffered because of the hospital's negligence. The court explained: "Plaintiff Thompson maintains that 'the facts of this case required modification of the law to allow . . . [her] an opportunity to recover for the severe emotional distress she experienced as a result of defendant's conduct.' We disagree. The trial judge's rulings on the theory of intentional and negligent infliction of emotional distress were consistent with the paucity of evidence of 'outrageousness' (see Savage v. Boies, 77 Ariz. 355, 358, 272 P.2d 349, 351 (1954); Restatement (Second) of Torts, § 46 and comment (h) thereto) and the lack of proof of damages to Thompson."[19]

The Emergency Medical Treatment and Active Labor Act

Cases like *Guerrero* and *Thompson* of outright denial of care and patient dumping based on a lack of insurance occurred so frequently in the United States during the twentieth century that by 1986 the federal government enacted the Emergency Medical Treatment and Active Labor Act,[20] which mandated that hospitals with an emergency room must examine patients to determine whether they have a life-threatening condition and provide care to those who do to stabilize them before transferring them to another hospital. The statute applies to hospitals that enter into Medicare provider agreements. On the surface, EMTALA established laws consistent with the moral principle that each human life is valued, but it did not stop all providers from acting immorally. Similarly, it did not attempt to address structural race and class biases. Moreover, even though the federal government passed legislation to address the issue, the problem of access to emergency care on an equitable basis remains unresolved.

The case described at the beginning of this chapter illustrates these points. Even though the nurses made the doctor on call aware of his obligations under EMTALA to provide care to a patient who was ready to deliver her baby, he refused. The hospital was held liable under EMTALA, and the attending physician on call was fined $20,000. Here, case law and morality were harmonized by the court based on the federal statute. But the question remains how and why this doctor could decide that he would not treat her when she was ready to give birth, leaving her at risk of injury to herself and her newborn by transferring her to a hospital 170 miles away.

Poor medical care or unethical treatment that does not result in physical injury may escape public attention because the victim lacks the resources to demand redress. Also, lawyers who most often get paid a contingent fee based on a percentage of the patient's compensatory damage award are unwilling to take a case in these circumstances because the award of money is likely to be small. In the case described above, a legal remedy made available by the federal Emergency Medical Treatment Act supported a lawsuit by the federal government against Dr. Burditt that resulted in a monetary penalty imposed against him of $20,000.

However, in many cases, dignitary injuries unaccompanied by serious physical harm pose substantial challenges to traditional tort remedies. Courts find it difficult to use resources to resolve conflicts over conduct that is offensive but does not cause physical harm. Besides, in a case like this, perhaps the emergency room doctor is not the villain he appears to be by the above recitation of facts. Giving Dr. Burditt the benefit of the doubt, his behavior may simply reflect the frailties of a human being operating in a healthcare system that is driven by an unclear and contradictory moral vision of entitlement. This vision includes a financial system underlying healthcare delivery that devalues individuals who lack sufficient personal finances and power. If one sees the world through the eyes of the emergency room doctor, overwhelmed by demands for care that is not adequately supported by the government or his community, would or should we hold him legally responsible for the inhumane treatment of this patient?

In the absence of a medical emergency in the United States, the law does not recognize a right to medical care. Instead, the person seeking care must first show an ability to pay for the care through insurance or personal resources. Since the passage of the Medicare and Medicaid statutes in 1965, only two groups of people were guaranteed health insurance: people over the age of sixty-five under Medicare, and children and disabled individuals who met a standard for poverty in states that participated in the Medicaid program.

EMTALA relies on a medical determination of the existence of an emergency and whether the patient is stable enough to transfer. It represents a huge step forward from the old common law rule that a hospital had no duty to render emergency care in the absence of a preexisting contract or promise. However,

EMTALA does not attempt to address the structural and racial biases that produce disparate care in hospitals located in rich and poor communities as described in the Johnson case recounted in chapter 8 of this book. EMTALA functions as an unfunded mandate that places the burden of providing emergency care on hospitals that receive any type of federal financial support.

Patient Dumping. Unfortunately, the denial of treatment to patients who need emergency care continues today despite the law. When hospitals comply with the law to admit, examine, and stabilize a patient who has a potentially life-threatening condition, the current system of healthcare financing provides an incentive to engage in "patient dumping."[21] An extreme example of the cruel treatment that may be given to patients who cannot pay for their hospital care was reported in 2018 when security guards in a Baltimore hospital dumped a twenty-two-year-old female patient on the street on a cold winter night.[22] A man who was passing by the hospital at the time saw the dumping and took a video of the event. He questioned why the hospital was doing this and called 911 to rescue the woman, who at the time seemed incapable of taking care of herself mentally or physically. The hospital later issued a statement explaining that the staff who dumped the patient onto the street on a cold winter night violated hospital policies. A later investigation by the Center for Medicare Services (CMS) resulted in findings that the hospital had violated several provisions of EMTALA.[23]

A patient dumping case in Washington, D.C., rivals the dumping in Baltimore for the most inhumane treatment of a patient. Howard University Hospital security guards were reported to have dumped a patient in a wheelchair on the sidewalk and walked away.[24] Video footage shows the guards stopping, the woman falling out of the wheelchair, one guard throwing a bag on the ground, and then the two guards walking away.[25] One security guard can be heard saying, "Leave her there," and no one coming to the woman's aid. Many bystanders were shocked and appalled.[26]

Dumping patients who are mentally ill has presented a special problem. In 2014 the United States Office of Civil Rights (OCR) issued a report on the problem, noting a finding by CMS that Rawson-Neal Psychiatric Hospital in Nevada adopted a systematic practice of getting rid of patients by sending them to other states by bus.[27] The CMS investigation found that the hospital sent most of these patients, some suffering from severe mental illnesses, to unfamiliar states and cities with no plan in place to ensure that they would receive adequate medical care. The hospital sent so many patients to California that the attorney general of California filed a lawsuit against the hospital. According to the OCR report:

Rawson-Neal dumped most of the patients in California. Three hundred twenty-five, of approximately 1,500 patients bused from Rawson-Neal, were sent to California. In September of 2013, the city attorney of San Francisco, Dennis Herrera, filed a class action lawsuit against the state of Nevada, Nevada's Department of Health and Human Services, and Rawson-Neal, among others. According to Herrera's complaint, patients did not have adequate food, water, or medication; nor did patients have instructions or arrangements for continued care once they reached their destination. Twenty of the patients required medical care shortly after their arrival in San Francisco—some within hours of getting off of the bus. Their medical care, shelter, and basic necessities cost San Francisco taxpayers approximately $500,000. According to the complaint filed by the city, one 36-year-old male bused to San Francisco—and diagnosed with psychosis, schizophrenia, and suicidal/homicidal ideation—had a history of 13 prior visits to Rawson-Neal. Another patient, who had three prior suicide attempts, was bused to San Francisco despite evidence that he lived and worked in Las Vegas. The hospital gave this patient a one-way Greyhound bus ticket to San Francisco and a day's worth of food.[28]

The solution to the problem of patient dumping obviously requires more than reflections on morality and ethics. The moral mandate must be supported and guided by financial support and caring for patients who lack insurance and resources. At the same time, penalties imposed on healthcare providers who engage in inhumane conduct should be severe.

In nonemergency situations, a threshold challenge to building a more equitable healthcare system requires a determination of the type of healthcare services that should be regarded as essential to human dignity. In part 3 of this book, I discuss alternative approaches to identifying healthcare services that should be regarded as essential in the United States in the twenty-first century.

Part 2

Power and Trust

Chapter 4

Professional Bias, Class Bias, and Power

Over the past fifty years, courts and legislators have underscored the right of a patient to decide what is to be done with her body. This is true whether the medical professional forms a good faith belief that it is in the best interest of the patient to provide or withhold medical care. Indeed, the most highly publicized cases that produced court opinions protecting patient autonomy involved decisions to withhold medical care that would entail inserting tubes to provide oxygen and nutrition to individuals who had lost the ability to breathe or eat without mechanical support and who were in a vegetative state with no hope of recovery. While courts sometimes disagreed as to the basis on which a guardian should make the medical decision, all have agreed that the primary goal of the law in these situations is to protect a patient's right to decide.[1] In short, a competent patient has the right to decide what is to be done with his body, and an incompetent patient also has a right to decide, even though the right must be exercised and protected by a substitute person such as a family member or a guardian.

American law is now well settled that a patient's need or desire for a diagnosis or treatment plan from a medical professional does not defeat a legal requirement of respecting a patient's decision-making authority. However, when the medical therapy selected is surgery, the reality is that once a patient consents, all power that was previously shared in the doctor-patient relationship shifts to the healthcare team. Rarely does a patient have a representative in the surgical suite to protect his interest. The patient must rely on trust, ethics, and morality to guide healthcare decision making at that point as to who does the surgery, what surgery is done, and how safely and effectively the surgery is performed. The stories that are told below reveal a variety of ways in which a patient may feel betrayed after giving consent to surgery.

Emotional Distress

Carol Canty[2] awoke around six in the morning, having difficulty breathing. She was sixteen years old and had enjoyed good health all of her life. Three days earlier, when she had first started feeling sick, she went to see her pediatrician, who diagnosed her with an infection in her lungs. When Carol awakened that morning struggling to breathe, her mother, Cheryl Canty, immediately took her to a nearby hospital. Carol was admitted to the emergency room with a diagnosis of adult respiratory distress syndrome. After undergoing a battery of tests, Carol had not improved after several hours of treatment and observations. Her attending physician in the intensive care ward of the hospital advised her mother that the doctors needed to perform an invasive heart procedure on Carol to find out what was causing the breathing difficulty.

The wanted to insert a catheter into Carol's heart to determine the cause of her difficulty in breathing. The catheter would be attached to a monitor that would measure both the breathing and the heart output, which in turn would allow the doctors to pinpoint whether Carol's illness stemmed from her inability to breathe or her heart's inability to pump sufficient blood into her system.

According to Carol's mother, father, and grandmother, all of whom were present in the hospital at this time, Cheryl Canty asked the attending intensive care doctor about the risks of the cardiac catheterization and *who would perform the procedure.* The doctor responded that the risks were small, and that if they did not do the procedure Carol would surely die, because without the information that could be gained from the test, they were practicing nineteenth-century medicine and had no clue about how to treat her effectively. *He further noted that the procedure would be done by a cardiologist* on the hospital staff who had extensive experience doing the procedure. Mrs. Canty responded that if the cardiologist was going to do the procedure, he was the person with whom they needed to talk.

The cardiologist was called to the floor and met with the family. He affirmed the need to perform the procedure and assured them that though the procedure had risks, he had performed it thousands of times on adults and children, with few problems. He told the family that the procedure would be done in the room and that it would take about an hour. Based on this conversation, Carol's parents gave their consent for the catheter procedure to be done on Carol.

After more than an hour passed, the family became concerned. Sitting in the waiting area down the hall from Carol's room, they heard loud noises and screams. They rushed down to the room but could not get in. Through the window, they saw doctors and nurses scrambling around Carol, and blood on the wall. The family complied with the request of a hospital employee to return to the waiting room. About thirty minutes later, a representative of the hospital came to the waiting room and asked Mrs. Canty, "Who is your minister?" Befuddled and in a state of shock, the family listened to the hospital representative announce that Carol was dead. She did not survive the catheter procedure.

As they were talking, the intensive care physician who had served as Carol's attending doctor approached the family and expressed his regrets. Mrs. Canty asked the doctor whether her daughter was in pain before she died. The physician responded that she was not in pain, because she had been anesthetized before he inserted the catheter used to conduct the test. Mrs. Canty froze and began to cry. She exclaimed: "What do you mean when you were inserting the tube? You said the cardiologist would do it." The attending doctor replied: "It was just like the cardiologist doing it. He was in the room watching the monitor as I inserted the catheter, and reading the monitor is the most important part of the procedure."

The family was stunned. They had asked to see the cardiologist because they were told that he had extensive experience in performing an invasive heart procedure that was required to save Carol's life. Four years later, Cheryl Canty had not recovered emotionally from the combination of the loss of her daughter and the willingness of a doctor who knew he lacked experience in performing a lifesaving procedure to attempt to do it on her daughter while the experienced cardiologist stood in the room looking at the monitor.

Carol's death precipitated a lawsuit that revealed two starkly different views of the power, authority, and responsibilities of doctors to patients. Carol's family believed they had been misled and betrayed by the professionals in whom they had placed their confidence and trust. Their lawsuit alleged that not only had the doctors killed Carol through negligent medical care; they had also committed fraud and intentionally inflicted emotional harm on Carol's mother. In addition, Carol's family pointed to the law's requirement that a doctor get a patient's informed consent to a surgical procedure and contended that informed consent was not obtained in this case. Instead, the doctor in training seized the opportunity to perform the catheter procedure in order to gain experience that would advance his career. Almost all of Mrs. Canty's legal claims rested on the contention that the healthcare providers had deliberately misled her and disrespected her right to make healthcare decisions on behalf of her daughter.

The doctors and the hospital defended the lawsuit by arguing that they had provided Carol with the appropriate medical care, performing all of the proper tests in an effort to diagnose and treat her illness. The hospital acknowledged that the catheter was inserted by the resident doctor, not the cardiologist. In the American system of educating and training doctors, physicians complete four years of medical school and may then qualify for a medical license in accordance with the laws of a particular state. If a physician wants to specialize in a particular aspect of medicine, she applies for a residency that will allow her to learn and train in the specialty for a designated number of years, as determined by the board of the specialty. In the Carol Canty case, the doctor who inserted the catheter was in a residency training program for intensive care.

The medical record suggested that the intensive care resident who inserted the catheter may have inadvertently inserted it into an artery. The record stated that the cardiologist who was reading the monitor at the time told the resident to stop inserting it because the monitor showed arterial wave forms, indicating that the catheter was in an artery instead of in the vein that was the intended target. On the other hand, the autopsy performed after her death suggested that she died as a result of a virus in her heart. The pathologist reported that he could not find a hole in the artery. In contrast, the cardiologist who testified that the doctors and the hospital had violated the standard of care also stated that the pathologist must have missed the hole in the artery because there was no way for the monitor to reflect arterial wave forms unless the catheter was in the artery.

In response to the argument as to violation of the standard of care, the hospital and the defendant doctors argued that it was standard practice to allow a resident to insert a catheter, even in a child, at this stage of the doctor's training. The presence in the room of an experienced cardiologist assured that the procedure would be done safely and effectively. The healthcare providers contended that the family misunderstood what the cardiologist intended to convey when he told them he would do the procedure. The inexperienced doctor intended to convey that *he* would insert the catheter into the child's heart while the experienced cardiologist would be present to monitor the procedure and ensure that it was performed correctly.

The ordinary medical malpractice case involves a claim that a healthcare provider made a mistake due to inadvertence, bad judgment, or lack of the required professional skill or knowledge. In recognition of the fact that most errors are not the result of bad intentions, the Institute of Medicine titled its report *To Err Is Human*.[3] A medical malpractice case based on a mistake relies on a legal theory of negligence where the court and the jury are asked to judge the conduct of a doctor or nurse based on the testimony of other professionals who have education and training similar to the defendant's.[4] Those professionals are deemed qualified to express opinions about the appropriateness of the defendant's conduct because they have specialized knowledge that assists the nonprofessionals—judges and juries—to make an informed and fair decision.

The Carol Canty case is different. It includes a claim of negligence but goes further to ask the judge and jury to socially condemn the professionals' behavior as a violation of community norms of decency. A claim such as this invokes community standards aimed at protecting a person's dignity from an abuse of power.

A core principle of human dignity that is protected by tort law in all contexts, including healthcare, is the right to be free of intentional invasions of one's body without consent.[5] This principle governs appropriate conduct for all physical encounters, including labor, sports, intimate sexual relations, and medical care. When presented with disputes about what medical care is appropriate for a specific patient, courts have relied heavily on the idea of autonomy as critical to the protection of human dignity. Courts have ruled that respect for individuals requires that a patient have an opportunity to decide what medical care is acceptable, to feel as though the options offered flow from a recognition that he is a valued person, and to believe that he is being treated in the same way that other members of the community would be treated if they needed medical care to treat the same illness. Affirmation of individual worth and a right to equal treatment represent the core components of dignity in the healthcare context. In addition to the requirement of consent, offenses to that dignitary interest are then identified in tort law on the basis of the motive or goals being pursued by any person who invades that interest. In clear and direct terms, Justice Holmes explained: "Even a dog distinguishes between being tripped over and being kicked."[6] Medical malpractice cases present special challenges to fairly determining whether a doctor or nurse has stumbled over a patient or deliberately kicked him.

There are, however, cases that identify facts that courts believe support the conclusion that the healthcare provider has crossed the line enough to warrant social condemnation of her conduct. The cases are usually centered on conduct that amounts to an abuse of power by the healthcare provider or blatant disrespect of the individual patient. The legal standard invoked in the Carol Canty case provides providers with a useful guideline for most of these cases. The question presented in these cases is whether the doctor has engaged in "outrageous conduct" that goes "beyond the bounds of decency."[7]

Abuse of Power, Intentional Torts, and Dignitary Harms

The term "intentional" has a broader meaning in tort law than in common usage. Tort law defines "intentional" to include not only a desire to harm someone, but also acting in a way that is substantially certain to harm another.[8] When the harm relates to a person's emotional condition, as distinguished from their physical health, the question is whether the person desired or knew with substantial certainty that his conduct would cause another to suffer severe emotional distress.[9]

Chapter 2 presented an illustrative case involving an obstetrician who promised his patient that he would come to the hospital to deliver her baby, and after making the promise, he made a conscious decision not to go to the hospital to deliver the baby. In that particular case, the baby was decapitated by residents who tried their best to deliver the child, but had no experience in delivering a baby under these circumstances. The obstetrician argued that it was customary for him to await a call from the hospital before going to the delivery.[10] On appeal, the Supreme Court of Arizona held that a jury could find that the obstetrician's conduct was outrageous and warranted an award of compensatory damages for intentional infliction of emotional distress.[11]

In a similar case in Alabama, a woman's obstetrician failed to keep his promise to attend the delivery of her child, despite telling the nurses in the delivery room that he would be "right on over." The nurses called the doctor at his home at 3 A.M., when he said he would come right away. The baby was delivered by the nurses at 11 A.M. The baby was either stillborn or died within minutes after birth. Despite the fact that the child was too premature to live, the Alabama court held that the mother could recover for negligent infliction of emotional distress, even without proof of any physical harm. In addition, the court ruled that the doctor could be held liable for mental anguish caused by breach of an implied contract.[12]

The courts in the above cases adopted the view that a patient's emotional health and dignity deserved legal protection even in the absence of conduct on the part of the doctor that reflected a desire to cause any physical harm. The fact that the doctor knew of the likely physical and emotional harm that the patient would suffer was enough, in light of the ability of the doctor to use professional skills and resources to minimize the potential harm.

In her lawsuit, Mrs. Canty contended that by misrepresenting that the experienced doctor would insert the catheter in her daughter's heart, and then allowing the inexperienced doctor to do so, the doctors had engaged in outrageous conduct that intentionally inflicted severe emotional distress on the child's mother.

The hospital and the doctors responded that there was nothing wrong with a teaching hospital allowing the less experienced intensive care doctor to perform a cardiac procedure if the experienced cardiologist was present and believed that this was an appropriate opportunity for the specialty training doctor to gain experience in performing a challenging and invasive cardiac procedure. After all, teaching and learning while providing medical care are the principal goals of a teaching hospital, and everyone should know that, understand it, and support it. Otherwise, medical education would face an untenable barrier if each patient—rather than the physicians—had the right to decide who would perform medical procedures. The hospital and the doctors argued that the public can and should trust the judgment of the medical staff to decide when it is safe and appropriate for a person in training to perform a procedure.

Troubling issues of race and class simmer just beneath the surface of this case. However, most courts will not allow parties to raise these questions directly in a medical malpractice case, concerned that the speculation and prejudicial effects of raising these issues far outweigh their usefulness in fairly resolving the legal claims. The Canty family was a middle class African American family. One question that they asked themselves—one that was never posed directly to the jury—was whether these same doctors would have concluded that they could tell the family that the experienced specialist would insert the catheter, and then proceed to have a person in training do it, if the patient were the child of a wealthy or powerful politician. They also wondered that if was Carol a white teenager, one who looked like the daughter of these doctors, the doctors would have taken the same or a different approach to her medical care.

There is substantial data on health disparities related to healthcare decision making generally to justify concern on the part of minorities and other subordinated groups that they are being treated unfairly by healthcare providers. For example, several studies showed that surgeons, presented with the same symptoms, were significantly less likely to recommend proven and accepted surgical procedures for treatment of African Americans than they did for white patients.[13] The researchers speculate that the different treatment decisions were explainable not by conscious discrimination, but by unconscious bias. The impact of unconscious bias on medical care decision making is gathering support from a variety of studies that have now been done on the brain and how it influences decision making of all individuals.[14]

It is likely that the doctors who treated Carol did not make decisions based on a *conscious bias* against her because of her race, gender, or class.[15] Most likely, the doctors believed that they could safely perform the procedure with the inexperienced physician inserting the catheter and the experienced cardiologist overseeing the procedure and watching the monitor to determine whether the catheter was going into the right vessel. This was likely routine practice and consistent with the culture and practice of teaching institutions of medicine.

And as Atul Gawande observes his book on medical practice titled *Complications*: "This is the uncomfortable truth about teaching. By traditional ethics and public insistence (not to mention court rulings), a patient's right to the best care possible must trump the objective of training novices. We want perfection without practice. Yet everyone is harmed if no one is trained for the future. So learning is hidden, behind drapes and anesthesia and the elisions of language. Nor does the dilemma apply just to residents, physicians in training. In fact, the process of learning turns out to extend longer than most people know."[16] However, because sixteen-year-old Carol Canty presented the team of doctors with a complicated medical problem and because the procedure was critical to diagnosing the source of the problem and adopting an appropriate treatment modality, the circumstances cried out for extreme caution. Expert surgeons testified on behalf of the family that this was a case that needed the hands-on performance of the most experienced doctor. To view the case as an appropriate situation for training, as argued by the hospital and treating doctors, is troubling because it suggests that the teenager did not need or deserve the best efforts of the healthcare team to save her life.

After Carol died, her parents believed that the life of their child had been marginalized and the promise to her mother had been ignored.. The jury agreed, concluding that the doctors had intentionally engaged in conduct that was outrageous and inflicted severe emotional distress on Carol's mother. The state supreme court ruled that Mrs. Canty should not have been allowed to recover based on a tort claim of intentional infliction of emotional distress.[17] The court reasoned that she learned that an unapproved doctor did the procedure after the procedure was done and was not in the room to immediately witness the outrageous conduct when it occurred. In the court's view, the mother had an opportunity to absorb the shock because she did not actually witness her daughter's death during the procedure, and a person who learns of outrageous conduct after it occurs does not have a tort action for intentional infliction of emotional distress.

The case was sent back for another trial based on other legal theories of wrongdoing that the family had asserted, namely, negligence, fraud, and lack of an informed consent. The lawsuit did not produce a definitive resolution of the central ethical question concerning the use of power by a hospital or a physician to pursue medical training and education in direct violation of limits set by a child's parents. The intermediate court held that the jury could find the doctors' conduct outrageous. The state supreme court did not rule on whether the conduct could be considered outrageous. Significantly, only one justice who participated in the decision expressed the view that the conduct could not be reasonably characterized as outrageous conduct. The cardiologist and the resident physician in training for an intensive-care specialty never accepted or acknowledged that there was anything wrong with the approach they took to performing the procedure on the teenager. They believed that they were unfairly targeted and sued by distraught parents and aggressive lawyers. The family ended the lawsuit with a firm belief that the doctors did not respect the life of their child or their right and authority to make important medical decisions on behalf of their child.

Most of the important legal issues presented in this case were never resolved through this litigation because the parties settled the case. The family and healthcare providers were emotionally exhausted by the judicial proceedings and decided not to go through another trial. Instead, they participated in mediation outside of court and reached a confidential monetary settlement.

The facts and legal arguments in factual circumstances presented by Carol Canty and the other cases discussed in this chapter raise important public policy questions that await resolution by future court decisions or legislation. What role should courts and juries play in resolving claims of emotional and dignity harm caused by decisions of healthcare providers related to the delivery of healthcare? I submit that the law of medical malpractice has a critical role to play in regulating and deterring conduct that causes serious physical or emotional harm to a patient due to conscious or unconscious bias of healthcare providers.

The current healthcare financing system frequently results in people getting specific tests or treatment modalities based on the type of insurance they have. Moreover, people with the same insurance may also be treated differently based on their race or social class. Sometimes the difference is prompted by conscious bias, and at other times unconscious bias impacts the healthcare decision making.

Consider the following statement by surgeon and writer Atul Gawande, acknowledging the vulnerability of patients to medical practice based on class: "When an attending physician brings a sick family member in for surgery, people at the hospital think hard about how much to let the trainees participate. . . . Conversely, the ward services and clinics where residents have the most responsibility are populated by the poor, the uninsured, the drunk, and the demented. Residents have few opportunities nowadays to operate independently, without the attending docs scrubbed in, but when we do—as we must before graduating and going out to operate on our own—it is generally on these, the humblest of patients."[18] Patients and families who become aware of the difference in care are usually indignant, and at times suffer severe emotional distress. Not every indignity warrants a legal remedy. Most should be handled by the healthcare profession and institutions based on professional standards governing the delivery of healthcare. However, when the conduct of the provider reflects a conscious or callous disregard of a patient's right to dignity, a legal remedy is appropriate.

Tort Law and Patient Autonomy

The development of legal rules in tort law in the twentieth century represents a shining example of how important it is for the public to have a means of meaningful input into the manner that any profession or business, particularly doctors, hospitals, and insurance companies, provides service to members of the public who lack the power and knowledge to influence industry practices. At least since the beginning of the twentieth century, American tort law has taken steps to protect the dignity of a patient by mandating that a doctor obtain the patient's consent to surgery. However, in the 1970s, the consent required by the law became more stringent, mandating that the consent must be "informed" to be legally valid. The legal doctrine of informed consent requires a doctor to disclose the material risks, benefits, and alternatives associated with rendering care so that the patient may make an intelligent decision as to whether to consent to treatment.[19]

The seminal case that launched the modern legal construction of the informed consent doctrine concerned a nineteen-year-old who underwent surgery to treat his back and was paralyzed following the surgery. He learned then that the specific surgery performed carried a 1 percent risk of paralysis even if done properly. In the landmark decision *Canterbury v. Spence*, Judge Spotswood Robinson, writing for the Court of Appeals in the District of Columbia, declared that failing to disclose the risks of the surgery violated the patient's right to an "informed consent."[20] A violation of the patient's right to medical information subjected the doctor to tort liability, even if the doctor's conduct conformed to the custom adhered to by other doctors acting in the same or similar circumstances. The *Canterbury* decision and its progeny had a profound impact on the practice of medicine, shifting the power of medical decision making for elective surgical procedures from the doctors to patients. State courts throughout the nation considered the issue of consent over the next few decades, and all agreed that informed consent was an essential requirement for validating medical procedures that posed a risk of harm to patients.

Adjustment to the new legal standard required a transformation in the culture of medicine to incorporate a demand for respect of the individual patient's right to decide what was to be done with her body, regardless of what the medical community thought was best to do in diagnosing and treating illnesses. The surgeon in *Canterbury* tried to defend withholding information about the 1 percent risk of paralysis from the patient, arguing that "communication of that risk to the patient is not good medical practice because it might deter patients from undergoing needed surgery and might produce adverse psychological reactions which could preclude the success of the operation."[21] Judge Robinson's opinion in *Canterbury* affirmed the decision-making rights of patients. He dismissed the paternalistic approach advocated by the surgeon that would allow him to make decisions he thought were in the best interest of the patient without the patient's approval. According to *Canterbury* and most courts who have addressed the question, a doctor has a duty to disclose "material risks, benefits, and alternatives" to a proposed medical procedure even if the disclosure may persuade the patient to make the wrong medical decision from the perspective of the physician.[22]

The bottom line is that the values and goals of professions and businesses do not always harmonize with the values of consumers and members of the general public. When these values clash, law matters more than ever.

Chapter 5

The Love Doctor

Sex and Gender Bias; Breach of Trust and Abuse of Power

James Burt believed that women were not properly constructed anatomically to gain maximum pleasure from sex. He theorized that they would get more pleasure from sex if their vaginas were reconstructed.[1] Unlike the ordinary citizen who might muse in such bizarre terms, James Burt felt empowered to fix the problem. He was a licensed physician in the state of Ohio who practiced obstetrics and gynecology.[2] In his practice hundreds of women came to him for delivery of their babies, for hysterectomies, or for a variety of other problems associated with their reproductive systems. Doctor Burt decided that when women came to him for medical care, he would improve their sex lives by reconstructing their vaginas.[3] He adopted an approach to this reconstruction that he dubbed "the surgery of love." He performed this surgery on hundreds of women without advising them of the true nature of the surgery and his purpose in doing it.[4]

Dr. Burt was a member of the medical staff of Saint Elizabeth Hospital and used his staff privileges at the hospital to perform this unorthodox and unproven surgery on hundreds of women.[5] The results of this surgery were devastating to many of the women, physically and emotionally. The surgery caused permanent disabilities, including sexual dysfunction, scarring, kidney infections, blood clots, and heart attacks.[6] Years later, a follow-up doctor who examined one of the women who had undergone the surgery said that he had never seen anything like it in terms of physiology and anatomy during his practice or his training.

Many members of the hospital medical staff, as well as others in the state of Ohio, were aware of what Dr. Burt was doing, but did not take definitive steps to stop him. The hospital decided that rather than prohibiting the surgery, it would have the women sign a consent form that read as follows:

Dear Patient:

The Executive Committee of the Medical Staff of St. Elizabeth Medical Center wishes to inform you that the "female coital area reconstruction" surgery you are about to undergo is:

1. Not documented by ordinary standards of scientific reporting and publication.
2. Not a generally accepted procedure.
3. As yet not duplicated by other investigators.
4. Detailed only in non-scientific literature.

You should be informed that the Executive Committee of the Medical Staff considers the aforementioned procedure an unproven, non-standard practice of gynecology.[7]

The hospital took the position that it had adequately discharged its duty to Dr. Burt's patients by disclosing the hospital staff's view of his surgery and having the patients sign this disclosure form.

Dr. Burt did not attempt to hide his surgery from the public. Indeed, he was so proud of it that he wrote a book titled *Surgery of Love*. Many of his patients did, however, assert that they were never informed by Dr. Burt of the specific nature of the surgery and its purpose. It does seem clear that none of the doctors, nurses, or other members of the hospital's staff ever reported him to the medical licensing authority. The first physician to file a report with the licensing authority was Dr. Bradley Busacco, a follow-up surgeon who examined one of Dr. Burt's patients twenty-two years after the latter had performed the surgery.[8] Dr. Busacco felt morally bound to report Dr. Burt to the licensing authority. When Dr. Busacco examined the patient, he was appalled. Her vagina had been so altered and mutilated by Dr. Burt's surgery that Dr. Busacco reported that he could not recognize her anatomy and had never seen anything like it in his medical practice or training.[9] The vaginal reconstruction surgery included vaginal redirection and elongation and a general restructuring of body organs, muscle, and tissue.

Dr. Busacco also concluded that he had a moral obligation to serve as an expert in the patient's medical malpractice case brought against Dr. Burt and the hospital.[10] The report to the licensing agency precipitated an investigation by the licensing authority that forced Dr. Burt to surrender his medical license and sign an agreement to never perform surgery again.[11] Dr. Burt then left Ohio and retired in Florida.[12] He also declared bankruptcy.

One of the attorneys who represented more than forty of Dr. Burt's patients in medical malpractice cases reported that the trial courts dismissed the first lawsuits brought by women against Dr. Burt because no doctor was willing to testify as an expert for the women.[13] No doctor was willing to state that Dr. Burt had breached the standard of care of the profession and that the breach caused the injuries to his patients.[14]

The facts set forth below are taken verbatim from an appellate court decision in Ohio describing the medical treatment and resulting injuries experienced by one of the women.

Moore's lawsuit stems from surgery performed by Dr. James C. Burt, then a physician with staff privileges at SEMC. Moore consulted Burt in 1976 and explained that she was experiencing urinary incontinence. She underwent a bladder suspension and vaginal reconstruction surgery the following year. Moore returned to SEMC throughout 1978 for restructuring because her incisions failed to heal properly.

In the following years, Moore developed a variety of ailments, including recurring kidney infections, bowel problems, worsened incontinence, backaches, and depression. Dissatisfied with her physical condition, Moore confronted Burt, who told her she had "inferior tissue" and that her problems would improve.

Still suffering, however, Moore contacted an attorney around 1980 and considered suing Burt. She also approached the Montgomery County Medical Society and inquired about any complaints on file concerning the doctor. Moore was "given the impression" that no complaints had been registered. She subsequently decided not to pursue legal action.

In October 1988, Moore viewed the "West 57th Street" television program regarding Burt's surgical practices and wondered whether Burt had performed his "love surgery" upon her. The following month, she also read a newspaper article recounting the doctor's unorthodox surgery.

Upon receiving this information, Moore consulted Dr. Bradley Busacco. The doctor conducted an examination and opined that Burt's surgeries caused Moore's physical problems. Consequently, Moore filed a complaint in April 1989, alleging, in relevant part, that SEMC negligently selected and retained Burt, negligently performed peer review, and fraudulently concealed its knowledge of Burt's surgery.[15]

Another woman who underwent Dr. Burt's surgery and brought suit against him after viewing the *West 57th* television program was Coney Mitchell.[16] Mitchell first saw Dr. Burt in 1985 due to bladder and pelvic pain during sexual intercourse. Dr. Burt informed her that a surgery to "'lift' her bladder 'out of the way'" would correct her condition and pain.[17] Mitchell signed a consent form for the surgery, and "apparently" signed the special consent form that Saint Elizabeth Hospital required for Dr. Burt's reconstruction surgeries as well.[18]

After her surgery, Mitchell's symptoms became worse. In addition to pain, infections, and bowel problems, after a failed attempt to resume sexual relations with her husband, Mitchell bled profusely and found that her vagina had been "sewn up."[19] After viewing the *West 57th* television program, Mitchell sought care from Dr. Busacco.[20] Dr. Busacco tried every corrective surgery he could, but ultimately "informed Mitchell that she had been surgically mutilated."[21]

Other women who underwent Dr. Burt's surgery also told their stories in public. One woman whose life was forever affected by Dr. Burt's surgical experimentation was Cheryl Dillon. Dillon was only thirty-six years old when Dr. Burt recommended that she have a hysterectomy as opposed to the minor bladder surgery that could have resolved her medical condition.[22] During the hysterectomy, Dr. Burt also relocated Dillon's vagina and removed her clitoral hood—two things that Dillon neither knew would happen nor consented to.[23] As a result, Dillon could no longer sit down, have sex with her husband, or even wear pants without experiencing excruciating pain.[24] Ultimately, the consequences of Dr. Burt's surgery ended Dillon's marriage. She found out about the unorthodox surgery only after she sought medical treatment from a different doctor who informed Dillon that she had been mutilated.[25]

Jimmie Browning was one of Dr. Burt's patients with a similarly devastating story. Browning first sought medical treatment for bladder infections and difficulty urinating.[26] Her doctor sent her to Dr. Burt for an "exploratory pelvic laparotomy with lysis and vaginoplasty," and Dr. Burt said that he would do the surgery with other cosmetic components.[27] Although the hospital contended that Browning had signed its consent form indicating that the procedure was unproven, Browning did not recall signing it.[28] After the procedure, Browning's symptoms became worse: she could no longer have sex without extreme pain, and she experienced severe kidney problems.[29] In an attempt to try to fix the mutilation, Browning had a series of sixteen surgeries, none of which fixed her condition.[30] Browning brought suit against Dr. Burt for medical malpractice and against Saint Elizabeth Hospital for negligence.[31]

Medical Ethics and Professional Power

In reviewing the James Burt case, it is frightening and appalling to see that he was permitted to perform unorthodox mutilating surgery on women for a period of twenty-two years with the full knowledge of hospital and medical staff. Neither the administration of the hospital nor doctors on staff reported him to the board of medical ethics. The medical profession is supposed to be the first line of defense for public safety, putting the best interest of the patients above that of their fellow professionals. Consequently, we delegate to the medical profession, and other professions, the authority to determine who is qualified to practice and to monitor their performance while they engage in practice. Each state can set its own standards for licensing, but in essence the medical profession defines the qualifications. Moreover, after one becomes a member of the medical profession, it is the medical custom that determines the standard of care to which its members must adhere.

One of the basic tenets of the Hippocratic Oath taken by all physicians is to first do no harm. The question arises as to what a physician or nurse should do if she becomes aware that another healthcare professional is causing harm to patients. The medical profession relies upon peer review to assess quality of care and to protect the public from unjustified risks. Effective peer review requires active and candid reviews and assessments carried out by professional peers. In modern-day medicine that means that they must review the medical services rendered by their peers as part of hospital care. Consequently, the medical and administrative staff of the hospital had a responsibility to review what Dr. Burt was doing and to protect the public from unorthodox and unsafe practices. Instead, the hospital chose to have patients sign a consent form that effectively waived their right to receive the established standard of care. If medical ethics do not protect the patient, the last line of defense is usually a medical malpractice claim, which I discuss below.

Law Matters

The first legal hurdle Dr. Burt's injured patients had to overcome in order to bring a medical malpractice lawsuit was to establish that it had been brought in a timely manner. By the time many of the lawsuits were filed, Dr. Burt had left the state of Ohio and moved to Florida. He had also filed for bankruptcy. The women sued the hospital, alleging that it, as well as Dr. Burt, was liable for the harm they suffered. The courts in Ohio had to decide whether to allow the lawsuits to proceed or to dismiss them because they were filed more than two years after Dr. Burt performed the surgery that caused the injuries.

Most states have a statute of limitations of one or two years for bringing a negligence claim against a physician or a hospital. The plaintiffs who wanted to sue Dr. Burt had to confront the fact that their surgeries had taken place many years beyond the two-year statute of limitations. The legal issue presented to the court was whether there was an exception to the running of the statute of limitations from the time of the surgery. The court found that there was an exception that allowed the statute to begin to run from the time the patients knew or should have known that they had been the victims of medical malpractice. Consequently, the court focused on when the television show that revealed that many women had been victims of Dr. Burt aired. Some of the patients were able to continue with their claims and get a judgment from the court or a verdict from a jury. Others were precluded from proceeding to a trial against Dr. Burt on the grounds that the statute of limitations had run before they filed suit.

As noted above, Dr. Burt had declared bankruptcy and left the state. He did not hire an attorney to defend himself, and he defaulted on most of the lawsuits by failing to file an answer to the legal complaints. The courts entered a judgment against Dr. Burt by default. However, in a civil case to collect money from a judgment, the litigant must find either insurance or assets to attach. It is unclear from the public records I reviewed whether Dr. Burt had insurance or assets. However, since the work had been done at Saint Elizabeth's Hospital, the plaintiffs chose to sue the hospital and hold it responsible. A rule of law adopted in most states provides that a hospital has an independent duty to a patient with respect to selecting and retaining only competent staff members. In addition, many states apply a legal rule that imposes a responsibility on the hospital to oversee the care that is rendered to patients in the hospital.

The issue in the cases brought against Dr. Burt centered on whether the hospital violated its duty to patients by allowing him to continue to perform the surgery in the hospital when it knew or should have known that his practices were not conforming to the standard of care. Those questions would have to be resolved by a jury in situations where the statute limitations had not run.

In the case of *Browning v. Burt* the court observed: "A [hospital] is not required to pass upon the efficacy of treatment; it may not decide for a doctor whether an operation is necessary, or, if one be necessary, the nature thereof; but it owes to every patient whom it admits the duty of saving him from an illegal operation [or] false, fraudulent, or fictitious medical treatment."[32]

In several of the cases that were tried, there were multimillion-dollar verdicts rendered against Dr. Burt and the hospital. The damages in such cases are measured by the loss of income of the individuals due to the injury and the medical expenses incurred, as well as the pain and suffering. These cases held that a hospital has a duty to oversee the practice of medicine that is going on within its walls.

In the cases brought against Dr. Burt, the court determined that the key legal consideration was whether the hospital had properly overseen Dr. Burt's surgical practice when they knew or should have known that he was not conforming to medical standards and was causing serious harm to parties. In *Browning v. Burt* the court concluded that it was for a jury to decide whether the hospital breached its duty to its patients to exercise reasonable care to ensure that the surgery being performed by Dr. Burt was not false or fraudulent.[33]

The law imposing a duty on a hospital to protect patients is even broader in most states. Courts have endorsed the view that a hospital has at least four duties to a patient to exercise reasonable care with respect to the following matters: (1) to provide adequate facilities and equipment; (2) to grant privileges to and retain only competent staff; (3) to oversee the care rendered by the staff in the hospital; and (4) to adopt and enforce policies to assure competent care.[34] If the court in Ohio had adopted these more comprehensive rules governing a hospital's duties to patients, there would have been no doubt that the hospital breached its duty to protect the patients from the risks and harm associated with Dr. Burt's surgery.

Modern healthcare usually relies on hospital facilities, equipment, and personnel to diagnose and treat serious medical problems. The hospital, consequently, stands in a unique position to identify, control, and report recurring breaches of medical standards of care and professional ethics that pose serious risk of harm to patients. It is especially important that lawmakers and community residents insist that hospitals make a good faith effort to protect against the dangers posed by healthcare professionals to the health and dignity of patients.

Chapter 6

Innovative Therapy and Medical Experimentation

The Maverick Surgeon: Medical Experimentation on Children?

On February 19, 2006, Dr. William Norwood, a renowned cardiac surgeon who specialized in performing surgery on children born with heart defects, was escorted from A. I. duPont Hospital for Children by a security guard. Dr. Norwood had just been fired as chief of cardiothoracic surgery in the special unit known as the Nemours Cardiac Center.[1] The U.S. Food and Drug Administration (FDA) and the Delaware Department of Health's investigations into the cardiac center had concluded that Dr. Norwood and his associates implanted a device in children's hearts that had not been approved by the FDA or the hospital's Institutional Review Board (IRB).[2] The surgeons had attempted to correct heart defects in several children by implanting a device, specifically a covered stent, in their hearts.

Federal statutes and regulations attempt to protect consumers who need medical devices and drugs by requiring the products to be tested in clinical trials before they are sold for use in medical care. One important procedural protection mandates that before the medical investigation occurs, the proposed clinical trials must be evaluated and approved by an IRB, an independent panel associated with the hospital or other healthcare provider.[3] Federal regulations mandate that the IRB must be an independent interdisciplinary group responsible for assessing whether the goals and design of the proposed study make the study worthwhile, and that the subjects of the study have given an informed consent to participate in the study.[4]

Dr. Norwood originally came to his position of renown in the medical community by pioneering a surgical technique two decades before his exit from the Nemours Cardiac Center. This original surgery was accepted by the medical community at large and was performed by Dr. Norwood in one stage. The medical community acknowledged Dr. Norwood's pioneering surgical efforts by calling the new procedure the Norwood procedure. Later, other surgeons and Dr. Norwood adopted an approach of performing the surgery in three stages, and the three- stage approach proved safer and more effective for the treatment of the heart defect. Other children who received the treatment given at the Nemours Cardiac Center submitted to a nonsurgical approach, one that Dr. Norwood hoped would be his latest advancement in medical treatment for the heart defect called hypoplastic left heart syndrome, or HLHS. This syndrome involves the severe underdevelopment of the left side of the heart and related structures, such as the mitral valve and the aorta. They are so underdeveloped that they are nonfunctional. The defect is uniformly fatal without intervention.[5]

The new approach, adopted by Dr. Norwood as an alternative to the surgical procedure and customarily used at the second stage, entailed inserting a stent to correct the blood flow in the heart. Dr. Norwood hypothesized that this new nonsurgical approach would be effective and safe for correcting specific heart defects in children. This chapter tells the stories of the legal cases brought on behalf of the patients who underwent either the surgical approach or the insertion of a stent. While several important cases cannot be discussed in detail due to confidential settlement agreements, others are part of public court records and provide a basis for understanding the regulatory approach to protecting consumers from unproven drugs and devices.[6] They also give us an insight into a system where medical practice is governed by the principles of a free market, with a hands-off approach by the government.

Law Matters

Federal law provides patients with three important protections from the abuse and misuse of power by physicians who plan to provide care that departs from standards adopted by the profession. First, if federal funding supports the healthcare being given to the patient, the law mandates that the doctor get an informed consent from the patient to the proposed treatment. Second, if the proposed treatment is a part of medical experimentation or a clinical trial, an IRB must review and approve the proposed plan. Third, if a new drug or device is employed, the person or company who supplies the drug or device to the doctor must secure the approval of the FDA to provide the drug or device for specific uses on patients. The parents or guardians of the children who underwent the attempted correction of their heart defects with the stents that Dr. Norwood and his associates implanted into the hearts of their infant patients alleged that they were not aware that the procedures were performed without complying with any of those federal mandates. In addition, some of the parents filed civil lawsuits against the company and its CEO who supplied the stents to Norwood and his associates, alleging that they violated the federal food and drug laws in supplying the surgeons with an unapproved device.[7]

In addition to the lawsuits brought based on the implanting of the stents, more than fifteen families filed lawsuits against Dr. Norwood alleging that the way he performed surgery on their children deviated from the established standard of care for surgically correcting these heart defects. Most of the lawsuits asserted that the specific act of negligence was that in preparing the infants for the surgery, their brains should have been "cooled" for significantly longer than Dr. Norwood allowed. The purpose of cooling the brain was to protect it against injury during the period that the patient's heart was stopped to permit the performance of the surgery. The patients who alleged negligence on the part of Dr. Norwood contended that the established standard of care was to cool the infant's brain for at least ten minutes. Dr. Norwood, however, followed a practice of performing the heart surgery as soon as the patient's temperature reached a specific level. In most of the cases that were brought against Dr. Norwood, the patients alleged they sustained brain injuries because the surgeon had allowed insufficient time for cooling.

Legal Cases

In addition to the civil lawsuits brought by the children and their parents, the FDA brought a criminal action against the company that supplied the stents used by Norwood and his associates, as well as the CEO of the company. The suit was resolved quickly through a guilty plea in which the company agreed to pay a fine of $2.3 million for distributing an unapproved device.[8]

The civil actions against the company met with less success. Emphasizing the legal requirement under Delaware tort law for an injured party to prove that the wrongful conduct was the cause in fact of the harm, the trial courts dismissed the children's claims of a right to compensation from the company and its CEO. The courts held that even though the company violated the federal statute, no compensation was due because the experts retained by the children acknowledged that the stents caused harm that may also have been caused if the doctors had performed surgery to correct the heart defects rather than implanting the stents. The courts did, however, rule that the children were entitled to recover from the company the financial cost of medical monitoring to assess and treat any illnesses or disabilities that may manifest in the future that were caused by the stents implanted in their hearts.

The civil lawsuits brought against Dr. Norwood based on allegations of negligence in the way he performed surgery to correct the heart defects extended over many years and resulted in some verdicts in favor of the children, some in favor of Norwood, and ultimately a settlement of most of the claims.

A significant legal hurdle to prevailing on the claims of negligence is the legal rule that requires a plaintiff prove that the negligent conduct was the cause in fact of the injuries for which he seeks compensation. The children were born with serious heart defects that placed them at risk of death. The correction of the heart defects involved a procedure that posed inherent risks even if the surgery was done in accordance with customary standards. Consequently, even though the jury was persuaded, based on medical evidence and expert testimony, that Dr. Norwood was negligent, they were challenged by the required legal determination of whether the negligence was the cause of the harm.

An initial case where a patient had severe brain damage was tried for several weeks before a jury and settled for a substantial sum of money before the jury reached a verdict. The amount of the settlement was subjected to a confidential settlement agreement. A second case was tried, and the jury decided it in favor of Dr. Norwood. A third case was tried resulting in a verdict for Dr. Norwood that was reversed on appeal, and then retried. At the retrial, the jury found that Dr. Norwood was negligent and that his negligence caused the death of the infant. Finally, the parties negotiated a settlement of all the remaining cases.

The pivotal question is aptly stated in a newspaper article reporting on Norwood's ouster from his position as chief of pediatric cardiac surgery: "Did Dr. Norwood go too far?"[9] The answer depends on the perspective, values, and priorities of the person answering the question. For reasons set forth below, I believe he went much too far beyond the medical, legal, and ethical standards that should guide the development and delivery of medical care to children.

Lessons Learned

The law plays a critical role in protecting patient health and the dignity of patients when doctors decide to employ new approaches to treating serious illness in patients. The governing law consists of statutes, regulations, and general tort law. A review of the facts and law applicable to the lawsuits arising out of Dr. Norwood's approach to the practice of medicine illuminates several important lessons relevant to law, medicine, and ethics.

The first lesson as to law is a recognition of the critical role that the statutes and regulations serve in protecting patient safety and dignity.

The second is that novel medical practices present special challenges to courts, lawyers, and juries as they attempt to assess the reasonableness of innovative therapy. From a trial perspective, a strong case of medical negligence accompanied by complex evidence of medical causation increases the uncertainty of the outcome. It is extremely difficult for courts to serve as fair and neutral gatekeepers who do not usurp the constitutional responsibility and power of jurors.

The core lesson applicable to the practice of medicine is the risk of allowing a consolidation of power in one doctor who can proceed to make life-and-death decisions without review or criticism from his peers.

The final lesson grows out of a recognition of the importance of providing children with the protection of the informed decision making of their parents prior to the implementation of new therapies. Moreover, some circumstances warrant a requirement of a review by an IRB or ethics committee to assure that the proposed therapy is in the best interest of the child.

Legal Regulation of Professional Medical Care

Doctors who perform new medical procedures are free from governmental regulation and guidelines, except when the new approaches to medical care entail the use of drugs or devices that have not been approved by the FDA. When new medical therapy is undertaken without using new drugs or devices, the law has taken a hands-off approach, relying on the standards of the profession to protect the consumer. The protection of professional standards usually works because doctors who deviate from the standard of care established by similarly trained and educated doctors are subject to both peer review in hospitals and medical malpractice lawsuits.

The hands-off approach, deferring totally to the professional standards and judgments of the industry regarding risks and benefits, stands in stark contrast to the governmental approach to consumer safety when drugs or devices are involved. Federal statutes authorize the FDA to establish and enforce standards governing what level of safety and effectiveness a drug or device must demonstrate—based on scientific studies—before a manufacturer can make the drug or device available to the medical community for therapeutic uses with patients. When the FDA approves a new drug or device for use, the manufacturer is permitted to market the drug or device only for the specific uses for which it has been approved.

Significantly, while the regulations govern the marketing conduct of manufacturers, the law does not apply to doctors, who are free to use the drug or device in treating a patient. This decision is instead based solely on the standards of the profession and the judgment of an individual practitioner. The freedom to use a drug or device for unapproved uses is known as "off-label use."[10]

Consumer protection from unreasonably dangerous off-label uses by the medical community lies in the standards and ethics of the profession and medical malpractice law.

In short, physicians who solely implement innovative medical treatment are not subject to FDA regulations, and when they engage in experimentation with a research protocol in order to test an innovative medical intervention, they must follow federal regulations.[11] However, a physician could *get around FDA regulations by going straight to implementing innovative therapy for an individual patient* as opposed to experimenting with that therapy beforehand.[12] This legal loophole is one that allowed Dr. Norwood to act as he did.

The difference between the approach used by Dr. Norwood and other surgeons was that the others cooled their patients' brains for at least fifteen minutes, while Dr. Norwood alone cooled his patients' brains as fast as possible—sometimes for as little as four minutes. Scientific studies, combined with the clinical experience of other surgeons, have concluded that the longer cooling period was a critical safety measure.[13]

Established tort law doctrine applicable to medical malpractice cases offers the following rules for determining whether a doctor has engaged in negligent conduct: The doctor is required to exercise the degree of skill and care in diagnosing and treating a patient that would be exercised by a reasonable doctor acting in the same or similar circumstances. To determine what a reasonable doctor would do, an expert witness is required to testify and express opinions as to what would customarily be done by other doctors in the same or similar circumstances.

There are two significant exceptions to reliance on custom. One is that the doctor must exercise his/her best judgment, and sometimes that leads to a justified deviation from custom. The other is that, in deciding whether to follow custom, the doctor must give due regard to the advanced state of medical knowledge. A review of Dr. Norwood's approach to surgery reveals the challenge of applying traditional tort doctrine to innovative therapy. The task is made easier if the court finds that federal or state statutes or regulations dictate what the doctor must do in the specific circumstances. It is much more difficult to assess the reasonableness of the doctor's conduct if the court and jury must rely on conflicting expert opinions.

Trying a New Approach with a New Device

Numerous mothers who gave birth to children born with HLHS and other heart defects entrusted Dr. Norwood and his associates to perform surgery on their children. For some of the children, in addition to the rapid cooling times for the brain, Dr. Norwood and his associates decided to try another new approach rather than using the established three-stage surgical repair. They decided to try to avoid the third stage of surgical repair by inserting a covered stent (via a catheter) in the child's heart, theorizing that the catheter could provide the final channel through which blood would flow. This final channel for blood flow had previously always been achieved by the performance of the third surgery, and use of the stent would allow the child to forego the trauma of a third heart surgery.

Dr. Norwood and his team faced several barriers to testing their hypothesis about the potential safety and effectiveness of the stent. First, a stent is a medical device that cannot be marketed by a manufacturer without the approval of the FDA, and the FDA had not approved the device they planned to use for the specific procedure they intended to perform. Second, the performance of a medical procedure on a human being as part of a clinical trial required the approval of an IRB. Third, the performance of the procedure would require that the doctors inform each child's parents of the risks, benefits, and alternatives related to the new catheter procedure.

According to the FDA's Modernization Act, devices implanted in or near a patient's heart are given the highest FDA classification and must meet the toughest regulatory requirements in order to be used, since they can cause significant risk to patients (as was the case with the new stent Dr. Norwood was testing).[14] In order to use experimental pediatric cardiovascular devices, a physician must first obtain premarket approval from the FDA.[15] Physicians and hospitals who are working toward medical innovations often have difficulty meeting these regulations since they are constantly trying to balance taking risks necessary to make medical advances in order to save more lives with following the rules to maintain patient safety.[16] It is precisely this difficulty that Dr. Norwood was faced with, and his solution ended in his ultimate departure from duPont and multiple lawsuits.

The Norwood team took the position that they did not need the permission of the FDA or the IRB to insert the catheter into a child's heart. While conceding that this was a novel approach to therapy, they noted that the FDA regulates the sale and marketing of drugs and devices, but it does not have authority to regulate the practice of medicine. Thus, they did not need FDA approval to use the device. As for the IRB, the surgeons believed that they had enough approval from the IRB because they informed the chair of the hospital IRB that they intended to use the device, and he informed them that they did not need IRB approval because they were not engaged in medical research. Finally, they contended that they had the consent of the children's parents to use the stent.

The need for consent of the parents, however, proved to be the requirement that was the undoing of the Norwood cardiac practice at Nemours. One of the hospital administrators tried to assemble the forms the parents purportedly signed to give consent for the catheter procedure, but he could not find all of them. He contacted one of the families, the Guinans, and asked them to sign a form and send it back to the hospital. The Guinans became suspicious and refused to sign the form, advising the administrator that this form had never been presented to them and that they had not signed it before and would not sign it then.[17] Mrs. Guinan contacted the FDA and the Delaware Department of Health, and the resulting investigation led to a decision by Nemours to revoke the privileges of Dr. Norwood and one of his associates to practice at Nemours.

The Legal Rules Governing Medical Malpractice Claims

As stated earlier in this chapter, medical malpractice law defers to healthcare professionals to determine what care is reasonable and what care is unreasonable. Several rules are routinely announced to juries. First, a doctor is not a guarantor of the results of medical care. Second, a bad result is not evidence of negligence. Third, an error of judgment does not amount to negligence unless another doctor says that it does. Fourth, and most importantly, doctors follow different schools of thought as to the proper way to provide medical care for an illness or procedure, and they can choose any one they prefer without being negligent for their choice.[18]

The last rule is especially problematic for a patient who receives care from a doctor who dances to the beat of a different drummer, and the patient does not find out until after the dance is over. In most of these lawsuits, parents alleged that they did not learn until after surgery was performed on their child that Dr. Norwood used an approach to heart surgery most other doctors saw as dangerous. However, in a medical malpractice case, the parents had to persuade a court and jury that the approach used was not only ill advised, but outside of the acceptable standard of care, and this presented a formidable challenge by itself. Added to the challenge was Dr. Norwood's reputation as an internationally famous pediatric cardiac surgeon who had been on the frontier of this kind of surgery, and who had initially played such a significant role in advancing the surgery.

The lawsuits against Dr. Norwood also raised complicated legal issues regarding the power of a surgeon to employ untested and/or innovative surgical approaches to treat children, and to include the children in projects that are aimed as much at medical research as they are in treating the child. Federal regulations prohibit making children subjects in research projects that do not have as a primary goal treatment of the children.[19] Pure medical experimentation aimed solely at advancing knowledge, with no expected benefit to the medical subject, is regarded as both illegal and unethical when applied to children. However, when the goals are mixed, that is, they both advance scientific knowledge and treat a disease or ailment of the patient, children may be included in the project provided the specific treatment can be selected because it is in the best interest of the child. If the treatment requires the use of a drug or medical device, FDA regulations also apply. If no drug or device is involved, physicians are expected to choose therapies in accordance with prevailing medical standards.[20]

The lawsuits against Dr. Norwood based on his use of a rapid cooling method, which differed from the prevailing approach of other pediatric cardiac surgeons, rested on arguments that he violated the right of the parents to give an informed consent and that his approach fell below acceptable standards of care as defined by other surgeons. The claims based on Dr. Norwood's insertion of an unapproved device in the children's hearts rested on arguments that he was negligent in not getting the prior approval of a hospital IRB. Additionally, to obtain legal consent from the parents of the children, he should have informed them of the experimental nature of the procedure he proposed to perform.

In one of the first death cases in this group, the jury reached a verdict that Dr. Norwood had failed to comply with the standard of care as required by his profession, and that this failure caused the death of the child. The jury awarded the family $650,000, a small sum considering the heartbreak they had suffered. The verdict represented only a symbolic victory. Yet, to the parents it represented a critical affirmation of the dignity of their son and the wrong that had been done. With respect to a judgment about what standard of medical care should have been followed, the verdict said to Dr. Norwood that what he was doing was wrong. Additionally, Dr. Norwood had been told many times by juries and his colleagues that the technique he was using to cool the children in preparation for surgery deviated from current medical practice standards. It is unlikely that this verdict had any impact on his state of mind and assessment of his work as a physician.

Each of the cases against Dr. Norwood and his associates for placing a stent in the hearts of children was dismissed by the trial court, notwithstanding evidence that the stents had not been approved by the FDA or an IRB and that the parents had not been informed of the experimental nature and purpose of using the stent instead of the established third stage of surgery. The court ruled to dismiss the cases because the plaintiffs' experts could not testify with certainty that the stent caused the ensuing complications. This meant that the claims could not meet an essential element of proof in a malpractice case, namely, that the negligence caused the harm.

The problem of proving causation in the stent cases was that some children who underwent the third stage of surgery experienced the same or similar adverse reactions or bad results as the children who had the stent inserted. Consequently, even if Dr. Norwood's use of the stent was unreasonable or violated the parents' right to give an informed consent, the parents could not recover in a tort case because they had to meet the burden of proving that more probably than not their children would be alive if the third surgery had been done instead of using the stent.

The doctors who used the stents for an unapproved purpose no doubt felt vindicated by the court's rulings dismissing the negligence claims. The parents, on the other hand, were emotionally devastated by the injuries and deaths of their children, and the court rulings added insult to injury. The court granted the defendants' motions in at least two of the stent cases, ordering the families to pay the litigation expenses allowed by rule to the prevailing party. Fortunately, two of the families had received monetary settlements of claims they had brought against the manufacturer of the unapproved stent who had supplied the stents to Dr. Norwood and his associates.

Lest there be any doubt about their feelings of indignation and mistreatment, Dr. Norwood and his associates who had been forced out of their medical practices at Nemours filed a lawsuit against Nemours, alleging that Nemours breached a contract with them and owed them money. The resolution of that lawsuit is not a part of the public record.

Medical Research, Ethics, and Law

In this chapter's final analysis, Dr. Norwood's career presents a complex puzzle of medical, legal, and ethical issues. Medically, he deserves credit for saving the lives of many babies who would have died if he had not discovered a surgical approach that enabled children with HLHS to live. In response to a two-part series in *Philadelphia Magazine* titled "Did Dr. Norwood Go too Far,?[21] one mother whose son was successfully operated on by Dr. Norwood twenty years earlier commented after reading media accounts of Dr. Norwood's being ousted from his position at duPont Hospital for Children, "Please do not lose sight of the fact that there are many children out there who would not be here if not for the wonderful care they received from Dr. Norwood."

Similarly, the CEO of the company that supplied the stents to Dr. Norwood was admired and respected by many in the medical community, and his criminal conviction for violating the federal regulations governing the distribution of medical devices evoked a public defense on his behalf, including an article arguing that punishing this CEO may end up killing children because doctors will not be able to get the customized devices they need to save their patients' lives.[22]

In contrast, a board certified pediatric cardiac surgeon who, after reviewing the medical records of many of the children on whom Dr. Norwood operated, was so disturbed by the high number of deaths and injuries associated with Dr. Norwood's surgeries on children spanning over a decade that he was willing to take time away from a busy and demanding surgical practice on infants to testify that Dr. Norwood's approach to surgery was unsafe and violated current medical standards. To make it clear that he was not motivated by personal gain, this surgeon insisted on not being personally paid for the time he spent testifying, but instead had the attorneys representing the families make contributions to charities that he designated.

Ethically, Dr. Norwood defended his use of an unapproved stent in children on the basis that he was providing innovative therapy to the children and had the authority and responsibility as a surgeon to use his experience and best judgment in selecting the therapeutic approach that he in good faith believed was in the best interest of his patients, and in these circumstances there was no need for approval of the FDA or an IRB at his hospital. Dr. Norwood offered the expert testimony of a highly regarded medical ethicist to support his position. The testimony of Dr. Norwood and his medical ethicist differed sharply from the views expressed by another highly qualified medical ethicist who expressed her opinion that Dr. Norwood's experimental surgery without the approval of an IRB and the informed consent of the parents was unethical.

Despite the laudable goals Dr. Norwood pursued in his approach to experimental or innovative surgery and medicine in the care of children, it is difficult to reconcile his actions with the categorical principle articulated by Immanuel Kant, which states, "No human being should be treated as a means to an end."[23] Experimentation or therapy that has the potential to benefit the child receiving the treatment may be reconciled with this ethical maxim where there is no established therapy to treat the child's condition. When children were dying from HLHS, the innovative approach used by Dr. Norwood was justifiable medically and ethically. However, once he and other surgeons developed a surgical approach that was safe and effective, the welfare of the child far outweighed the potential benefits that could flow to the child from the use of an untested experimental technique. At a minimum, ethical and legal standards mandated that the parents of Dr. Norwood's pediatric patients be fully informed of the innovative or idiosyncratic surgical approach he planned to use, as well as the risks and benefits of the proposed surgical approach and the customary alternative approaches employed by other surgeons.

The medical and legal communities have responded in a conflicting manner to Dr. Norwood's approach to medical practice. He began his career as a researcher and a pediatric cardiac surgeon at the Boston Children's Hospital, where he conceived and developed the Norwood procedure that saved the lives of children who, prior to that time, would have died shortly after birth due to a heart defect. In the 1990s he served as head of pediatric cardiac surgery at Children's Hospital of Pennsylvania (CHOP). During his tenure at CHOP, Norwood, according to an article in *Philadelphia Magazine*, faced more than twenty-five medical malpractice lawsuits, including one that resulted in a verdict of $55 million in favor of a severely injured child: "During surgery, Norwood stopped Stephen Jr.'s heart using a rapid hypothermic cooling technique he had been investigating in his chop [sic] research lab. The morning after surgery, Stephen Jr. had a devastating seizure. He's now a quadriplegic and partially blind. The [parents] sued, and in 2000 the jury announced a verdict of $55 million—at the time, the biggest malpractice award in state history. (As it turned out, the parties had reached a settlement of $7.5 million just before the verdict was read, so the verdict didn't stand.)"[24]

That same magazine article described the legal troubles Norwood encountered with personal injury lawsuits by his patients while he was at CHOP and offered an explanation for his long-term employment at various hospitals:

> During Norwood's decade-long tenure at chop [sic], he was sued at least 25 times, according to court records.
>
> The lawsuits—most settled, some dismissed, and some won by Norwood—didn't seem to sully his professional reputation. The field of pediatric heart surgery is small, and there are maybe 15 big-name surgeons worldwide. Norwood was—is—one of them. Cardiac centers bring in big bucks for children's hospitals, so hospitals try to attract name players like Norwood. "He was a huge moneymaker," says Norwood's friend, former hospital administrator John Walsh.[25]

Dr. Norwood left CHOP after a decade and opened a cardiac unit in Switzerland, which he jointly headed with his mentor for a few years. He then returned to the United States to build a pediatric cardiac surgery unit where he was the sole head and was given complete autonomy. It was with this complete autonomous control that he met his downfall, ending with him being escorted from the hospital by a security guard. Although Dr. Norwood has left duPont behind, the medical, legal, and ethical issues raised by his approach to practicing pediatric surgery continue to beg for resolution. While devices and drugs are subject to FDA approval and regulations, medical professionals have comparably free rein. They are largely unsupervised by the government, and legal options can be unsatisfactory, to say the least. While we want medical professionals to have the power and option to innovate, as a society we cannot allow them to insulate themselves from public outcry and scrutiny. As we look toward a future where healthcare law is shifting and uncertain, we must reflect on and remember the lessons offered by clinical trials and innovative medical care provided by doctors like Norwood.

Lessons Learned

Dr. Norwood's approach to providing healthcare to children in the Nemours Cardiac Center offers critical lessons for hospitals, doctors, nurses, and lawmakers. The core lesson is that no one person should be empowered to make isolated decisions about whether innovative therapy or pure experimentation should be carried out on human beings, particularly children. Indeed, one court, after reviewing a lead paint study at Johns Hopkins Hospital done on children in Baltimore, invoked ethical principles that led to the adoption of the Nuremberg Code—an ethical guideline authored in response the atrocities committed in the name of science by the Nazis—to support a legal holding that parents do not have the authority to consent to a child participating in an experiment that offers no benefit to him, and thus is conducted solely to advance scientific knowledge.[26]

Moreover, I submit that even when the study has the potential to benefit a child, balancing the pursuit of new scientific knowledge and the best interests of a patient is too complex and sensitive to allow one person to make that decision. Dr. Norwood's clinical approach, designed to allow him to have exclusive control over all the employees and staffers who were involved in providing care to his patients, did not have the dialogue and critical assessment necessary to balance those important interests that sometimes clash in fundamental ways.

Existing legal rules and procedures aimed at promoting safe and effective treatment of patients are effective only if medical practices and procedures are subjected to critical review by both healthcare professionals and laypeople. The law is adequate as it stands to produce protection for patients and to allow the advancement of science, but it must be followed. Norwood's approach to providing care, by conducting clinical trials on children, evaded all the major third-party reviews that usually protect patients from exposure to unjustified risks.

Consumers are supposed to be protected from untested drugs and devices by reviews conducted by the FDA before the products are used. Norwood was able to use a loophole that enables a physician to avoid restrictions by FDA regulations when using a product in a way that, in his professional judgment, best suits the clinical situation. Furthermore, before a new drug or device is tested on an individual in a hospital, the hospital's IRB is supposed to assess the potential risks and benefits of the proposed study. The IRB review was avoided by Dr. Norwood, who claimed that the hospital administrator told him that this was not necessary for the implantation of the stent in the hearts of the children.

Finally, courts rely on the medical profession to provide appropriate protection for consumers by using the professional group's collective experience and knowledge to establish the appropriate standard of care. However, Norwood avoided the standard of care established by his peers by deliberately departing from it. In this situation, courts are left to rely on expert testimony as to whether it was a reasonable departure. In tort law, custom serves as evidence of what a reasonable person would do, but it is not controlling. The tort litigation against Dr. Norwood pitted his expertise and his claim that he knew more than his peers against the collective judgment and practices of others who were competent and conscientious pediatric cardiac surgeons.

When a doctor decides to engage in innovative therapy, the doctrine of informed consent plays a critical role in protecting patient dignity. When presented with risks and benefits about standard medical treatment, patients are empowered by information that enables them to make a choice to engage in or avoid the proposed medical treatment plan. When the treating doctor has deliberately decided to depart from the established standard of care, both he and his patient are confronted with a higher level of uncertainty about the actual risks and benefits of the innovative therapy than would be faced if the established therapy is given.

The seriousness of the risks of using an unapproved and untested product, as well as the loophole left open for doctors by current law, is starkly revealed in the stent cases by the strict application of the device approval regulations to Numed, the company that manufactured the stents. The drug manufacturer pled guilty to a criminal violation of the Food and Drug Act, paid a substantial criminal fine, and entered a confidential settlement with some of the families in the civil cases.[27] In contrast, while the physicians were fired by the hospital, they faced no criminal charges because the Food and Drug Act does not restrict their conduct. They also avoided paying damages in the civil cases because the experts who had to formulate opinions about an untested device could not meet the legal requirement of stating with reasonable certainty that the harm was caused by the device.

In the absence of an emergency, innovative therapy should be preceded by more scrutiny and advice from third persons than is ordinarily invoked for standard care. The review by the FDA of a new drug or device that is being used in connection with a new therapy should be regarded as an essential requirement before the treatment is rendered. Moreover, the IRB is legally and ethically bound to the task of assessing whether the patient is competent and that his consent is voluntary and informed. Legal rules requiring third-party reviews and informed consent cannot protect patients if the hospital adopts a structure and process that concentrate the medical decision-making power in one person or department.

Part 3

Racism in Healthcare: Practice, Policy, and Law

Chapter 7

Perspectives on Racism

Racism in America is permanent. So declared law professor Derrick Bell after devoting many years of his professional life to the civil rights struggle.[1] In lectures, articles, and books published in the 1990s, Professor Bell confessed that he realized that he and others had pursued legal strategies for several decades that were destined to fail because they were based on a false premise that American racism was an aberration that could not continue to exist in a modern democracy that embraced equality as a predominant value.[2]

The civil rights movement of the 1960s was fueled by faith in religion, morality, and law. Professors and reformers believed that educating individuals and the public at large about the immorality and destructiveness of racism would eventually result in the elimination of racial bias as a significant force in American society.[3] Surely, American citizens would eventually insist that America provide equal opportunity to all persons, unrestricted by racial identity. Civil rights advocates also believed that law would serve as a potent weapon for eliminating racism, particularly after the momentous 1954 Supreme Court decision *Brown v. Board of Education*,[4] which rejected the argument that separation of the races was a fair and legal way of educating children.[5]

Three decades after *Brown*, Professor Bell concluded that the evidence of the continued strength and pervasiveness of racism was too powerful to ignore in connection with the strategies and tactics being employed in the civil rights struggle. Schools, residential neighborhoods, and jobs remained segregated, with black citizens being treated as inferior to whites. White supremacy remained a core value of the American political, economic, and cultural landscape. Rather than vesting the future of the country in a dream of a transformed society, it was better to be realistic and acknowledge that American racism is permanent. Strategies to address racism should reflect a recognition that racism is not "an anomaly on our democratic landscape."[6]

Professor Bell's "racism is permanent" thesis provoked widespread and vigorous debate.[7] For one thing, the permanence characteristic flew directly in the face of the professed beliefs of some of the most respected civil rights leaders and thinkers, who held steadfast to a dream that we would one day enjoy a "beloved community" built on values of mutual respect, equality, and human dignity.[8]

Sadly, the evidence of racism that has accumulated during the first two decades of the twenty-first century—particularly the racial bigotry encouraged by Donald Trump—supports Professor Bell's "racism is permanent" thesis.[9] Despite the *Brown* decision condemning government-enforced racial segregation of schools, over sixty years later schools and residential neighborhoods are more segregated than ever.[10] Income and wealth disparities based on race continue to grow.[11] Criminal law enforcement that effectuates arrests and imprisonment and police violence reflects racial bias.[12] Life expectancy and quality of life can still be projected based on race and zip code.[13]

While the manifestation of racism is sometimes pushed beneath the surface of everyday interactions, it eventually surfaces to remind us that it continues to influence thought and behavior. As the arrest of two African American men waiting for a business meeting in a Starbucks coffee shop in 2018 demonstrates, American racism is omnipresent, whether emanating from conscious or unconscious bias. The two black men were arrested because they declined to buy anything while sitting in the store waiting for a third person to arrive for a business meeting. The manager called the police, who then arrested the men for trespassing.[14] While one can debate whether American racism is permanent, there is no doubt that it continues to impact and shape individual relationships and public policies.

Social science has helped us to understand that racism is not always conscious. If one lives in a country that has built economic, political, and cultural systems that establish group hierarchies based on skin color, it is a rare individual who lives there for any length of time who does not psychologically absorb the messages denoting racial superiority and subordination.[15] In good economic times when the need for racial subordination to govern the distribution of resources is less acute, the expression of conscious racism is condemned and the struggle for social justice is more efficiently targeted toward unconscious bias. In addition, studies of fundamental institutional structures and procedures reveal that racial bias has been built into the system.[16] Identifying effective strategies for achieving racial equality requires an examination of how the system operates and of ways to eliminate structural bias.

In my view, the most haunting aspect of Professor Bell's "racism is permanent" thesis is how well it prophesied the vibrancy and rebirth of public racism after America's first African American president completed two terms in office. Professor Bell had presciently identified the driving political force of the perpetuation of American racism: "[I]t is a critically important stabilizing force that enables whites to bind across a wide socio-economic chasm. Without the deflecting power of racism, masses of whites would likely wake up to and revolt against the severe disadvantage they suffer in income and opportunity when compared with those whites at the top of our socio-economic heap."[17]

It is sobering and disturbing to note how well Professor Bell's assessment of American racism explains the coalition of conservative politicians and working-class whites who are emotionally driven to repeal the Affordable Care Act (ACA, popularly known as Obamacare), the first healthcare reform bill to pass in over fifty years to expand financial coverage of millions of Americans for access to healthcare. Racism is not the only factor that drives opposition to the ACA, but it serves as a potent political tool for inducing people who are the primary beneficiaries of Obamacare to support and demand the repeal of the statute.

Neither the Bell thesis that racism is permanent nor the observations of social scientists that racism is omnipresent today makes an argument that all whites, blacks, or any other racially defined group are racist. While the interaction and communication between individuals from different races remains limited, many white citizens abhor racism and devote energy to eliminating its operation and effects. Indeed, if the majority of voting Americans were motivated primarily by racism, Barack Obama could not have been elected twice. However, polls and social science studies reveal that the ideology of white superiority remains at the core of the American economic, political, and cultural systems for many white Americans.[18]

Addressing the distinct ways in which racial bias is manifested and causes injury represents a monumental challenge that entails, at a minimum, identifying the factors that influence individual decision making about politics, economics, law, and morality. Once factors contributing to bias emerge, we must ask if the law can play a constructive role in controlling or eliminating the operation of bias and consider different remedies to achieve social justice and protect human dignity.[19]

Given the overall continued operation of bias and racism, it is no surprise to find bias and disparities in the current healthcare system.[20] The cases described in part 3 of the book provide examples of racial bias in the healthcare system that reflect three manifestations of racial bias: individual bias on the part of a doctor in one instance; structural bias in the healthcare system; and political bias in law and policy making as revealed in the fight over Obamacare. Addressing these distinct manifestations of racial bias requires different strategies and remedies. Law has an important role to play but cannot by itself resolve the problems.

"Black People Just Don't Understand"—The Botched Hysterectomy

Shirley Johnson sat motionless in a chair across from me in the conference room, staring intently into my eyes. She had retained my law firm to represent her, and I had just spent several minutes making an argument to her that emphasized the importance of keeping an appointment she had with a gynecologist. She turned away from me and sat silently for a moment, staring into space as though I were not there. Finally, fighting to hold back the tears that had welled up in her eyes, she responded: "I want you to listen again, and hear what I have been saying. It does not matter how sick I get, or how bad I feel, no doctor is ever going to touch me down there again." I passed her a box of tissues as she began sobbing.

Shirley was a thirty-three-year-old woman with radiant brown skin and piercing dark eyes that made you feel she was looking into your soul. A year before our meeting, while she was in the prime of her life, she learned that she had cervical cancer that would require a radical hysterectomy, meaning that it was necessary to remove not only her uterus, but also the cervix and part of her vagina. Based on a referral from her primary care doctor, she agreed to allow Dr. Mark Morris, a general surgeon, to perform the hysterectomy. What she did not discover until after the surgery was that Dr. Morris was trying a new technique for performing a radical hysterectomy. Rather than performing the open surgery using the traditional approach of making an incision in her abdomen and removing the uterus that way, Dr. Morris decided to include Shirley as one of the early patients in an investigational study he was conducting at the hospital to determine whether he could safely perform a radical hysterectomy by using a laparoscope. With this new approach to surgery, he would use a tube with a camera and insert surgical tools through a small incision in the abdomen. He would then use the camera to view the operation on a video screen and perform the hysterectomy.

Today, a laparoscopic hysterectomy has been developed into a safe alternative to open surgery. However, at the time Shirley underwent the surgery, performing a radical hysterectomy with a laparoscope was a novel and untested technique. The results of the surgery Dr. Morris performed on Shirley were disastrous. Ten days after the surgery Shirley remained in a hospital bed, suffering pain in her lower back, passing flatus and feces through her vagina, and leaking urine through her catheter. When she complained to Dr. Morris and asked him why this was happening to her, what stood out most in her mind was a statement that Dr. Morris made to her: "Black people just don't understand."

I asked Shirley if she was certain that these were the words that Dr. Morris used. She responded firmly: "Yes, that is exactly what he said. I was lying on the bed in pain, feeling as though I was going to die, and this white doctor who operated on me was now telling me that he could not explain to me why I was suffering, because I was Black and could not understand."

Shirley's nightmare continued the next day when another doctor who worked for the hospital came to her room and told her that she had a blocked right ureter that was preventing the drainage of her right kidney. Three days later another hospital doctor, the chief of the hospital's urology department, informed Shirley that her right ureter had been either stapled or nicked during the hysterectomy. To treat this condition, the doctors inserted a temporary stent into the blocked ureter to allow urine to drain from the kidney. Five days after the insertion of the stent, Shirley was discharged from the hospital.

Shirley returned to the hospital two weeks later to have her sutures replaced. Two days after replacing the sutures, the urologist informed Shirley that she now needed more surgery because she had a fistula (a surgically made passage between a hollow organ and the body surface), which needed to be repaired, and that her bladder had dropped. Alarmed at the medical treatment she had received up to this point, Shirley checked herself out of the hospital, refusing to undergo any further medical care in that hospital.

A week later, Shirley's primary care doctor referred her to a doctor affiliated with a different hospital. After examining her, this new doctor told Shirley that her bowel and bladder were joined at the top of her vagina due to the laparoscopic hysterectomy that had been performed on her. He recommended bladder reconstruction surgery to repair the hole in her bowel and her damaged ureter. After this recommendation, Shirley decided that it was time to see a lawyer. Her decision to seek legal counsel is what caused her to sit across the table from me and declare: "No other doctor is ever going to ever operate on me again. I will die first."

Fortunately, Shirley later relented and underwent reconstructive surgery recommended by the last doctor. The surgery was successful. At the time Shirley was deciding whether to have a radical hysterectomy and selecting a doctor to do the surgery, the law gave her a right to be informed by the surgeon of material risks and benefits of the surgery and any viable alternatives to treat her disease. The duty to convey the information is imposed on the doctor who agrees to do the surgery.[21]

Most jurisdictions mandate the disclosure of "material risks, benefits and alternatives" to proposed treatment.[22] Under this standard, when a surgeon plans to do something that is new, the fact that a proposed procedure is new and untested is material information that should be disclosed to the patient. According to Shirley, Dr. Morris never informed her that he was trying a new surgical approach. In addition to the question of whether the surgeon violated the duty to obtain an informed consent, the case presents the question of what effect the law should give to his conduct if he was motivated or influenced by racial animosity or prejudice.

The legal remedies available when a patient experiences racial discrimination in the context of healthcare are important and complex, particularly when the person alleged to have engaged in the discriminatory conduct is a private actor. The present chapter focuses on the impact that race has on a tort claim based on informed consent or intentional infliction of emotional distress.

Race, Healthcare, and Human Dignity

Shirley Johnson's case of a botched hysterectomy illustrates common features of the doctor-patient relationship of power, dependency, and trust. The doctor is powerful because he has healthcare knowledge and skill that the patient lacks and needs. The patient is dependent on the professional to share and apply that knowledge and skill in accordance with professional standards, with the goal of promoting the best interest of the patient. Some patients are active in acquiring information and making decisions, while others are passive. Ultimately, all patients who have access to a healthcare professional or institution must trust in the honesty and good faith of the professional and the institution. Only after the care has been rendered do most patients and their families apply a critical eye to the care and the decision-making process. In most cases, a patient's trust is rewarded by good faith adherence to professional standards of ethics, knowledge, and skill. However, when things go wrong, a patient usually wants to know why—which is when the conduct of the healthcare provider may be subjected to critical assessment.

When Ms. Johnson agreed to undergo a laparoscopic hysterectomy, she was not in a position to evaluate whether that technique was better for her than the established open surgery. She was at the mercy of her doctor to advise her of the risks, benefits, and alternatives. While she and most women in her position would likely have agreed to undergo a hysterectomy rather than risk death from cancer, she may certainly have decided not to submit to a novel surgical approach. In addition, if she chose the novel laparoscopic surgery, she certainly may have decided to have the hysterectomy done by a surgeon who had more experience with the procedure than Dr. Morris. Yet Dr. Morris chose not to share information with her about the untested nature and his surgical inexperience with the procedure.

When she was suffering in the hospital for eight days after the surgery, Ms. Johnson understandably wanted to know why. The explanation she got from her doctor sought to deflect responsibility from him and make Shirley doubt herself, if not *blame* herself, for not understanding the risks of the procedure.

Shirley Johnson's treatment by her surgeon is, unfortunately, a common example of how racism continues to taint relationships among individuals in America, and in that regard many studies demonstrate differential treatment in healthcare delivery.[23] Most often issues of class and race remain under the surface, and patients do not confront healthcare providers with their concerns about bias. While implicit bias may impact the care given, patients are not sure and do not want to complicate decision making that is critical to their health. In Shirley's case, issues of race and class boiled to the top when Dr. Morris made an explicit racially biased remark to her. It is critical that the healthcare and legal systems provide effective means for both patients and healthcare providers to address both conscious and unconscious race and class biases.

History has demonstrated that dignity is an essential attribute of the human species, and perceptions of equality have a profound impact on individual human dignity. The validity of social organization and community goals is undermined if there is not a certain level of respect accorded to every member of the community on the basis of his membership in the human species.

The systems of slavery and racial segregation in America, apartheid in South Africa, and the Holocaust in Europe provide chilling examples of the potential cruelty and destruction of a society that fails to recognize every human as entitled to a minimal level of respect and treatment as a human being. The U.S. Supreme Court's decision in *Dred Scott v. Sandford*,[24] holding that black people were property and not persons within the meaning of the U.S. Constitution, and in *Korematsu v. United States*,[25] holding that it did not violate the Constitution to arrest and intern persons of Japanese descent based on their race, represent low-water marks in American jurisprudence when measured against a standard of social justice and the principles upon which our society has been built.

Today, conscious racial bigotry is regarded as socially unacceptable by the clear majority of Americans.[26] Thus, cases where parties expressly state their racial prejudices as justification for conduct are rare. The more common manifestations of racial bias in the healthcare context flow from unconscious biases, or at least conscious efforts to conceal biases and beliefs about distinctive differences between racial groups that have continued despite the end of Jim Crow and the passage of civil rights laws that outlaw intentional discrimination. Participants in, and observers of, the legal system and the healthcare system are compelled to wrestle with a much more complex situation than that presented by explicit acts of racial discrimination.

Recent medical and social studies have demonstrated the complexity of the problem of persistent racial bias in America. Health disparities show that recognition of race may be useful in addressing medical, social, and environmental factors that have an impact on health.[27] The Harvard Implicit Association Test,[28] available online, has repeatedly proven that even well-intentioned and socially conscious individuals react with unconscious bias. A landmark publication authored by Shankar Vedantam, entitled *The Hidden Brain*, reports on numerous studies that reveal how stereotypes continue to influence behavior.[29] Indeed, a recent study of the brain showed that white and black individuals identify with victims of pain who are the same race as they are, and have less empathy for individuals of a different race who undergo the same pain.[30]

The fact that we are all influenced by factors that prompt us to manifest unconscious racial biases is further complicated by the continued effects of systems of structural bias that perpetuate inequality. Disparities in health, education, employment, and housing perpetuate inequality despite the lack of conscious racial bias on the part of the majority of Americans. Public policy and laws aimed at correcting structural racism or reducing unconscious bias are often met with resistance by white Americans who view the policies labeled as affirmative action as "reverse racism."[31] Others who see the policies as necessary and justified to promote social justice have tried to raise awareness of "white privilege" created by hundreds of years of racial discrimination.[32] The challenge of promoting and protecting human dignity in healthcare in light of these complexities will be addressed more fully in the final chapter of this book. For now, I seek to focus the reader's attention on the impact of racial bias in ordinary healthcare situations that do not receive public attention.

Shirley was particularly vulnerable to physical and emotional harm. She had just learned that she had cancer and that the treatment required an operation on her reproductive system. All patients struggle with dignity issues when a disease or proposed medical procedure threatens their sexual organs. However, African American women have good reasons for special concerns based on the many published and publicized examples of mistreatment by doctors.[33]

An open and honest communication about the risks and alternatives to the proposed surgery was not only legally owed to Shirley, but was essential to maintain her dignity. From a dignity perspective, whether legally required or not, Dr. Morris should have discussed with Shirley, prior to the surgery, the risks, benefits, and alternatives to the proposed novel laparoscopic hysterectomy he wanted to perform as a part of a clinical study.

Evidence produced after the medical malpractice lawsuit was filed revealed that not only was the procedure new and unproven at that time as to its safety and effectiveness, but that Dr. Morris had very limited experience performing the laparoscopic hysterectomy. The evidence of his experience was contradictory. He testified in a deposition that Shirley was only the second patient he had performed the procedure on as the chief of surgery. However, he had published a paper indicating that prior to Shirley's surgery, he had participated in fourteen such operations, and four of the fourteen patients had suffered serious injuries to their bladder, bowel, or vagina. In his paper, Dr. Morris wrote that the rate of injury associated with this procedure based on his personal experience was "alarming." Yet none of this information was communicated to Shirley when she purportedly gave consent to the laparoscopic hysterectomy.

Tort law makes a person liable for harm that he caused to another person if the harm was caused intentionally or negligently. When racism motivates the actor, courts have determined that the aggravating circumstance of racism warrants characterizing the touching of another person as a battery because it understandably causes an offense to the dignity of the person being touched. A well-known case of an offensive battery occurred when a waiter in a restaurant snatched a plate from the hands of an African American customer as the waiter shouted a racial slur.[34] Another example involved a supervisor who made racial slurs and insults to an employee, causing the employee to suffer severe emotional distress.[35] In both cases, the courts ruled that the conduct would be treated as committing an intentional tort. The waiter's conduct was viewed as a battery, and the supervisor's conduct was characterized as intentional and so outrageous as to support a claim of intentional infliction of emotional distress.

Shirley filed a medical malpractice claim against Dr. Morris and the hospital that employed him, alleging that they should compensate her for bodily harm and emotional distress because Dr. Morris violated professional standards of medical care, failed to inform her of the risks and benefits of, and alternatives to, the laparoscopic hysterectomy, and engaged in conduct intentionally aimed at causing her emotional distress. In addition, she alleged that Dr. Morris had made derogatory racial comments toward her that were unprofessional, unethical, and immoral.

Shirley was understandably most concerned with her personal health and well-being. She settled her medical malpractice case against Dr. Morris and the hospital before trial under terms of a "confidential settlement" that precluded the parties and their lawyers from disclosing the terms of the settlement or the specific allegations in the lawsuit. It is for this reason that the names Shirley Johnson and Dr. Morris will forever remain pseudonyms.

An important feature of the tort system is that it allows private parties to decide whether to initiate the legal process and whether and when to terminate the process. In contrast, criminal laws and many public interest laws, such as civil rights or environmental protection statutes, rely completely on the judgment and discretion of public officials as to whether and how to invoke the legal system to resolve complaints and concerns about improper conduct. Thus, Shirley had the option of settling this case by looking primarily at what best served her interest, even if the public interest may have been better served at trial.

While the public interest may have been better served if the conduct of Dr. Morris was exposed through a trial before a jury, such a trial would also have required Shirley to discuss her medical history and physical injuries publicly. This process risked causing her additional emotional harm. She chose a course that allowed her to begin a healing process immediately by putting this nightmare behind her.

Shirley's case received no public attention because a clause in the settlement mandated that both parties maintain confidentiality about the terms of the settlement. In this regard, it falls into a category that includes many medical malpractice cases that could reveal serious flaws in the operation of the healthcare system, but never receive public scrutiny because the patients, providers, and insurers conclude that their individual interests are best served by a confidential settlement. The task and responsibility of preventing a recurrence of the event are left with the medical profession. Rarely does the public learn what action, if any, a licensing board or hospital has taken to protect patients from the risk of substandard care provided by a particular doctor or nurse. With the frequent reliance on confidential settlements, the legal system also leaves the problem and the potential solution buried with the victim.

The physical injury Shirley suffered would last a lifetime, and so would the hurt caused by the racial insult. After Shirley filed a medical malpractice case, Dr. Morris denied that he ever made a racial slur. He admitted that he discussed her complications with her, and may have said she did not understand, but certainly did not say, "Black people do not understand." Had the case gone to trial, the jury would have been empowered to decide whether Ms. Johnson or Dr. Morris was telling the truth about Dr. Morris having made a derogatory racial comment. Seeing the world through the eyes of an African American attorney who had been the target of such statements on several occasions, I was both outraged and determined to bring this issue to a jury for resolution. Credibility rested more on Shirley's recall of the conversation than that of Dr. Morris. It seems highly unlikely that a person in Shirley's position, struggling to understand why she was suffering following surgery, would have imagined a racially derogatory comment.

In the absence of a verdict or some official action by a court or licensing authority, the question remains as to how many other patients suffered physical and emotional injuries caused by the medical care and inhumane conduct rendered by Dr. Morris. Patients and lawyers often conclude that holding a negligent doctor publicly accountable comes at too great a cost to the dignity of the patient or the patient's need for privacy to protect her dignity.

Private civil actions based on state tort law and civil rights law should continue to be available to individuals who suffer serious physical and emotional harm prompted by racially motivated healthcare decisions. In many cases, corrective justice, social justice, and deterrence of this heinous conduct depend on the availability of a legal remedy that a private citizen can invoke and control. However, widespread reduction of racially biased conduct requires governmental action and effective monitoring of professional associations. Proposals for strategies and tactics that should be considered by government and professional associations will be set forth in the last chapter of this book.

Chapter 8

Healthcare Disparities as a Lived Experience

One Family's Story

James Johnson awoke at 6:00 A.M., experiencing severe chest pain and having difficulty breathing. He had a heart condition and high blood pressure that required daily medication. He stopped taking the medication because he had no insurance. During most of his adult life, Mr. Johnson was covered by health insurance offered by his employer, Keystone Mechanic Company. He had worked for Keystone until his health started to fail and he was laid off. For three months after losing his job he continued to pay for health insurance, but his savings were soon depleted. He dropped the insurance because he could no longer afford it. He then applied for Medicaid insurance under the state statute where he lived in Alabama. Unfortunately, Alabama did not expand coverage under Obamacare for Medicaid patients, and he did not meet their poverty guidelines for state-sponsored Medicaid insurance. For several months after losing his insurance, Mr. Johnson would sporadically buy his prescription medicine and take lower portions of it to extend its longevity.

Mr. Johnson lived with his three children, ages six, nine, and twelve, and had been divorced a few years earlier. When he woke up in the morning having difficulty breathing, he screamed for help, and the oldest child telephoned his aunt, who lived in the neighborhood. The aunt came to the house within fifteen minutes. When she saw her brother struggling to breathe, she called 911, and twenty minutes later an emergency medical team arrived in an ambulance. The emergency medical technicians put a breathing mask over Mr. Johnson's nose and mouth to oxygenate him. They carried him into the ambulance and transported him to the nearest hospital in the urban area in which he lived.

When he arrived at the hospital, an emergency room nurse examined him, and he was placed on a cot to await an examination by the emergency room physician in charge.

One half hour after Mr. Johnson arrived in the emergency room, the doctor in charge examined him and found him in severe distress, with his heart beating rapidly. The doctor was immediately upset when he saw Mr. Johnson because earlier that morning, he had asked that the ambulances not bring any more patients to the emergency room that day because the ER was already overloaded, and the hospital did not have beds to take care of new patients. He examined Mr. Johnson, inserted a breathing tube in his trachea to assist his breathing, and ordered medication and close monitoring of his vital signs. The emergency room doctor then sent a request to the cardiology unit to send a cardiologist to the emergency room or to arrange for Mr. Johnson to be transferred to the cardiac unit as quickly as possible. The chief of cardiology responded immediately that there was no cardiologist in the hospital who was free to come to the emergency room, and no bed was available in the cardiac unit or the intensive care unit.

The emergency room doctor directed the nursing staff to pay close attention to Mr. Johnson and move him close to the nursing station to monitor him. However, the nurses were also extremely busy. Five hours later, Mr. Johnson still had not been seen by a cardiologist. His sister, who had called 911, immediately came to the emergency room after she made arrangements for someone to take care of the children. She was sitting by Mr. Johnson in the emergency room when he sat up, pulled the breathing tube out of his nose, and then began to gasp for air. She called for help, but by the time the emergency room nurses and doctors got there he had stopped breathing and lost consciousness. Unfortunately, the medical staff was unable to resuscitate Mr. Johnson, and he died of a heart attack in the hospital.

One year later, the Johnson family retained a lawyer who had the medical records reviewed by two experts, one in emergency medicine and the other in cardiology. Both experts informed the family that the standard of care required that Mr. Johnson be examined and treated by a cardiologist on an urgent basis, and both experts believed that the treatment rendered to Mr. Johnson violated the standard of care. Mr. Johnson's estate filed a medical malpractice lawsuit against the hospital, doctors, and nurses, alleging negligence in not providing Mr. Johnson with the timely care that he obviously needed when he arrived at the hospital. The hospital, nurses, and emergency room doctor responded that they did the best they could under the circumstances. They claimed that they had limited resources and had to make decisions about how to prioritize the treatment of patients on that day.

The emergency room physician responsible for the care of Mr. Johnson testified that even if a hospital bed had become available for a patient who needed it on an emergency basis, there were two other patients sicker than Mr. Johnson who were waiting for treatment in the cardiology unit. None of the patients could be transferred in a timely manner for treatment in another hospital in the community. The emergency room doctor recalled that he had directed the staff to call several other hospitals in the area to request that they accept the transfer of Mr. Johnson, but the other hospitals were also overloaded with emergencies. Consequently, he could not transfer Mr. Johnson to another hospital.

A case such as this raises troubling legal, moral, and ethical issues. Who, if anyone, can or should be held accountable for the fact that people who live in different communities experience disparate healthcare that causes serious injuries and sometimes costs them their lives? Is it fair to hold hospitals, doctors, and nurses who serve communities populated by poor people, many of whom are uninsured, responsible for failing to provide the quality of care given to members of affluent communities on a routine basis?

Tort law defers to judges and juries to answer these questions on a case-by-case basis, offering the guidance of a vague legal standard that a healthcare provider must provide the care of a reasonable hospital or professional acting in the same or similar circumstances. When the decision that exposes community members to a danger to their health involves a financial judgment about efficient allocation of resources, it is difficult for a court or jury to conclude that the hospital's decision amounts to negligence.

Dr. David Ansell, in his book titled *The Death Gap*, describes a decision by the University of Chicago Medical Center to close its trauma center located in the predominantly black and poor South Side of Chicago, while keeping the trauma centers in other middle-class and white neighborhoods.[1] The rationale for closing the trauma center on the South Side was that the hospital was losing large sums of money every year operating it. And yet, it was known at the time that the South Side was the geographic area with the greatest need for the trauma center, given the concentration of poverty and the high rate of gun violence.

Closing the center would mean that an increased number of residents of the South Side would die because it would take longer to transport them to a trauma center in the event of a serious injury caused by an accident or a crime. The financial decision was consistent with a recognition that the cost of care was having a significant negative financial impact on the hospital. However, if the decision were to be made on a moral basis, it would lead to keeping the trauma center open. Moreover, a nonprofit hospital has a mission that usually includes serving the public good as a central part of its rationale for existence. The public service mission and moral duty usually elude legal enforcement.

It is extremely important to note that the devastating impact on the community that Dr. Ansell and others describe flows not from the closing of an entire hospital, but from the closure of a specific service provided by the hospital that the people residing in poor communities desperately need. For another example, in 2017 the *Washington Post* published a story with this headline: "Closure of two D.C. maternity wards hurts low-income women most."[2] The article reported that as a result of the closures, "no labor and delivery services exist on the east side of the city."[3] The closures of the prenatal and obstetrical services left the low-income pregnant women who resided in the northeast section of DC to scramble to find alternative care in a healthcare system that is already producing disproportionate deaths of newborns and their mothers based on race and ethnicity. The article noted: "Using data from 2013, the city found that the infant mortality rate among white mothers was 1.7 per 1.000 births. For Hispanic and black mothers, it was, respectively, 6.4 and 9.9 per 1,000 births."[4]

As noted in chapter 3, which discusses emergency care, tort law does not often formulate and apply rules that are driven by morality. Instead, it accepts economically rational decision making as persuasive evidence as to what a reasonable person would do acting in the same or similar circumstances. And while accrediting agencies and public financing sources purport to place a high value on serving people who are poor and uninsured, rarely is there an effort to legally enforce the public service obligation.

Dr. Ansell has argued persuasively that addressing harm caused by inadequate healthcare due to structural racism requires community activism to transform the legal duties of the federal, state, and local governments, as well as healthcare providers and insurers, to acknowledge the harm caused by "structural violence." He explains that structural violence "exists when some groups have more access to goods, resources, and opportunities than other groups, including health and life itself."[5] He argues that structural violence is different in kind from interpersonal violence and more thorough and deadlier: "This kind of violence is called structural violence, because it is embedded in the very laws, policies and rules that govern day-to day-life. It is the cumulative impact of laws and social and economic policies and practices that render some Americans less able to access resources than others."[6] Over the past two decades, many researchers have identified the disparities in health and healthcare in America. The challenge today is to fashion effective remedies to reduce and eventually eliminate the dominant factors that cause the disparities.

Unequal Community Access

Historical and economic data show that group-based disparities are primarily the result of conscious policies and practices bestowing wealth and opportunities on white Americans, while excluding African Americans and other people of color from gaining access to the same wealth and opportunities.[7] Discrimination on the basis of race, class, and gender was a joint project of federal, state, and local governments and private white citizens that was carried on under the color of law until the 1960s, when the practices were struck down or prohibited by federal and state courts and legislatures.[8] By the time governmental and private race and gender discrimination was declared unconstitutional, poverty was concentrated in geographic areas occupied by African Americans.[9]

A lower life expectancy and quality of life were hallmarks of a community composed of a high percentage of African Americans. The same is true in the twenty-first century, and the health disparity has expanded to engulf most people of color, accompanied by disparities in income, wealth, housing, and educational opportunities. Today, communities with large numbers of the working class, the poor, and/or people of color have higher percentages of sick and uninsured people who rely on hospital emergency care as their primary means of accessing the healthcare system.[10] Hospitals serving poor communities have insufficient resources for meeting the high demand for emergency room care. Consequently, a person living in a poorer community has difficulty getting the same quality of care that others obtain in a different class of hospital and another community.

America lives with and accepts a system of two-tiered medical care.[11] Not only is there a two-tiered system for medical care, but the individual who lives in a working-class or poor community has little choice as to where he can access care and the quality of care he receives, particularly when emergency care is required. Most communities in the United States are segregated based on race, and people of color are disproportionately affected by the two-tiered medical care system.[12] Consequently, two people may suffer from the same treatable medical illness, and one will live and the other will die due to the disparate availability and quality of healthcare providers, institutions, facilities, and equipment. Dr. Ansell offers the following observations concerning hospital care in Chicago: "What hospital you attend is literally a matter of life and death. In general, hospitals and clinics where many minority patients receive care are lower quality than those that serve white populations, whether for medical or surgical conditions. Further, hospitals treating a higher proportion of black patients have higher mortality rates for many surgical procedures. In addition, those hospitals have higher mortality rates independent of race: both black patients and white patients have higher mortality in hospitals with mostly black patients [than] their racial counterparts in other centers."[13] David Ansell, like other scholars who have researched health disparities, presents many disturbing statistics that reflect the gap in the quality of healthcare and other vital community resources, which, in turn, produce vastly different life expectancies of people who live within miles of each other.

Like Chicago, communities in Pennsylvania present vast disparities in quality of health and life expectancy correlated to race and class. For example, when comparing Chester, Pennsylvania, with Swarthmore, Pennsylvania, the life expectancy differs by seventeen years with only a 4.3-mile geographic distance between the two cities. Further comparisons showed that the per capita income in Swarthmore as of 2010 was 3.5 times greater than that of Chester. Residents of Chester primarily used basic Medicare and Medicaid for health insurance, while most residents of Swarthmore had supplemental Medicare and private insurance. The factors leading to the poorer health outcomes and lower life expectancy in Chester include where people live and work, socioeconomic factors, less access to healthy food and exercise, and higher crime rates.[14]

I agree with Dr. Ansell that the correlation between a shortened life span and racism cannot be ignored if we are ever going to fix the problem. People of color and poor people are trapped in environments that shorten their lives. This book relates stories reflecting experiences of individual consumers and patients who view the healthcare system from "the bottom of the well"[15] and who have suffered the consequences of structural violence. The stories are based on both publicly reported cases and unreported cases from my professional experience in representing individuals and families in cases arising out of healthcare that caused death or other serious injuries. Sometimes a premature death caused by inadequate healthcare comes from the structure itself, as Ansell points out. Other times it comes from the unconscious bias or lack of caring produced by a healthcare system or institution that is inadequately staffed or funded.

A tragic example of a premature death is reflected in a Pennsylvania case where a pregnant woman who was past her due date went to a hospital. When she was admitted to the hospital, members of the medical staff knew she was suffering from pregnancy- induced hypertension. Notwithstanding the established medical knowledge that inducing the birth of the child was the standard care required, the woman sat in a waiting room for thirteen and a half hours, and her delayed admission resulted in the necessity of an emergency cesarean section. The hospital offered no explanation for leaving her in the waiting room all day. It was as though she was nobody in the minds and eyes of the doctors and nurses until the emergency demanded their attention. The baby lived, but the mother died in the hospital a few weeks later.[16]

People who live in working-class, poor, rural, and minority communities encounter some of the same problems residents of upper-class and predominantly white communities face when they seek access to healthcare. However, people from poor and minority communities must also contend with behavior based on race and class biases of individuals and institutions, as well as the long-standing practices and structures that perpetuate "white privilege."[17] Studies have also shown that even among individuals in the same economic class, race plays a role in producing disparities in healthcare.[18]

As noted earlier in this chapter, tort law, as traditionally formulated, lacks effective tools to address structural race and class biases. Civil rights laws offer little help, particularly considering the Supreme Court's conservative interpretation of the laws as requiring victims of discrimination to prove that the perpetrator of the harm intentionally discriminated based on race. A legal requirement of evidence of intentional racial discrimination provides a shield against claims based on implicit bias and structural bias.

In most circumstances of discrimination today, there are too many layers to roll back to prove intentional discrimination. A look beneath the surface of an established structure or policy that has a clear discriminatory impact usually reveals a history of racial discrimination by government, private institutions, and individuals, followed by an explicit endorsement of the current discriminatory effects by many people presently in power who argue that the policies, practices, and structures are neutral. The disparate effects, in their view, are not appropriately addressed by law.

The factors that produce the inequities are so widespread and entrenched that a radical transformation of the approaches to providing and paying for healthcare is necessary to reduce the disparities. As the country learned after the failed efforts to remedy the effects of government-backed racial discrimination in education by judicial decree, success through integration requires a radical change in the minds of the dominant community members who enjoy the benefits of a segregated white privilege. I believe that the core value that we should invoke to guide the development of new strategies and programs is the promotion of the human dignity of everyone who seeks healthcare in America. To do this, we will need a diverse coalition of community members to develop, market, and implement the message of human dignity.

A promising approach to improving the delivery of quality of healthcare by hospitals to members of their local communities has emerged in recent years. A Los Angeles hospital, previously dubbed "Killer King Hospital" by local residents, was torn down and replaced by a new building with a new philosophy. The sad irony is that the original hospital was built after the riots in the 1960s and was named after Dr. Martin Luther King Jr. and Charles Drew, a pioneering African American doctor who is credited with developing blood banking techniques that enabled the first safe and effective blood transfusions. The hospital at first served as a source of pride to the poor black community, but by 2007 it had become a disgrace and a source of shame. Its primary mission was to serve the poor in the adjacent southern Los Angeles neighborhood.

In 2004, the *Los Angeles Times* published a Pulitzer Prize–winning series of articles describing the shocking cases of substandard care that had occurred in the hospital.[19] A story reported by CBS in 2007 gives the flavor of the type of abysmal medical care that compelled the closing of the hospital. King Hospital was on the brink of collapse:

> When Edith Isabel Rodriguez showed up in the emergency room of an inner-city hospital complaining of severe stomach pain, the staff was familiar with her. It was at least her third visit to Los Angeles County's public Martin Luther King Jr.–Harbor Hospital in as many days. "You have already been seen, and there is nothing we can do," a nurse told her. Minutes later, the 43-year-old mother of three collapsed on the floor screaming in pain and began vomiting blood. Employees ignored her, and soon she was dead.
>
> Now state and federal regulators are threatening to close the hospital or pull its funding unless it can be improved, and Rodriguez has become a symbol of everything wrong with the facility derisively known as "Killer King." After she collapsed, surveillance cameras show that Rodriguez was left on the floor.[20]

The CBS report continued with descriptions of additional horrendous cases that eventually resulted in a decision by government regulators to close the hospital: "In February, a brain tumor patient languished in the emergency room for four days before his family drove him to another hospital for emergency surgery. A pregnant woman who complained of bleeding was given a pregnancy test and left, only to return three days later and have a miscarriage after waiting more than four hours to see a doctor."[21] The sad story of a dream turned into a nightmare was also underscored by a study of the hospital by the U.S. Centers for Medicare and Medicaid Services that found that in the sixty cases it reviewed, more than 25 percent of the patients received substandard medical care.[22]

Ten years after King Hospital closed in 2007, leaving hundreds of thousands of South L.A. residents without access to healthcare, an article appeared in

Politico with the headline "How 'Killer King' Became the Hospital of the Future."[23] The article describes the opening of a new hospital building adjacent to the old "Killer King" Hospital that is being guided by a unique public-private partnership with a new vision. The hospital aims to address the health needs of the community through a network of community health providers and to reserve in-house hospital care for patients who are acutely ill. The new hospital chose not to include a trauma center because of the cost and chose instead to refer the community to a nearby county trauma center.

A core part of the strategy that radically departs from the traditional role of a hospital is to reach out to the community and act as a partner in addressing the social determinants of poor health. The new hospital has elected to take a wellness approach to its primary mission and to assist the community in developing sources of fresh food, senior citizen centers, and safe environments for exercise.

The jury is still out on the new hospital's ultimate effectiveness and sustainability, but the community and the management and staff have hope that the hospital will become a safe and effective facility for providing healthcare to a local community populated primarily by people of color.

Another program that earned its creator a McArthur "genius grant" is operating in Camden, New Jersey, under the auspices of Cooper Hospital. The program, the Urban Health Institute, was implemented to improve the delivery of care to underserved populations and Medicaid and Medicare recipients by coming up with outpatient primary and specialty care options for those in serious need.[24] The institute has two outpatient practices with twenty-three specialties and primary care medicine. The goal of these outpatient services is to increase face-to-face time with clinicians, usually nurses.[25] Nurses are available for weekly appointments to help with diabetes and hypertension management to help reduce the number of emergency room visits by this population.

The Camden Coalition is also run out of the Urban Health Institute by Dr. Jeffrey Brenner. Dr. Brenner collected data that showed that 90 percent of hospital costs in Camden stemmed from 20 percent of patients, known as "super-utilizers," and that many of the visits were for minor illnesses such as colds and sore throats.[26] In order to help fix this problem, Dr. Brenner developed a "care management team," comprising a social worker, a nurse, a community health worker, and a health coach, who visit patients with complicated medical and social needs in the hospital. They review medications, consult with the patient's doctors, and help plan the patient's discharge. Members of the team then visit the patient's home to provide continued support for up to nine months following discharge in order to connect the patient with a primary care physician, go with the patient to appointments, and help line up social services.[27] Camden hospitals have seen positive results, improving the health and welfare of the super-utilizers and reducing the hospital's costs.

The lessons that we are now learning from the study of disparities of health and healthcare make it clear that, to solve the problems, we must carefully examine the structures, practices, and policies that contribute to race, class, and gender disparities, and engage in bold and innovative methods to address the problems that biased structures often conceal. Without a doubt, intelligent decisions about the way we pay for healthcare are critical to building a sustainable system. However, human dignity must remain at the core of our concerns, or we risk adopting an approach to healthcare that destroys an existential community value.

Chapter 9

Catastrophic Injuries

Protecting and Restoring Human Dignity

On the morning of Harriet's fortieth birthday, her mother, Ruth Cooper, chirped good morning and sang happy birthday to her. Ruth then began the daily routine that she had followed almost every day during the past thirty-nine years. She bathed Harriet, dressed her, and then fed her. She performed these tasks while listening to music and singing Harriet's favorite songs.

Ruth loved Harriet and did not resent caring for her. In fact, she believed that the opportunity to take care of Harriet was a blessing, not a curse. In her words: "Harriet is a 'total need' child, and fortunately, God has blessed me with the disposition and support that enables me to care for her. Harriet's older brother and sister will come to the house that night to celebrate Harriet's birthday, as we have done every year. Other family members, neighbors and friends will also attend the birthday celebration."

Yet, Harriet's severe brain damage was not an "act of God," as that term is used in the law. She was the victim of a medical error that occurred when she was nine months of age.

Harriet was born in March 1971. Her parents, Charles and Ruth Cooper, greeted her with love and took her home, where she was smothered with hugs, kisses, and loving care from her parents and two siblings. Except for a rare blood disorder that causes anemia, Harriet was healthy and vibrant. She developed normally for nine months, growing, putting on weight, and starting to crawl, lift herself up, and babble.

On December 2, 1971, when Harriet was eight months old, Mrs. Cooper took her to Carson Community Hospital for a blood test aimed at determining the cause of the anemia. The physician who performed the test was a hematologist, a specialist in diagnosing and treating blood diseases. To perform the test, the doctor took a sample of bone marrow from Harriet's right hip bone, referred to in medicine as the right posterior iliac crest. Prior to inserting the needle to remove the bone marrow, he injected a small amount of a local anesthetic called Medicaine, generally called lidocaine hydrochloride.

The test took place in a laboratory room located on the pediatric ward. When the test was done, the student nurse who was responsible for caring for Harriet after the test asked whether there was anything she should look out for. The hematologist replied that there was nothing to be concerned about. He had done thousands of these tests, and nothing ever happened after the test is done. Unfortunately, that was not true in Harriet's case.

The nurse took Harriet back to her room and began feeding her orange juice from a bottle. Suddenly, Harriet's arms began to twitch and jerk, and her eyes rolled back in her head. The nurse laid Harriet on a bed and screamed for help. An intern and a resident responded to the call for help. Upon seeing the baby, the resident exclaimed that the child was not choking on orange juice but was experiencing convulsions. The child stopped breathing, and her heart stopped. The resuscitation effort was successful in restoring her heartbeat and breathing, but not in time to avoid Harriet sustaining severe brain damage. Harriet has not been able to walk, talk, or feed herself since December 2, 1971.

When Mrs. Cooper returned to the hospital, the doctor presented her with the horrifying news of Harriet's condition. The treating doctor, a hematologist, explained to Ruth that it would take some time to determine both the cause of the accident and the extent of Harriet's injuries. At that point, the hospital staff thought that Harriet had choked on the orange juice that she was drinking from a bottle after the test had been done. They also thought she would recover.

For months after the accident, Ruth Cooper believed that Harriet would soon recover and begin to walk and communicate. Harriet was Mrs. Cooper's third child, and, based on her observations as a mother, Harriet was progressing wonderfully in her development. Believing that recovery was possible, Mrs. Cooper dutifully took Harriet back and forth to the doctors for examinations, and to the therapists for physical therapy. Each week she would perform the tasks and rehabilitation exercises in accordance with the instructions given to her by the doctors and therapists. As the months passed, it began to sink in that Harriet was not getting better, and that the accident in the hospital had severely and permanently damaged Harriet's brain. The doctors still had no explanation other than that she choked on the orange juice.

Had Mrs. Cooper not had a conversation with George, a lawyer who lived in her neighborhood, she probably would have accepted this explanation and continued with the belief that this was a rare accident that was no one's fault, and that it was now her duty to take care of Harriet with the support of her husband, Harriet's father. The family was buoyed by their religious faith as devout Muslims and relied on their family and religious values to keep moving ahead.

But something about the story that Mrs. Cooper had been told did not make sense to her neighbor. Although he was a new lawyer, practicing real estate law, George had always had a knack for science and medicine. It did not make sense to him that a baby being cared for in a teaching hospital could choke so badly from drinking orange juice from a bottle that she would end up with a cardiac and respiratory attack that was so severe and lasted so long that she would become permanently disabled. After asking several law firms to investigate the case and being rejected, he decided to get the medical records and evaluate the case himself. He called me, a law professor with no trial experience, to help.

The investigation, which included months spent reading medical journal articles and painstaking reviews of drug reaction reports in the drug manufacturer's warehouse, led to the production of evidence that convinced three internationally recognized medical experts that the local anesthetic used in connection with the bone marrow test was the cause of Harriet's medical accident. In addition, serious questions arose as to why the hospital personnel were unsuccessful in resuscitating the infant after she exhibited signs of choking and ensuing cardiorespiratory arrest.

Finally, the investigation of the adverse reactions to the drug revealed that, contrary to the requirements of the Federal Food, Drug and Cosmetic Act, the drug manufacturer, Medico Pharmaceutical Products, Inc., had not filed adverse reaction reports with the Food and Drug Administration. Instead, Medico had taken the position, supported by a legal opinion from its lawyers, that Medicaine, the local anesthetic administered to Harriet, had been on the market in the United States since 1948 and, in Medico's view, that meant that Medicaine was no longer a "new drug" that the FDA had authority to monitor and evaluate for safety and effectiveness.

Even after the discovery of the scientific and other evidence related to the explanation for what caused Harriet's injuries, the perspectives and feelings of those who provided healthcare services and products to the patient/consumer clashed with the view of the patient's family. The doctors and the hospital viewed this catastrophic injury as no one's fault. Rather, it was one of those rare incidences where a patient suffers an unexpected reaction to a prescription drug. After all, it is well known in medicine that the same drug that cures may be the drug that kills. The drug company shared this view and asserted that the drug did not cause the child's injuries; more likely, it was the child's rare blood disease that caused her to convulse and sustain a heart attack. Moreover, if the child did suffer an adverse reaction to the drug, it was an unusual event that was far outweighed by the good that this local anesthetic had done for millions of patients.

All the parties, their lawyers, and the court agreed that the medical case was complicated. Mrs. Cooper decided that she would rely on her lawyers and the expert doctors they retained to unravel the mystery. What she did know was that she took a healthy nine-month-old child to the doctor and left her in his hands for what was supposed to be a minor procedure to perform a blood test. When Ruth Cooper returned to the hospital to retrieve her robust and energetic nine-month-old baby, she found a severely brain damaged child who would never be able to walk, talk, or engage in normal life activities.

The Lawsuit That Lasted Ten Years

The investigation ultimately produced a lawsuit against the physician who administered the local anesthetic, the drug company that manufactured and sold the local anesthetic, the doctors who unsuccessfully tried to resuscitate Harriet, and the hospital that failed to effectively train and prepare its staff to care for an infant who suffered an arrest. A recounting of the lawsuit spawned by the medical care and the drug administered to Harriet requires much more time and space than is allocated for the present book. The litigation lasted for ten years, required three trials for a final resolution, and resulted in a groundbreaking legal decision in a federal court that Medico had sold and distributed Medicaine in a manner that deprived the medical community of important information about the drug's risks.

The jury that heard the evidence in the case against Medico rendered a verdict awarding the child $2.3 million. Prior to the trial of the case against Medico, the doctors and hospitals settled the medical malpractice claims brought against them alleging negligence in properly preparing to recognize and treat the adverse drug reaction Harriet suffered.

In cases where multiple healthcare providers and product sellers have each engaged in conduct that fails to meet professional or governmental standards, tort law provides that all the parties who contributed to the harm may be held responsible for compensating the injured party. This is known as joint and several liability, and in some states it means that each party may be liable for the entire harm (although the injured party may only collect once). In other states, the parties are held proportionately responsible, and the court or jury will allocate damages to each defendant on a comparative basis.

Life after a Catastrophic Injury

Long before the lawsuit finished its ten-year voyage, Mrs. Cooper decided she would take care of Harriet. Her husband and their two older children, along with friends and relatives, chipped in to help care for Harriet. While Harriet was young, and more easily transported, the family took her to events and on vacations as much as possible. When Harriet grew to adulthood, transportation presented a greater challenge, and most care and activities took place in the home.

A conversation with Mrs. Cooper today would not lead one to conclude that she has endured any extra burdens as a result of a lifetime of caring for Harriet. She has benefited from the settlement of the personal injury lawsuit, invested her money wisely, and lives a normal life, taking care of and raising three children. She emphasizes that because Harriet requires "total care" it is not difficult for her to take care of her—bathing, feeding, clothing, and taking her for hospital visits. She has sufficient funds to buy the medical equipment necessary, visit the doctors, purchase the medicine, and take care of all of Harriet's needs. In addition, she can afford a babysitter when she needs to take a day off or to go on a vacation for a week with her family and friends, which she does once a year.

Clearly, the character, personality, and values of Ruth Cooper deserve the major credit for the quality of her life. In fact, she feels sorry for others who now must take care of aging parents who have no experience in taking care of others—an experience she declares she would never trade considering what it has meant to her for her personal development. It is also clear, however, that freedom from worry about the expense required to keep Harriet at home and care for her as a part of the Cooper family has allowed her to continue living her life with dignity.

Reflections on Healthcare, Law, and Catastrophic Injuries

In the absence of a legal system that provided the tools to discover what happened, and to mandate compensation, the Cooper family would have faced a serious struggle to care for a child as severely dependent on medical and social support as Harriet has been. Even with a tort system, they could have lost their claim and turned to the government, charities, family members, and friends for support. As things developed, they won their case, and Mrs. Cooper continues to care for her daughter in her home and to live a life that allows her to engage in social and civic activities and hold her head high when she cares for Harriet, at home and in her community.

In reflecting on the way in which the current legal system resolves a claim of compensation for a devastating injury caused by an accident, I have several concerns and thoughts about the process as it impacts the dignity of patients and healthcare providers. I begin with concerns about patients.

As a lawyer who was involved in sharing the responsibility of representing a family in the scenario described in this chapter, I have formed a firm belief that the healthcare and other basic needs of a severely injured and disabled person should not depend on proof that someone was at fault in causing the injury. The basic human needs of the victim should be met regardless of the cause of the injury. But special concerns arise if the injury results from medical care. The emotional impact on patients and families involved in the litigation process is a high price to pay for a decision about compensation, unless we are unable to come up with other sensible alternative approaches and processes. The uncertainty of outcome and time required to reach a resolution inflicts tremendous emotional and, in some cases, financial pain on families who must take care of an injured party, particularly if the person suffers neurological or orthopedic injuries that render her unable to take care of personal needs such as eating, bathing, and using a toilet. Indeed, if the injured party remains sufficiently intact mentally, the indignities may seem unbearable.

Turning to a consideration of the impact of the medical malpractice lawsuit on a doctor or nurse, a claim of negligence may destroy the healthcare provider's spirit. Even if the individual believes he may have made a mistake, the question remains whether he should experience a reliving of the accident for three to ten years after it occurs. The basic claim that the injured party has to prove goes to the healthcare provider's sense of self-worth because the former patient must offer expert testimony not only that the medical care rendered caused the harm, but also that the doctor or nurse failed to live up to the professional standard of care required of him.

For political reasons, the Obamacare statute did not address the process of resolving medical malpractice claims. It did, however, include a provision that encourages states to explore innovative approaches to resolve medical malpractice claims.[1] In the past thirty years, well before the passage of Obamacare, states began exploring a variety of alternative processes for handling medical claims. Arbitration, mediation, and no-fault compensation schemes have been the most popular.[2]

In reflecting on the needs of a person who suffers a catastrophic injury, I believe that providing that person with access to medical, rehabilitative, nursing, social, and other essential supportive services should be the highest priority.

One way to achieve this goal is to provide universal access to medical and nursing care through a national catastrophic injury compensation fund that offers the combined insurance coverage now available under Medicare and Medicaid. The difference would be that coverage would be automatically available. If the facts underlying the potential tort case are egregious enough to warrant litigation, that litigation should be pursued separately, and we should explore effective means of moving it forward that may include reliance on private lawyers, government lawyers, or public interest lawyers.

Healthcare and supportive services needed by the injured party or his/her family should not depend on the outcome of litigations seeking to deter unreasonable conduct in the future, based on proof of fault and an award of damages for loss of income, pain and suffering, and the ability to enjoy life. With universal access to healthcare, states could revise tort law damage awards to omit medical care expenses, as is done in many states today where medical expenses are covered by a government program. The need to recover for loss of income, pain and suffering, and ability to enjoy life will then guide determinations of whether to bring a medical malpractice action based on fault.

Chapter 10

Orthopedic Health Disparities

Grappling with Socioeconomic Factors That Affect Health and Healthcare

Kathy Jones has been unable to walk more than a few steps for the past two years due to arthritis in both knees. She did not attend her daughter's high school graduation because she was in too much pain to handle the stairs that she would have had to navigate at her home and her daughter's school. She is fifty-five years old, 5 feet, 4 inches tall, and weighs 210 pounds. Her daughter is now in her third year of college, and Kathy is determined to attend her college graduation.

She went to see a doctor who specialized in orthopedic surgery, focusing primarily on knees, and was told she needed both knees replaced but had to lose weight to increase the chances of success of the operation and rehabilitation. Over the next six months after her visit with the orthopedic surgeon, she lost twenty-five pounds, and the surgeon agreed to perform the knee replacements on her. However, when the surgeon sought approval of the surgery from Kathy's insurance company, the surgeon discovered that Kathy's Medicaid insurance company had recently reduced the reimbursement rate for knee replacement surgery so much that the doctor could not perform the surgery on Kathy without incurring a substantial financial loss for her and the hospital.

Kathy is an African American single mother who worked for twenty years as a cook in a small restaurant. She stopped working in the restaurant because of her severe knee pain. She has worked off and on at various part-time jobs over the past two years, but none of the jobs offers health insurance coverage. Kathy now feels trapped in a lifetime of pain. What are her options? We will return to Kathy's story at the end of this chapter.

Being Human: Joint and Bone Health

"Greetings, my fellow humans." Augustus White, MD, a distinguished orthopedic surgeon and professor at Harvard University, often uses this greeting to
initiate a group discussion about healthcare. For a large part of the past decade,
I have had the privilege of serving with Dr. White on Movement Is Life, a national
steering committee that conducts research and collaborates on strategies to
reduce the disparities in joint and bone health based on race and gender in the
United States. I have always found his "fellow humans" greeting to be a calm-
ing reassurance that we will eventually figure out that it is futile to make decisions about human relationships and distributions of goods and services based
on characteristics such as skin color, gender, sexual orientation, national origin, and other superficial traits. As Dr. White reminds us: "Beneath the skin we
are all the same."

Humans of all races, ethnicities, and nations are capable of biologically
reproducing future generations of humans. To the chagrin of many people in
America, we are all capable of falling in love with other human beings who may
be socially constructed and viewed as being from a different race. The fundamental social problem is that we use social constructions of race to divide people
from one another. In the worst-case scenarios, parents teach children to discrim-
inate and hate at such a deep level that bias impacts each generation.

In the United States, the political and cultural classification of black people
as inferior human beings is so entrenched that interracial marriage was classified as a crime until the landmark ruling in 1967 of the U.S. Supreme Court in
Loving v. Virginia, which found that the interracial marriage prohibition violated
the United States Constitution.[1]

In his book *Seeing Patients*, Dr. White writes about his decision to devote
a prestigious lecture, which he was honored to give to the American Association of Orthopedic Surgeons in 1971, to a direct and frank discussion of racism
in medicine.[2] He began the lecture by pointing out the history of doctors performing medical procedures and experiments on African Americans that were
rationalized on the basis that black people were not human. He offered the audience a blunt, direct, and honest declaration: "Inferior medical care (or no care
at all) has accompanied inferior treatment of black Americans across the board
from the earliest colonial period through slavery and segregation—all of it
impelled by propagandistic identification of blacks as something less than fully
human."[3] Later, in a discussion of the continuing racial discrimination in healthcare, Dr. White highlights the key the findings of an Institute of Medicine study
in its report titled *Unequal Treatment*. The Institute of Medicine reviewed

hundreds of research studies done in the 1980s and 1990s that show that not only racial disparities, but also racial discrimination in healthcare, continue to plague the country. Dr. White observes:

> It might be a commonplace that poor people often didn't have private doctors, that lack of insurance meant it wasn't easy for them to see specialists, that they might not be able to afford medications. But why was it, then, that black cardiac patients in the same hospitals and with the same insurance as white cardiac patients received less catheterization, less angioplasty, less bypass surgery? They were even less likely to receive common heart disease medications such as beta blockers, anticlotting drugs, or aspirin. Why was it that, in one of the country's top teaching and research hospitals, black emergency room patients were more likely to be referred to doctors who were still in training as residents while whites were more likely to be referred to experienced staff specialists? And in my own field, just why in the world was it that African Americans brought into ERs with long bone fractures were less likely to receive opioids and other analgesics?[4]

Disparate treatment in healthcare based on race, whether from conscious, unconscious, or structural sources, reveals the profound nature of the reference to common humanity as a standard for rendering medical care and making healthcare research and financing decisions. Science clearly shows that we are all the same beneath the skin, and that skin color cannot account for differences or disparities that manifest in later life in the development of the musculoskeletal system of people in America. How, then, did it turn out that African Americans and other people of color experience a lower quality of life based upon musculoskeletal systems once they become adults? The answer lies in socioeconomic data, explaining the way in which people of color and poor people are forced to live and the way in which they are treated.

The story of Kathy Jones illustrates how the disparities develop and multiply daily on a person-by-person basis. In addition to experiencing the effects of structural bias, individuals of color and those who are poor are frequent victims of the unconscious racial and class bias described in many of the research studies published in the past decade.

There are good and bad uses of race.[5] Medicine proves that point in important ways. For example, identifying the need for research on a disease that predominantly affects African Americans, such as sickle-cell anemia, may lead to an equitable increase in research funding to pursue a cure for that disease. On the other hand, experiments on African Americans to determine the effects of untreated syphilis reflect the lack of a moral compass. There are also many bad uses of race that produce a lower quality of healthcare based on race, such as delayed diagnosis and treatment of diabetes that leads to amputations of limbs that could have been avoided. "My fellow humans" shines a spotlight that assists our sorting out the good uses of race from the bad.

America's response to disparities in joint and bone health provides a useful lens that highlights factors that contribute to health disparities, particularly laws, policies, and practices. These same factors affect other aspects of health, but orthopedic health offers a prism for understanding bias and health disparities because joint health affects the quality of life for large portions of the population regardless of race, gender, or age. When an individual suffers a joint or bone injury or disease, the whole family is adversely impacted, as are many others in the community who frequently interact with the injured person.

When I first joined the steering committee of Movement Is Life, Verona Brewton, the creator and executive director of the organization, urged the committee members to go to any black church on Sunday morning and pay attention to how many people come in on canes or are obese. She also suggested that we pay attention to the church's identification of the "sick and shut-ins" who could not come to church because of illnesses or disability. I could immediately visualize the African Americans who struggle up the stairs to get into the churches I attended, but thereafter I became more conscious of making these observations when I went to any black church. I remain troubled by the disparities and have joined with others to conduct research and explore strategies to reduce them. In an article I co-authored with James Wood, a prominent orthopedic surgeon, and attorney Sherin Fahmy, we reported:

More than one in four Americans suffers from some form of musculoskeletal disorder, making musculoskeletal disorders the leading cause of disability in the United States. As in other areas of health care, minority and female populations within the United States experience disparities in musculoskeletal care. Researchers have documented such disparities in spine surgery, joint replacement, pain management, treatment for osteoporosis and fragility fractures, diabetic foot management, amputations, rehabilitation after a stroke, management of congenital and developmental disorders, and treatment for metastatic prostate cancer.

African Americans, Hispanics, Pacific Islanders, and American Indians experience disparate health outcomes and decreased access to effective operative procedures as compared to other Americans. For example, despite a higher incidence of osteoarthritis, African Americans and

Hispanics receive proportionally fewer total knee and total hip replacement procedures than non-Hispanic white patients. Studies have revealed that "African Americans were nearly 50% less likely than whites to perceive the benefits of total joint [replacement] and 70% more likely than whites to recognize barriers to total joint [replacement]." In fact, lower extremity amputation for the management of diabetic foot ulcers is the only surgical intervention in which minorities receive treatment at a disproportionately high rate.[6]

Poor joint health affects not only the person who is immobilized or who has limited mobility, but also his/her family, friends, and co-workers. In addition, the ability to prevent or ameliorate the bone or joint pain may be significantly influenced by physical activity, which, in turn, is substantially impacted by where a person lives and works. For that reason, the socioeconomic factors that influence joint and bone health require attention in connection with the development and implementation of any strategy aimed at cure or prevention. In addition, in most situations, prevention and treatment strategies are optional, and thus dependent on the mental, emotional, and financial resources of the individuals involved. The factors that influence joint and bone health show that law and policies prove critical to the success of any strategy aimed at promoting health equity in the prevention, restoration, and improvement of a person's orthopedic health.

Joint and bone disease and injuries are the leading cause of disability in the United States, affecting more than twenty-two million adults each year.[7] Many of the people who are struggling up the church stairs on canes and walkers, or who stayed home because they could not get out of the house, are not just the victims of an unfortunate accident or disease. Rather, they are the representatives of the results of the structural violence and social and racial biases discussed earlier in this book and in the references cited. Law and public policies can play a pivotal role in guiding or constricting the strategies that are employed to address this serious problem. The law addresses the relationship between doctors and patients and the decision-making process. The policy most impactful is the funding or reimbursement rate that determines access to healthcare. The discussion below addresses fundamental legal doctrine that applies to decisions about orthopedic care from the patient's decision-making perspective.

Informed Consent and Shared Decision Making

The tort law doctrine of informed consent generates most of the rules that guide the communication process between a doctor and a patient. That doctrine requires doctors to inform patients of the risks, benefits, and alternatives relevant to a proposed medical treatment before instituting medical therapy. It is noteworthy that the seminal case that fueled the tort doctrine of informed consent involved orthopedic care. *Canterbury v. Spence*, previously discussed in chapter 4, is the case where an eighteen-year-old man underwent a surgical procedure to correct his back pain, and after the surgery he was paralyzed from the waist down.[8] He had not been told about the risk of paralysis associated with the surgery. The court held that he should have been told of the risk and that the failure to inform him constituted negligence. Courts who have considered similar medical decisions after *Canterbury* have agreed that informed consent of the patient is required prior to implementing a treatment plan for an orthopedic disease or injury.

Good faith efforts on the part of the medical community to comply with legal requirements for informed consent have revealed that more than information is necessary if we are to correct disparities. Counseling, motivational interviewing, and reform of insurance coverage may prove critical to reducing disparities. In an article reviewing the law of informed consent in the context of joint and bone healthcare, Dr. Wood, attorney Fahmy, and I argued that the law needs to be reformed to encourage the active participation of healthcare providers, family, and community members in assisting the decision making of individuals who must decide how to prevent joint injuries and pain or whether to seek surgical intervention.[9] Because self-help on matters such as diet and exercise is often important in terms of preventive or restorative strategies, many people can avoid surgery if they are diligent and disciplined with exercise and diet. On the other hand, hip or knee replacement surgeries are safe and effective remedies for some people. Often, the decision making is improved by sharing feelings and information between patients and providers.

While the law does not prohibit shared decision-making practices aimed at respecting the autonomy of the patient, privacy mandated by HIPAA (the Health Insurance Portability and Accountability Act of 1996) may discourage the inclusiveness that benefits patients. We have advocated a "safe harbor" established by state law to address these concerns. But even in the absence of formal legal protection, the standard of care of shared decision making, if adopted by healthcare professionals, should induce a change in practice patterns.

New approaches to promoting informed decision making by patients and doctors are essential to reduce health disparities in orthopedics. A few approaches that merit scrutiny and replication are described below.

Toward Patient-Centered Care

In the first decades of the twenty-first century, we dispensed with the medical model of decision making that rested on the premise that the doctor knows best. But we still have a long way to go. A brief review of the evolution of the dominant decision-making models for medical care will help launch the discussion. Prior to the "informed consent" era that emerged in the 1960s, the model relied on the doctor who stood at the top of the medical hierarchy, acquiring the profession's latest medical knowledge and using his skill to treat a patient's illness or injury. This was a world that the preeminent scholar Jay Katz, MD, described and critiqued in a book titled *The Silent World of Doctor and Patient*.[10] In this world, the doctor needed only to use his scientific knowledge to do what he thought best to cure disease, and he had no need to inform the patient of the risks, benefits, or alternatives to the medical intervention he selected. The doctor was legally required to get the patient's consent to surgery, but it need not be "informed."

This model of medical decision making ended during the consumer and civil rights era of the 1960s when the law in the United States was changed by court decisions and state statutes, and legal rules were established to protect a patient's right to decide what was to be done to his/her body. The informed consent model conceptualized the patient as an autonomous decision maker about medical therapy, with the doctor's duty being to provide the patient with enough information to make a knowledgeable decision. The informed consent model emphasized the content of the conversation and paid almost no attention to whether a patient understood the information imparted.[11]

The first two decades of the twenty-first century produced substantial research on the socioeconomic factors that impact health, leading to a public recognition that medical care offered by doctors and hospitals in the traditional manner represented a small percentage of the factors that determine the health and well-being of individuals. With an acknowledgment that environment, place of residence, employment, income, and emotional health impacted heavily on an individual's health, the public policy makers have shifted to an effort to develop more effective models for promoting good health.

What follows is a brief presentation of specific concepts and projects addressing musculoskeletal health. The patient-centered approaches aim to consider the values and needs of a diverse patient population for maintaining, restoring, or improving health. These programs are conceived and implemented on a common belief that an understanding of the patient's needs for specific healthcare requires information about and respect for the community, economic conditions, and social relationships that impact the individual.

Operation Change is a program based in Chicago that was initiated by Movement Is Life, a national caucus focused on musculoskeletal health.[12] Operation Change began as a pilot program to assess the needs of two groups of women who were experiencing limited mobility. One group was Latino, and the other was African American. The initial program lasted for six weeks during the summer and entailed weekly meetings of each group with time for exercise and education through materials and speakers from a variety of disciplines, including orthopedics, law, sociology, and psychology. Reviewers who assessed the program described it as "a community-based, culturally sensitive program to stimulate behavioral changes in activity level and improve musculoskeletal health in African-American (AA) and Hispanic/Latina (H/L) women with obesity and early-stage osteoarthritis."[13]

Many of the participants were socially isolated and experienced depression due to limited mobility. The regular meetings enabled them to connect and communicate with peers and to learn more about medical and community resources that enabled them to exercise, lose weight, and have better nutrition. In addition, they learned about medical options for addressing the pain they were experiencing from aching knees, hips, and backs. The results of the program were summarized as follows: "Participation in Operation Change increased physical activity, resulting in improvements in pain and function scores. This supports a new paradigm for behavioral modification that helps AA and H/L women take an active role in living with osteoarthritis."[14]

Operation Change, like many of the innovative approaches to healthcare that have been adopted in the past two decades, focuses on a strategy of educating and empowering community members to take charge of their health and make better decisions about activities that promote good health, and to learn about medical services available to protect and enhance wellness.

In addition to seeking expertise from medical professionals, many programs invoke the sharing of the knowledge and experiences of patients and consumers who have already elected, and completed, a specific approach to managing a health problem such as cancer or obesity. A program focused on HIV/AIDS has operated in Philadelphia for several decades. It is called Project TEACH and is a component of an array of services offered by an organization called Philadelphia FIGHT.[15] The program consists of several weeks of classes where individuals diagnosed with HIV and their families are educated on medical therapies and clinical trials available to treat their illness. The students who successfully graduate from the program return to help teach future classes.

Another strategy that has met with success is to use the services of professionals as navigators.[16] In this role, the professionals assist the patient or consumer in making a choice about insurance coverage as well as the primary doctors and hospitals they will rely on for their medical care. Navigators proved critical to educating and assisting consumers who were enrolling in Obamacare.[17] They are also effective in helping patients navigate the healthcare system. For example, Cooper University Hospital in Camden, New Jersey, established a program to enhance the care given to patients who frequently rely on the emergency room for their healthcare.

A hospital study revealed that 20 percent of the emergency room patients produced 90 percent of the hospital's medical costs.[18] The approach taken was to identify what the hospital called "medically complex" patients. The healthcare staff determined that because of the social conditions in which the patients lived or their limited health literacy, the patients were failing to take their medicine or adhere to other important therapeutic regimens. To assist the patients with their healthcare, hospital navigators visited the patients in their homes and neighborhoods and established relationships that enabled them to monitor the patients and assist them in addressing their medical needs.

Other hospitals have developed medical-legal partnerships, setting up teams of healthcare providers and lawyers or law students to identify and address legal barriers that prevent patients from getting good medical care.[19] Under this arrangement, the legally trained participants are integrated into the healthcare team, often working out of offices in the hospital.

Another barrier to healthcare has been a developing shortage of primary care doctors. One potential remedy for this shortage may be the expansion of medical services provided by nurse practitioners, who practice in connection with or independent from physicians. Currently, each state has specific licensing requirements and limitations on the medical services that a nurse practitioner can provide, but there is growing recognition of the skill, knowledge, and patient needs that nurse practitioners can provide.

Finally, hospitals are exploring new approaches to offer medical services and form new relationships with the communities in which they reside, as well as with other healthcare professionals. Reducing reliance on emergency rooms is a critical strategy that will reduce costs and enable more efficient administration of high-quality care to patients. A key part of a hospital's approach to care in the future is likely to be partnering with other healthcare providers, social service providers, and community leaders to take a multidisciplinary approach to providing healthcare to the community.

To be effective and sustainable, the healthcare system of the future must develop more efficient methods of delivering healthcare while at the same time respecting the dignity of individuals with widely varying resources and knowledge about health. A focus on the importance of treating people with dignity will throw light on options that meet the health needs of patients, while at the same time enabling healthcare providers to develop programs and strategies that make the delivery of healthcare more equitable and financially sustainable. Difficult financial decisions will still have to be made. But these decisions are more likely to be accepted and viewed as moral and equitable when made with transparency and input from the community members directly affected. If the concept of patient-centered care is going to have a positive and lasting impact on the quality of healthcare, it must rest on the moral and ethical mandate that everyone is entitled to be treated in a way that makes each person feel as though his life matters.

Revisiting Kathy Jones

Imagine if we met Kathy Jones two years after she had lost weight and was rejected for the knee replacement surgery she needed to eliminate her pain and regain her mobility. How would we respond to her on a personal level, as well as a political level, when learning that she is still in pain and more immobilized— unable to attend her daughter's college graduation? Would we just say we are sorry and wish her good luck in the future, knowing that she is unable to enjoy most of the activities that bring her meaning and happiness in life? Do we start a GoFundMe campaign on social media or send her church or other charitable organizations financial contributions? Or do we expect doctors, hospitals, and other healthcare providers to fix her knees at a financial loss to themselves?

This chapter ends with a series of policy questions that we must resolve as a nation in the twenty-first century. The first question relates to osteoarthritis, but it should be asked and answered with respect to all disabling diseases that medicine can treat or prevent. If twenty million people suffer from disabling osteoarthritis, can we afford to take care of all of them? Or, stated differently, can we afford not to take care of them?

If we strive to build a health system that provides "essential health services" to everyone, should osteoarthritis and other joint and bone disabling conditions be included among those essential services? If medical care is available to everyone, should it include prevention as well as restoration? Should insurance coverage be limited to pain medication or should it extend to exercise facilities, physical therapists, psychologists, and surgeons?

Should the answers to these questions be the same for every human being, or should the healthcare available be determined based on wealth, class, age, race, ethnicity, national origin, gender, religion, or sexual orientation? Does an economic analysis lead to the same conclusion as a moral analysis? Should healthcare be classified as a privilege or a human right?

The initial chapters of this book related stories about emergency care. The answer to the question of whether we have an obligation to provide emergency care in order to save a human being from imminent death or a disabling injury was an easy one for me to answer. But once we answer that question, we must then decide whether healthcare in America can and should be a legally protected human right. And if healthcare is a human right, which I contend it is, we can begin to wrestle with the hard questions of what we mean by healthcare and how we pay for the minimum that ought to be available to all members of our society.

I think, ultimately, these are moral questions that each person must answer for herself. And in answering these questions, it is critical to have a moral compass to guide you. To paraphrase the Cheshire cat in Lewis Carroll's *Alice in Wonderland*, if you don't know where you are going, any road will take you there. The road I am urging us to take heads toward embracing healthcare as a human right. We may disagree on which road will take us to that destination, but if we agree on the destination we will eventually get there.

Chapter 11

Paying for Healthcare

Lessons from a Fifty-Year-Old
Government Program Called Medicare

"Keep your government hands off my Medicare," yelled a senior citizen attending a town hall meeting in South Carolina in 2009. In a July 30, 2009, article titled "Health Care Realities," Paul Krugman reported the incident with humor, but then noted the serious underlying problem.[1] Representative Bob Inglis of South Carolina, the congressman to whom the remark was addressed, "tried to explain that Medicare is already a government program—but the voter, Mr. Inglis said, 'wasn't having any of it.'"

To anyone familiar with just the basics of healthcare financing in America, that was a funny demand, and it became one of the most quoted statements of the year. But if you get beyond the laughter, the vehement demand that reflects a passionate opposition to government is scary, particularly because it shows a fundamental lack of understanding that the Medicare program is not only a government program, but one of the most successful social service programs ever conceived and implemented. It works so well that even conservative senior citizens demand to keep the benefits that the program provides to them. AARP summarized the impact of Medicare on access to healthcare in a recent report:

Medicare provides health coverage to more than 57 million Americans. Over 18 percent of the nation's population relies on Medicare for health security. As more baby boomers turn 65, enrollment will reach 64 million in 2020 and 81 million in 2030. In 2016, over one-third of people receiving Medicare benefits were ages 75 and older. **Medicare is not just for those 65 years old and over**. In 2016, about one in six beneficiaries (16 percent) qualified for coverage before turning 65, on the basis of permanent disability. These individuals tend to have lower incomes and higher rates of health problems than older beneficiaries, including cognitive impairments and limitations in activities of daily living.[2]

In addition to providing access to medical care for all Americans over sixty-five years of age for more than fifty years, the federal government used the spending power of Medicare to eliminate racial discrimination in hospitals. David Barton Smith, in his book *The Power to Heal*, describes how the federal government used the financial power of government spending under Medicare to integrate both patient care and hospital medical staffs. Within one year of active enforcement of the Medicare program, which refused to fund racially discriminatory conduct, hospitals ended their practices of segregating or refusing to admit African American patients for treatment and of refusing to hire African American doctors and nurses. Unlike the battles in the halls of state governments and the streets of the South and the North over integration of schools and public transportation, the primary weapon used to transform the policies and practices of healthcare institutions was the power of the government's purse. With the federal government making it crystal clear that it was serious about integration, the dignity of African Americans both to receive nondiscriminatory admissions to hospitals as patients and to become members of the medical staff was protected.

The design and implementation of the Medicare program have made it one of the healthcare insurance programs that produces the highest satisfaction from its beneficiaries, beating the consumer satisfaction ratings of private health insurance companies.[3] Medicare provides access to care for all seniors and for people who suffer disabling conditions such as kidney failure. It is important to note, however, that Medicare does not cover catastrophic injuries. The basic medical benefits include Part A coverage of hospital expenses and Part B coverage of doctor expenses. In addition, supplemental coverage is available for medical care under Part D. With this design, the program offers both guaranteed care and choice for additional services and products. A Center for Medicare Services (CMS) report explains the coverage available:

> The three components of Medicare are Parts A, B, and D. Part A, or hospital insurance (HI), provides coverage for inpatient hospital services, skilled nursing facility services, hospice services, and post-institutional home health care. Covered services and items under Part B—one component of supplementary medical insurance (SMI)—include physician services, durable medical equipment, laboratory services, outpatient hospital services, physician-administered drugs, dialysis, and certain other

home health care services. The other component of SMI, Part D, princi-
pally provides access to prescription drug coverage through private insurance plans beginning in 2006.[4]

Medicare derives its revenue from several sources, including a trust fund that
earns interest and federal government transfers of funds from the general budget. Another key source of revenue is taxes on workers' earnings, either as a payroll tax or a tax on independent earnings. Some have argued that a tax on
earnings is unfair because benefits are the same for everyone, and do not consider the amount a Medicare beneficiary contributed to the fund. CMS explains:
"In practice, the role of participant income in Medicare is convoluted: workers
pay the HI payroll tax on their earnings, but all participants qualify for the same
HI benefits regardless of the total amount of taxes they have paid. Part B is voluntary, with the same benefits regardless of income, but, starting in 2007, high-
income beneficiaries will pay higher Part B premiums. Low-income Part D
beneficiaries can qualify for Medicare assistance with Part D premiums and cost-
sharing requirements."[5]

Some critics of Medicare argue that the program is unfair to the younger
generation who must support an increasing number of aging citizens who are
living longer and consuming a disproportionate amount of healthcare resources
at the end of life. A CMS report acknowledges this concern: "Medicare also
raises important intergenerational equity questions. The retirement of the post–
World War II baby boom generation will substantially increase the ratio of
Medicare beneficiaries to working-age persons. Since Medicare is financed on
a pay-as-you-go basis, the demographic change will have a sizable effect on the
cost of the program relative to workers' earnings and the GDP. Proposals to
address Medicare's financial status can have markedly different impacts on one
generation's Medicare value compared to another's."[6]

Sustainability Issue

An essential question that must be answered about the Medicare program is
whether it is sustainable, financially and politically. As CMS recognizes, the
answer depends in part on economics and in part on the predominant values
that Americans endorse in the twenty-first century:

> Medicare general revenues are projected to increase from 13.6 percent of
> Federal income taxes in 2010 to 57 percent by 2080. The figure gives an
> illustration of the projected impact of current law Medicare growth on the
> Federal budget. Implications of this sort of growth could include reduced
> spending on other Federal programs, increased Federal borrowing, or

increased taxes. While some of these outcomes may be undesirable, their impact would have to be considered in relation to the effect of slowing the growth of Medicare spending. Again, society will ultimately be the judge of Medicare's sustainability.[7]

The Medicare program is constantly changing in an effort to meet concerns about financial sustainability and fairness. An economic analysis of the program finds critics and supporters on both sides. However, no one can dispute the fact that the program has provided care and saved the lives of millions of seniors for over fifty years. Despite the success of the Medicare program, it attracts vehement criticism from people who want to limit the role of government based on their political and economic philosophies.

Medicare is also opposed by citizens who believe that government programs primarily benefit minorities and poor people who are unwilling to work.[8] The facts do not support that view. According to an estimate by the Kaiser Family Foundation, based on Census Bureau data from 2016, 76 percent of the beneficiaries were white, 10 percent black, 8 percent Hispanic, and 6 percent other.[9]

Another source of misunderstanding is that many people do not know the difference between the Medicare program for seniors and the Medicaid program for the poor and disabled. The racial and ethnic distribution of Medicaid benefits to people of color does include a higher percentage than the Medicare distribution, but this is not surprising given the disparities in wealth and employment among white Americans and people of color.[10] The Kaiser Family Foundation reported that in 2016 Medicaid was nationally distributed among nonelderly as follows: 43 percent white, 18 percent black, 30 percent Hispanic, and 9 percent other. Medicaid coverage eligibility is based on poverty or low income, and blacks and Hispanics, as groups, bear the burden of lower-paying jobs and underemployment when compared to whites.[11] Nevertheless, the Medicaid program cannot fairly be characterized as a minority benefit health insurance program. It benefits the poor and the disabled of all races and ethnicities. This is important to keep in mind when considering the political forces seeking to deny the expansion of Medicaid under the Affordable Care Act (ACA) or to repeal the ACA completely.

The administrative structure of Medicare relies on the federal government as a single-party payer to develop and implement policies. In comparison, the Medicaid program operates through a federal-state partnership, allowing each state to decide whether it will participate and what income level will qualify a resident in that state for participation in Medicaid. Empowering states to make the Medicaid healthcare coverage decisions for the poor opens the door for political decisions based on the culture and values that dominate a particular state. "States' rights" has historically served as a rallying cry for people who want to perpetuate a system that privileges whites over others, and that continues today. Notwithstanding this history, the U.S. Supreme Court ruled in response to a constitutional challenge to the ACA that compelling states to expand Medicaid coverage under the ACA or lose federal funds violated traditional powers allocated to the states under federalism.[12] The political result was predictable. Drawing a map of the ex-slaveholding states almost completely coincided with the states that refused to expand Medicaid coverage to allow state residents to qualify for Obamacare.[13]

Payment Models and Human Dignity

The choice of whether and how to pay for healthcare has both a financial and dignitary impact on individuals who need healthcare. While every government must set limits on the healthcare it will pay for, the varying impact on different populations is not always transparent. Take, for example, the impact of the decision to enroll in managed care and the differing impact that the decision has on a young person just entering the workforce and a senior who has retired.

A Personal Story

I will use my father as an example of how a payment model affects an elderly person in need of healthcare for chronic illnesses. My father worked fifteen hours a day for forty-five years. He had two full-time jobs: one as the owner of a barbershop that served the black community with two other barbers employed full-time; and another full-time job as a steelworker. Having migrated from rural South Carolina to Pittsburgh, he was determined to make a better life for his family than was available to blacks in the Jim Crow South.

By the age eighty-three, he had been retired for fifteen years and devoted a substantial portion of his time to seeing doctors for himself or taking my mother to see a doctor. At the age of eighty-three, he faced the choice of continuing in Medicare under a fee for service plan or switching to managed care. In 1999, I described in a law review article[14] how his experiences in the American healthcare system affected his views of doctors:

> Similar to other retired persons in my father's age group, health care
> looms large in their lives. The most significant trips he and my mother
> now make are visits to an array of doctors. The trips to the doctor are pre-
> ceded by detailed preparation regarding the route of travel and the matters
> to be reported to the doctor after they arrive. Usually my sister or brother

transport[s] them to the various doctors' offices and participate[s] in the discussions, when they are allowed to do so by the doctors.

For my parents, the choice of whether to enroll in a managed care plan has immediate consequences as to which doctors they are able to see. At this stage in his life, my father has formed some rather firm opinions about doctors. He does not trust young doctors because they are inexperienced and always in a rush. He does not trust white doctors because they do not really care whether black people live or die. He has many personal experiences, as well as stories told to him from the time he was a young boy, for those who want to dismiss his distrust based on skin color as racist. He does not trust foreign doctors because he cannot understand them and they cannot understand him. Indeed, he had been victimized by a foreign doctor who exceeded the scope of the consent my father gave for limited surgery. After my father complained about the violation of consent, the doctor asserted that "there must have been a misunderstanding." He does not trust young black doctors because too many of them have forgotten where they came from and only care about making money. The only doctors he really trusts are African-American doctors around his age, but there are few of them still practicing. So he does the best he can with the doctors available but stays on the alert. He is highly suspicious of the motivations of every doctor and skeptical of all of their diagnoses and advice. Yet, he depends on them to keep his now fragile body functioning.[15]

For my father, adopting a managed care plan would mean he would have to find a new doctor. It would also mean a change in where he traveled to see the doctor. At the age of eighty-three, my father still had a driver's license, but we discouraged him from driving, and my brother and sister who lived close to my parents undertook the responsibility of transporting him to his many doctor visits. Alternatively, he sometimes took public transportation or a taxi, both of which were burdensome. The taxi was expensive; the public transportation was difficult to navigate if you walked slowly on a cane with a bad back caused by forty years of physical work. He asked me what he should do.

As I reflect on this period of my father's life, I understand much more fully now than I did at the time how important it is to human dignity to have the power to make decisions about your everyday activities in general, but, particularly, to make decisions as to whom to trust with your healthcare. A person who lives to the traditional age of retirement around sixty-five begins to lose control over many of the experiences that shaped him or her as a person. My father spent most of his life as a solid rock in a family that he was committed to caring for. Whether it was money, love, or discipline, he was much better at dispensing than receiving. The notion of having someone tell him what to do—particularly outside of an employment setting—was totally unacceptable to him. He also had undergone enough experiences wherein he felt his trust had been betrayed and was on guard to protect himself from those types of encounters. At age eighty-three, he knew he could not protect himself physically, but was determined not to yield his emotional and mental powers to tell people what to do and to draw limits on what they could do for him. For the protection of his dignity and decision-making power, it seemed in my father's best interest to remain in a fee for service Medicare plan, and I so advised him.

While my father's story is unique to his life situation, it is representative of the experiences of many seniors. In important ways, my father reaped the privileges and benefits that all deserve, but many fail to receive, after a lifetime of hard work. He had a pension, a house, post-employment healthcare supplemental insurance, and, most importantly, Medicare. In truth, he needed each of those benefits to continue to live his life with dignity. He was also fortunate to have children willing to support and help him, but nothing provides dignity like the ability to take care of your own financial and personal needs.

At a certain age, as Atul Gawande artfully describes, almost everyone begins to appreciate what it means to be mortal, and so do others around you.[16] Your bones begin to deteriorate, your physical strength wanes, and your mind is not as sharp. Fortunately, for the past fifty years in America, one thing you do not have to worry about as you get older is whether you will have health insurance that gives you access to doctors, nurses, and hospitals. That explains why, even through ignorance of the source of his health security, a man would scream to a congressman, "Keep your government hands off my Medicare." It is vital that you have the assistance and guidance of healthcare professionals and access to prescription drugs, hospitals, and nursing care or home support. If you have the security of access to the core components of healthcare in the twenty-first century, the next challenge is to exercise good decisions as a consumer. From the supply side, the challenge is to make rational decisions as to what healthcare to cover and how to make the system economically sustainable.

Lessons from Managed Care

At the time my father requested my advice on whether to enroll in a managed care Medicare program or to remain in the traditional Medicare fee-for-service plan, many governmental bodies and policy makers viewed managed care as offering an effective approach to containing medical costs. It would soon become clear, however, that this strategy of cost containment posed a threat to the dignity and health of patients and to the dignity of physicians.

One of the many disturbing cases that resulted in a reported court decision involved a woman insured in California under the Medicaid program who underwent complicated surgery on her legs and was required by a managed care company to leave the hospital four days after the operation, even though her surgeon had requested that she stay in the hospital for eight days for treatment and observation.[17] The patient, Mrs. Wickline, a woman in her mid-forties, was sent home with her husband, where the pain and discoloration in her leg increased over several days. By the time she and her husband decided she should return to the hospital, it was too late to save her leg. The surgeon amputated her leg and later testified that the insurance company's rejection of his request for an extended hospital stay was unreasonable, and had she been allowed to stay in the hospital for the time he requested, she would not have lost her leg. The extended stay was rejected based on a review of the request by a doctor employed by the insurance company who never examined the patient and made his decision based on a review of the medical records. Notwithstanding what appeared to be a bad decision on the part of the insurance company, the court held that the company was not responsible to Mrs. Wickline for the loss of her leg because it had in place a process that would have allowed her treating doctor to appeal the initial rejection of his request for an extended stay, and he failed to process an appeal.

The court did comment, however, that if an insurance company used a process of decision making that corrupted the treating doctor's medical decision making or did not supply reasonable means of appealing medical treatment requests, the insurance company could be held liable. This legal analysis allowed managed care companies to use procedures aimed at containing healthcare costs that encouraged or required medical care and treatment that was different than the care a treating doctor believed was best for her patient. Nevertheless, the U.S. Supreme Court explained in another case challenging the healthcare dictates of another managed care company that containment of costs is a legitimate goal for federal government–authorized managed care companies to pursue in accordance with what Congress considered to be sound public policy. The Court explained:

> Since inducement to ration care goes to the very point of any HMO scheme, and rationing necessarily raises some risks while reducing others (ruptured appendixes are more likely; unnecessary appendectomies are less so), any legal principle purporting to draw a line between good and

bad HMOs would embody, in effect, a judgment about socially acceptable medical risk. A valid conclusion of this sort would, however, neces-
sarily turn on facts to which courts would probably not have ready access:
correlations between malpractice rates and various HMO models, similar correlations involving fee-for-service models, and so on. And, of
course, assuming such material could be obtained by courts in litigation
like this, any standard defining the unacceptably risky HMO structure
(and consequent vulnerability to claims like Herdrich's) would depend
on a judgment about the appropriate level of expenditure for health care
in light of the associated malpractice risk. But such complicated factfind-
ing and such a debatable social judgment are not wisely required of
courts unless for some reason resort cannot be had to the legislative process, with its preferable forum for comprehensive investigations and
judgments of social value, such as optimum treatment levels and healthcare expenditure.[18]

The role played by managed care companies differs significantly from the
role played by the traditional health insurance company that offers an indemnity insurance plan. Under the indemnity plan, the doctor makes the medical
decision considering, as best he can in a nonemergency situation, what the
insurance company has agreed to pay for, and the final approval of payment
takes place after the medical care has been rendered. Under the traditional
indemnity plan, the insurance company reviews the propriety of the medical
care after it has been rendered. In contrast, the review that denied Mrs. Wickline's care took place prior to the provision of the specific medical care preferred
by her doctor, namely, an eight-day stay in the hospital for treatment and observation. This is referred to as a "prospective review" of proposed medical care.
Under this arrangement, the insurer informs the doctor or hospital, in advance,
whether it will pay for the proposed plan of treatment.

It is unrealistic to expect the average layperson to understand the procedures
and options described above at the time they select a plan and sign numerous
insurance company documents. Young people who learn that they have made a
mistake in selecting the best insurance plan for their current situation have an
opportunity to change, usually before the selection has a serious impact on their
health. Many seniors live with concurrent illnesses that require chronic care and
treatment, so that a year under the wrong plan can have consequences that seriously affect their health and their lives. This foreseeable lack of understanding of
the legal and medical consequences of selecting a particular plan cries out for
providing navigators to assist seniors who are selecting insurance plans.

Setting Limits

On both an individual level and a broad policy level, limits to medical care are required to make any system sustainable. Both the standards employed and the process used to set the limits should be subjected to critical social, political, and moral analysis to control or limit the biases in healthcare that we have explored throughout this book. I have provided references to studies and literature that demonstrate how these biases affect personal and professional institutions and policy decision making. Critical components of effective approaches to minimizing healthcare bias include transparency of conscious factors supporting the proposed limits and a willingness to probe beneath the surface to identify unconscious and structural biases in operation.

I offer two examples of transparency that I believe deserve appreciation, and perhaps duplication. Both involve policy making. One is the argument that Daniel Callahan made several decades ago, in his book entitled *Setting Limits*:[19] that the elderly have a moral duty to future generations to limit their consumption of resources, including healthcare. This proposition evoked strident opposing arguments, but what I like about it was the transparency and willingness to defend a specifically articulated value system. I agree with Dr. Callahan's argument that people who have enjoyed a long life on earth have a moral duty consider how their consumption of healthcare resources affects the future of generations that follow. However, translating that moral concern into policies and practices is likely to confront insurmountable moral and practical barriers. Morally, it is difficult to defend an explicit policy that relies on age alone as the basis of denying healthcare to individuals who want and need healthcare. Whatever age is selected will not produce a uniform picture of the person's past and future enjoyment of community benefits, consumption of resources, and continued contributions to the community. The wide variations of health and socioeconomic circumstances produce a great deal of examples where making a healthcare decision to deny care based solely on age is both illogical and morally repugnant. To whom do we say that you have lived long enough, and can we say it on a categorical basis of age? Probably not. It may, however, promote sound economic and moral decision making to encourage patients and providers to consider the benefits of proposed healthcare in light of the cost of the care to their immediate family and community members, as well as future generations.

The other example of transparent healthcare rationing decision making that warrants consideration is the Oregon Plan, adopted to determine the medical care that would be available to Medicaid beneficiaries in the state of Oregon.[20]

A commission was established to conduct public hearings to get input on how to rank health services that should be prioritized. The premise was that by agreeing to limits on a collective basis, a plan could be adopted that enabled a larger number of people to have healthcare coverage. Kaiser Permanente took a similar approach when it was met by HIV/AIDS protests against its limitation of medical care coverage. In a series of broadcasts critically assessing American medicine, journalist Mark Shafer praised the approach Kaiser Permanente took to the AIDS crisis:

> Our broadcast focuses on the original home to Kaiser Permanente, the Northern California region, principally the San Francisco Medical Center. That is where on World Aids [sic] Day 1995, AIDS activists converged to protest Kaiser's conservative approach to treating HIV and AIDS. Rather than shrink from the pressure, Kaiser Permanente took the bold step of bringing its harshest critics inside the organization, making them leaders of its unique HIV advisory board.
>
> Despite the fact that people with HIV and AIDS are among the most costly patients—averaging close to $20,000 a year in drug costs alone—Kaiser launched a public ad campaign touting its beefed up HIV program. "Most health plans would never do an advertisement saying, 'We take good care of HIV,' because they would then get HIV patients who are expensive and they'd lose money on them," says health care analyst Dr. Thomas Bodenheimer, a San Francisco physician who works outside Kaiser.[21]

This approach of transparency reflects respect for individual dignity and prioritizes dignity as an essential component of a healthcare program that must set limits.

Medicare for All?

With fifty years of experience with Medicare as a government-run single-party payer healthcare system, it is fair to ask the question whether it is time for America to recognize healthcare as a human right and adopt a plan based on the Medicare model that provides healthcare insurance for all. In an illuminating article written prior to the adoption of Obamacare, Professor Barry Furrow argues that it is time to directly confront the negative impact of the free market ideology on efforts to achieve universal access to healthcare.[22] He points to three significant barriers to extending Medicare to all as a way of achieving universal access to healthcare in the United States: "The evidence—as to what will work, and what will be most efficient and fair—is increasingly uncontroverted, but the path to reform is impeded by three bramble bushes: the history of our health care system and its resulting fragmentation; the entrenched interests tied to employment-based insurance; and ideology."[23]

Professor Furrow and other scholars have noted that by providing health-care insurance to seniors through Medicare, to the poor through Medicaid, and to the working and middle class through their employers, the United States adopted an approach to healthcare coverage that fragmented the political will of the country as a whole for universal access to medical care.[24] Professor Furrow argues that it is irrational and cruel to direct people who lack the personal resources to purchase health insurance on the private market when it is obvious they cannot afford the insurance being offered on the private market.[25] While the free market system preserves the important right of consumer choice, that right is meaningless if you lack the money to make a choice. From a moral perspective, one cannot defend strict devotion to a free market approach to access to healthcare when the income inequality among those who need care varies dramatically. So long as one person can buy fifty homes and eat at an expensive restaurant every night, and another cannot afford to even rent a room or buy a hamburger, the notion that the free market is a fair way of determining who gets healthcare is not only ludicrous; it is inhumane. Nevertheless, ideology remains a dominant force that must be addressed in order to construct a healthcare system that honors the importance of individual human dignity. A brief review of the events preceding and following the adoption of Obamacare offers a perspective on the role of ideology in propelling and resisting America's movement toward Medicare for all citizens of the United States.

The Fight over Obamacare

On March 14, 2017, the *New York Times* reported that the Congressional Budget Office (CBO) had reviewed a proposed Republican healthcare reform bill and concluded that it would mean twenty-four million more Americans would be uninsured under the GOP plan.[26] The story summarized the CBO's assessment of the Republicans' proposed statute, crafted by Speaker of the House Paul Ryan, and supported by the newly elected president, Donald Trump. The forthright purpose of the new plan was to repeal the ACA. The ACA was by now popularly known as Obamacare," a name given to the statute by Republicans opposed to the ACA because it had been enacted under the leadership of President Obama.

At the beginning of President Obama's first term as president, Senate Majority Leader Mitch McConnell and other Republicans announced that their highest priority was to oppose Mr. Obama on every score and assure that he was a one-term president. To support their attack on the ACA, Republican opponents of the law sought to invoke animus from citizens who did not like President Obama. In response, President Obama and others embraced the name "Obamacare" as a source of pride rather than shame. The Affordable Care Act represented the first major federal bill offering health insurance to U.S. citizens since the adoption of Medicare and Medicaid in 1965 and provided insurance coverage to over twenty-five million people who were previously uninsured. Enacting the healthcare reform bill was the signature accomplishment of President Obama during his first term as president. As I listened to and read the arguments about repealing Obamacare, I thought about how quickly political gamesmanship buries concerns about the suffering of Americans who live without healthcare. This book offers stories and legal cases that remind us why we need universal access to healthcare as well as a sustained national program to build a viable and equitable healthcare system.

The approach taken by a national government to providing or denying healthcare reveals the core values of the nation. The United States is the only developed country that does not provide universal access to healthcare. Many Trump supporters oppose universal access to healthcare because they embrace a free market ideology that posits the best way of producing and distributing goods and services. In their view, access to healthcare is just another good or service that the free market can handle. Other Trump supporters oppose Obamacare based on racism. Negative feelings about race were deliberately unleashed by Trump's rhetoric, which legitimized expressions of group-based biases centered on race and religion.[27] Donald Trump motivated his base who clamored for the "repeal of Obamacare" by rhetoric suggesting that what the America white citizens valued was being taken away from them by Latino immigrants coming across the border, Muslims flying into the country, and people of color living in urban communities who were unfairly benefiting from Obamacare.

During President Obama's first term, Republicans could not muster enough votes to repeal Obamacare. They also failed to defeat his reelection bid. President Obama's election to a second term did not, however, stop the Republicans from trying to repeal Obamacare during the next four years. During his eight years as president, Republicans in Congress made over seventy attempts to repeal Obamacare, but none was successful.[28]

While campaigning for the presidency, Donald Trump proclaimed to cheering supporters that one of the first things he would do if elected would be to repeal Obamacare. The Republican Party spent six years, starting immediately after the passage of the ACA, criticizing the statute and trying to repeal it. Oddly enough, the statute drafted by Speaker Ryan to abolish Obamacare did not get enough votes in the House of Representatives to pass because the self-named

Freedom Caucus, an ultraconservative group within the Republican Party, thought that the bill Ryan drafted was too liberal, even though it was projected to take away coverage from an estimated twenty-five million people. Contending that the draft bill did not save enough money, the seventeen members of the Freedom Caucus refused to support the bill drafted by Ryan, and no Democrat voted to support it, leaving it short of the votes necessary to pass. Despite the projections of the nonpartisan CBO that the proposed bill will take away insurance from millions of citizens, politicians advocating the repeal of Obamacare expressed almost no concern about the consequences to individuals who would be excluded from healthcare coverage under the Republican plan. They chose, instead, to blame Obamacare for rising health insurance premiums and to argue that rising healthcare costs and premiums proved that the ACA was not sustainable.

Although rising healthcare costs represent a serious problem, Obamacare was not the cause of the rising costs, and the Republican arguments were part of a campaign of misinformation that gave rise to confusion about the ACA on a national scale. An article in the *New York Times* in February 2017 reported on a survey that found that 35 percent of respondents did not know that the Affordable Care Act and Obamacare were the same thing.[29] The survey also found that 45 percent of respondents did not know that if Obamacare was repealed, the ACA would also be repealed. Furthermore, 61 percent did not know that repealing the ACA would result in lost coverage under Medicaid and loss of subsidies for private health insurance.

Unfortunately, the public has shown that it is easy prey for those who want to spread false information, particularly on social media. In addition, proponents of healthcare reform bills such as Obamacare failed to educate the public on the core features of the law and the reasons the reforms were necessary. Nor did proponents explain how the reforms would stem the tide of rising healthcare costs, control premiums, and increase access to healthcare. One component of Obamacare was well explained and was embraced by the public: insurance companies could no longer reject an applicant because he had a preexisting condition. Unfortunately, a significant number of Americans thought that this important health reform would still exist even if Obamacare was repealed.

The Trump administration continued to undermine the effectiveness of Obamacare by reducing the budget for navigators to educate members of the public about enrollment options, reducing the enrollment period, and eliminating subsidies. Undoubtedly, the efforts to destroy Obamacare will continue, notwithstanding the absence of a healthcare financing plan to replace it.

The vehement efforts to repeal Obamacare are odd, considering the coverage it brought to millions of uninsured people and the way in which the plan accommodated the conflicting claims of diverse parties with vested interests. Obamacare allowed employment-based insurance for the majority of workers to continue. It also left Medicare covering people over sixty-five undisturbed and sought to expand coverage of the poor under Medicaid by providing monetary support to the states' Medicaid programs. Finally, Obamacare accommodated the interests of private insurance companies motivated by potential profits in the marketplace and consumers who either wanted a choice of insurers or who did not qualify for existing insurance plans to buy health insurance in a newly created market with a variety of plans. The Obamacare statute was far from perfect, making it a target for criticism from both progressives and conservatives. However, the new healthcare plan had enough merit, followed by success in increasing access in its first few years, to warrant support and efforts to revise and improve it. Instead, the cry from Republicans has been for repeal, even in the absence of a plan to replace Obamacare.

Given the ideological divisions, the changes in the population in terms of age, race, and immigration, and the increasing income and wealth inequality in America, it appears to me that we have reached a winner-takes-all conflict over healthcare, among other critical public policy issues. If that is the case, there may be no better time than the present for proponents of a more equitable and sustainable healthcare financing system to muster the evidence and arguments that the best healthcare reform approach for America in the twenty-first century is Medicare for all.[30] While it will probably take several years for politicians to support a single-party payer on a national level, evidence is mounting that the public and important constituencies in the healthcare industry may be willing to support a system that allows universal access to healthcare.[31]

The enactment and implementation of Obamacare provide a source of both hope and despair for advocates of universal access to healthcare. The last chapter of this book reviews our latest political fight over healthcare and healthcare reform. The hope is that our fifty years of experience with Medicare and Medicaid and our experience with increasing access to care for millions under Obamacare will encourage a coalition of diverse people and communities to demand healthcare for all. The despair is that the emotions and false information that have fueled opposition to Obamacare and encouraged piecemeal repeal will succeed in paralyzing the U.S. Congress or impelling it to block the path to universal access.

Chapter 12

Healthcare and Human Dignity in a Diverse and Changing World

The Critical Role of Empathy, Compassion, and Humility

In 2010 reports emerged revealing that American scientists conducted research on people in Guatemala that entailed injecting the research subjects with syphilis.[1] The Tuskegee Syphilis Study on the effects of untreated syphilis in black men was horrible. But the study in Guatemala was even worse. *Researchers actually injected the syphilis in these human beings* so that they could conduct scientific research. The research was conducted decades earlier, but the public disclosure of this inhumane study emerged only in the past decade.

Another article published in 2013 told the story of research conducted on poor men in New York in the 1950s and 1960s.[2] The article describes clinical trials conducted on poor men living in the area known as the Bowery. The men in the study were tested for prostate cancer and then operated on if they were found to have cancer. The men were induced to participate in the study, which involved undergoing surgical biopsies of their prostates, by promising them food for a few days, a clean bed, and medical treatment if the test revealed they had cancer. The men were not carefully informed of the risks of prostate surgery, including impotency and other side effects such as laceration of the bowel. Unlike modern prostate biopsies that use a thin needle, the biopsies done in this study required cutting and removing a small slice of the men's prostates, often resulting in serious complications.

As the article observes, despite the poverty of the participants, "Dr. Hudson himself makes no apologies for recruiting impoverished alcoholics." Now ninety-six and living in South Pasadena, Florida, he has said in recent interviews that the men volunteered, they were not paid, and they got "the best care in New York." Doctors in private practice "would never have allowed their patients to get biopsies since they assumed the disease was fatal, he said."[3] Many men who participated in the study suffered serious complications, including impotence and incontinence.

Once again, just as in the Tuskegee Syphilis Study, a medical practice was adopted and implemented by a healthcare professional who did not see the humanity of the individuals with whom he was interacting. A person who empathized with these men could not have implemented the study and later fail to see that it constituted an assault on human dignity. The sad truth is that we have only a limited knowledge of how many studies like this have been conducted on poor people in the United States and around the world. The need to continue enacting and applying laws that increase access to healthcare and protect the human dignity of individuals who interact with healthcare professionals is reinforced by new reports that reveal abuses that have been hidden from the scrutiny of the general public.

While we should recognize the importance of the law, we should also remain aware of its inherent limitations. Laws cannot address the myriad circumstances that produce inequitable policies and practices. The protection of human dignity in healthcare requires a cultural reinforcement of the values the community holds dear. The cultural reinforcement that I have identified in relating the cases and stories in this book highlights the importance of empathy, compassion, and humility that should accompany decision making.

This book has also acknowledged that American consumers have influenced policy making in a way that injures members of their own communities because of group-based biases and fear. Racism, sexism, homophobia, xenophobia, and other biases operate as major forces that undervalue empathy and compassion. As David Livingston Smith argues in his book aptly titled *Less Than Human*, "Dehumanization probably is, despite appearances to the contrary, always bound up with racism. In fact, the concept of race is the place where psychological, cultural and ultimately biological dimensions of dehumanization all converge."[4]

A well- researched and thought-provoking book published in 2019 presents a persuasive explanation of why it is so difficult to enact and implement healthcare law in the United States that protects and promotes wider access to healthcare by working-class and poor people. This book, written by Jonathan Metzl, a sociologist and physician, is titled *Dying of Whiteness: How the Politics of Racial Resentment Is Killing America's Heartland*.[5] Based on in-depth interviews of white people living in the South and Midwest of the United States, and on a thorough review of studies of the impact of various laws such as the Affordable Care Act on them, Metzl concludes that preserving the place of whites as a group in America's racial hierarchy is so important to large numbers of working-class and poor whites that they are literally willing to die rather than support healthcare laws and policies that they perceive primarily benefit people of color. Summarizing the views and beliefs of one person identified as Trevor, Metzl explains that Trevor, an uninsured forty-one-year-old white man who suffered from an inflamed liver, opposes government programs that would protect and promote his health because of dogma—"dogma that, as he made abundantly clear, aligned with beliefs about a racial hierarchy that overtly and implicitly aimed to keep white Americans hovering above Mexicans, welfare queens, and other nonwhite others. Dogma suggesting to Trevor that minority groups received lavish benefits from the state, even though he himself lived and died on a low-income budget with state assistance. Trevor voiced a literal willingness to die for his place in this hierarchy, rather than participate in a system that might put him on the same plane as immigrants or racial minorities."[6]

This concluding chapter offers cases and stories to demonstrate the critical role that humility, empathy, and compassion should play in influencing healthcare law, policies, and practices. From a legal perspective, empathy, compassion, and humility are essential to the promotion of social justice and should be reflected in legislation, in regulations, in the voting booth, and in the courtroom. To appreciate a person's hopes, dreams, disappointment, and pain requires a conscious effort to see the world through that person's eyes. This perspective, shaped by the life experiences of the individual, enables an outside observer who has never shared those experiences to see matters that were previously totally overlooked or underappreciated. It is not surprising that many of the cases I draw upon involve women whose treatment leads us to more fully appreciate the dynamics of power relations. The abuse of the female Olympic athletes discussed in the introduction to this book stands as a prime example of a need to invoke humility, empathy, and compassion to protect human dignity. Additional examples are presented throughout this book and in this final chapter.

Humility

I start with humility because I believe this is a valuable attribute of decision making that people in power often do not employ. The general definition of humility is the state of being humble. However, the aspect of humility that I want to emphasize reflects the opposite of arrogance. One can be confident in relationships and decision making affecting healthcare without being blinded by arrogance. Indeed, I believe that the capacity to act and think with humility reflects that highest level of confidence and competence. A person who is able to approach a project or challenge by, first, acknowledging that he/she may not have all of the answers and, second, is aware that others may have important information to impart, is acting with humility and employing an approach to decision making that is likely to produce better results than that of the person who approaches the project with an attitude that he/she knows more than everyone else. Humility is especially important in a diverse and rapidly changing world. Encounters with unfamiliar people can produce both frightening experiences and richly rewarding experiences and are affected by the attitudes of the people interacting. Healthcare doctrine and protocols related to the interaction of professional decision makers with patients already have started down a path that requires participants to adapt to a diverse and rapidly changing world.

In a thought-provoking book titled *The Spirit Catches You and You Fall Down*, Anne Fadiman describes the troubling and frustrating encounters experienced by a Hmong family from Laos as they sought care for their epileptic child from doctors and nurses at a hospital in California.[7] A highly educated and caring medical staff found themselves unable to provide effective medical care to a Hmong child because they did not understand or appreciate the culture of the family, who accepted only part of Western medicine as appropriate for their child's treatment. Instead, the family interacting with healthcare professionals followed instructions, but filtered and altered the care of their child when they returned home by following some of their core beliefs about medicine and health, based on their culture. Notably, the family's departure from the medical instructions led to frequent visits to the emergency room, and eventually the hospital invoked legal proceedings to take the child from his parents based on charges of neglect.

This heart-wrenching story leaves no doubt that the parents had deep love for their child and were making decisions about healthcare following in good faith their cultural beliefs. Similarly, the doctors' directives were based on good faith assessments of the welfare of the child according to knowledge gained from studying Western medicine. Therein lies the clash: Whose views should prevail? American law vests decision-making authority about health and healthcare in a child's parents except where the parents' decisions can fairly be classified as constituting neglect. When science clashes with culture or religion, courts err on the side of medical science if the decision poses a risk of significant injury or death of the child.

While the preference for decisions guided by Western medicine is understandable in making decisions for children or incompetent adults, it presents an inherent and indisputable threat to the dignity of parents and families in these situations. There is a disrespect of parental authority and the sanctity of family privacy when the state orders a parent to comply with decisions or consent to care in the manner the state thinks is in the best interest of the child. At the same time, we must keep in mind that children do need protection from healthcare decisions by doctors and parents that threaten their health and lives.

An alarming example of the need for courts to protect children grew out of a decision by physicians at Johns Hopkins Hospital to conduct a research study in Baltimore to determine the impact of partially abated lead in houses occupied by children.[8] The Institutional Review Board in the hospital approved the study, and the parents consented to live in the houses after being told that the purpose of the study was to measure the lead in the blood of their children after the lead was partially abated in the house. The rationale of the study was that the families were too poor to live elsewhere, so it may have been of some benefit to learn if partial abatement produced a safe living environment. The court in Maryland declared the study unethical and illegal, offering a stark rebuke:

> It is not in the best interest of a specific child, in a nontherapeutic research project, to be placed in a research environment, which might possibly be, or which proves to be, hazardous to the health of the child. We have long stressed that the "best interests of the child" is the overriding concern of this Court in matters relating to children. Whatever the interests of a parent, and whatever the interests of the general public in fostering research that might, according to a researcher's hypothesis, be for the good of all children, this Court's concern for the particular child and particular case, over-arches all other interests. It is, simply, and we hope, succinctly put, not in the best interest of any healthy child to be intentionally put in a nontherapeutic situation where his or her health may be impaired, in order to test methods that may ultimately benefit all children.
>
> To think otherwise, to turn over human and legal ethical [*sic*] concerns solely to the scientific community, is to risk embarking on slippery slopes, that all too often in the past, here and elsewhere, have resulted in practices we, or any community, should be ever unwilling to accept.[9]

Careful attention to the process employed to make these healthcare decisions can encourage a level of empathy that promotes and protects the dignity of all the participants. The process must allow and encourage dialogue that enables each side to better appreciate the values, benefits, and burdens that produce these clashing choices. For that to occur requires humility. Professionals with superior medical knowledge, wealth, and experience must be willing to accept that patients often know more about what is going on with their bodies than the professionals appreciate. Moreover, the professional is charged with caring for a person, not just a body. To care for a person requires respect for and acknowledgment of the patient's values, beliefs, goals, and culture. In many instances, the most effective strategy to guide the professional will be obtained by shared decision making that accommodates the patient's values to the maximum extent possible, without unreasonably jeopardizing the life and health of the patient.

Empathy

Valuable lessons about the importance of empathy are offered by some of the landmark court decisions in cases involving requests to withhold or remove life-sustaining medical support from patients who are severely brain-damaged or terminally ill. One of the most instructive decisions was the one that gained national attention, the case of Karen Quinlan.[10] For undetermined reasons Ms. Quinlan stopped breathing for a long enough period to cause her to suffer severe brain damage. She was taken to a hospital in a coma, where she remained in a vegetative state. She was not totally brain dead, because her brain stem, which controls vegetative functions such as blood pressure, still worked, although her ability to breathe was compromised. Moreover, she did not have any awareness of her environment. She was kept alive by the insertion of a breathing tube for respiration. Her doctors believed that if they removed the respirator she would die quickly.

Her parents wanted to remove the breathing tube, but the hospital was concerned about its civil and criminal liability because there was almost no legal precedent to guide them. The court's opinion affirmed the authority of the parents as guardians to make the decision to remove the tube. If the prognosis supported a conclusion that she was unlikely to regain a conscious state, the parents were authorized to make the decision as guardians. Standing in for Karen Quinlan, her father, as her guardian, was authorized to make the decisions that he believed Karen would have made if she were competent. In addition, the court's opinion defined the role of the doctors as making a prognosis of the likelihood of her regaining a conscious state and recommended that hospitals set up ethics committees to aid in such decision making. Importantly, the *Quinlan* court ruled that in the future, the dignity of a patient and his/her family would be protected by privacy, and further held that no court order was needed to make the decision to withdraw mechanical respiratory support for their loved one.

Subsequent decisions on withdrawing and withholding artificial life support raised the question of the standard that should guide those decisions. The courts have declared that the preferred standard is to make the decision that the patient would have made if she were competent to decide. In the absence of evidence as to the patient's preference, the guardian should make the choice that he/she believes is in the patient's best interest. Decisions about withholding or removing extraordinary medical care reflect the need for empathy at an extremely intense, heart-wrenching level.

Compassion

Empathy must be accompanied by compassion. An article in the *New York Times* in 2018 set forth a frightening statistic: "African-American women are nearly 3.5 times more likely than white women to die from pregnancy-related conditions."[11] The article commanded my attention, particularly considering cases that I have litigated, such as *Whittington v. Episcopal Hospital.*[12] That case involved a pregnant woman who died at age twenty-six after being left unattended in the waiting room of a hospital for nearly fourteen hours. She arrived at the hospital and was admitted at 7:30 A.M., for induction of labor and delivery because she was overdue and had pregnancy-induced hypertension. After admission, she was kept in a waiting room and ignored until 9:00 P.M., when she complained of headaches. It was noted at that time that she had an elevated blood pressure, and she was finally transferred to the labor and delivery area for induction. Despite assessments that showed consistently elevated blood pressure throughout the night, no blood pressure–lowering drugs were ordered until 7:00 A.M. the following morning, and none were administered until 8:40 A.M. Finally, at 11:30 A.M. on Christmas Eve, she was "rushed" to the operating room for an "emergency" cesarean, which was delayed for at least another hour. The baby was born healthy, but her mother died in the hospital on January 4, 1994, because of the negligent care she received, including the failure to order and administer deep vein thrombosis prophylaxis, resulting in the formation of blood clots in her lungs, pulmonary edema, and other complications. The mother's death could have been easily avoided by standard humane and equitable healthcare.

Kim Brooks, the author of the *New York Times* article reporting this occurrence that caught my attention, explained her motivation for interviewing pregnant women in search of some answers to the statistics about their poor treatment. She wrote: "I wanted to know what it is like to experience this— to face one's death during childbirth in the richest country in the world in the second decade of the 21st century." Ms. Brooks continues to tell many heart-breaking stories of pregnant women whom she has interviewed who described not being listened to, whose complaints have been trivialized or not believed by the healthcare providers who have attended to them during their pregnancy. The take-home message from her interviews is that the women felt dehumanized.

One woman featured in Brooks's article was forty weeks pregnant and in good health when she went for an examination. She was told that her amniotic fluid was low and that, although the baby's vital signs were good, she needed to have the baby delivered by inducement right away. When she asked about the success rates for induction versus a C-section, she was informed that she had no choice. When she asked if she could go home to get an overnight bag, she was told that she would be arrested for endangering the life of the baby if she tried to go home.[13]

Many studies have been conducted to better understand the reasons for the surprisingly high rate of pregnancy-related maternal deaths in the United States and the racial disparity in pregnancy-related deaths.[14] However, as Brooks's article informs us, most of the studies deliberately choose not to carefully examine the medical practices that may be contributing to the deaths and disparate outcomes. The failure to address a severe problem that is causing avoidable deaths of large numbers of women is just the latest example of healthcare and illness that could be effectively addressed if policy makers and practitioners responded with empathy, compassion, and humility. As with the HIV and AIDS epidemic, the problems will only be addressed when people in power see them as affecting them and their families.

I finish this chapter and this book by describing a case that I believe everyone interested in issues related to healthcare and human dignity should read. The case is *In re A.C.*,[15] a caption used to protect the privacy of the pregnant woman who was the subject of the court dispute. Tragically, this pregnant mother suffered untreatable cancer that was predicted to result in her dying prior to carrying her child to full term. Her doctors had to make critical medical decisions that determined whether they would offer palliative treatment designed to extend her biological life to increase the chances of the fetus being born alive and healthy. They administered pain medication, but her condition continued to deteriorate; as a consequence, she faded in and out of consciousness and was unable to communicate her view as to whether or when a cesarean section delivery should be performed. While her husband and her parents stayed at her side, the hospital asked the court to decide what to do. The trial court ordered that a cesarean be done. Sadly, the mother died after the surgery, and the child died a few days later.

Recognizing the importance of the public policy issue presented by the facts of the case, the appellate court heard an appeal of the lower court's decision after the mother's death. The appellate court issued an opinion declaring that the trial court had used the wrong standard for making its decision. The appellate court explained that the trial court should not have decided the case based on what the judge thought was in the best interest of the mother. Instead, the court should have decided what the mother's wishes would have been if she were competent to decide. The appellate court decision and preference to decision making resting in the pregnant woman underscored the importance of protecting and affirming her dignity. The appellate court reasoned that she retained her right to decide what was to be done to her body, even after becoming pregnant.[16] The opinions and decisions of both the trial court and the appellate court reflect a high level of empathy, compassion, and humility warranted by such complex and sensitive healthcare decisions and how bodily autonomy interplays with these interests particularly in pregnancy.[17]

Conclusion

Law in a democratic society should reflect the core values of the community with respect to how people in positions of authority and power must behave when interacting with others affected by their use of power. Controls and standards for the use of power are particularly important when the power derives from a position within government. Legal standards often offer important protections to people who struggle to obtain the minimum values distributed in a community when the source of power flows from wealth, education, religion, or social status.

As this book has shown through a recitation of statistics, stories, and cases, healthcare is an area where the use and misuse of power because of disparate knowledge too often cause severe harm to the dignity of individuals who are the target of explicit, implicit, and structural biases. American healthcare law tries to define the boundaries of acceptable treatment afforded to people who find themselves in need of care from healthcare professionals and institutions. The United States has faced and continues to face vigorous forces that challenge healthcare policy makers and practitioners to make decisions that reflect empathy, compassion, and humility. Among those forces are changing demographics as to age, ethnicity, country of origin, religion, culture, gender, sexual orientation, and race. Policies and practices that aim to wall off or trivialize those forces represent a strategy akin to placing a finger in a dike or burying one's head in sand. It is my view that the infliction of indignities on individuals in the context of healthcare delivery and practices will continue to be challenged and that their efforts to attain equal respect in these times of prodigious societal changes will inevitably prevail. The undervaluing of their humanity conflicts with fundamental values of America and most countries in the developed world linked to the protection of human rights.

An alternative strategy has been offered by civil rights leaders and educators such as Dr. Martin Luther King Jr. and Vincent Harding, to name only two. That strategy is to envision and strive to build a "beloved community."[18] This vision of a beloved community that welcomes people of diverse backgrounds and beliefs is not a utopian twenty-first-century dream. Rather, it is the fundamental idea and vision that spurred the founding of the United States. From the time of the founding of the United States the key challenge has been whether all human beings will be recognized as human and treated equally and fairly. I believe that projecting the vision of the "beloved community" shines a light on the most precious core values that must be vigorously protected and preserved, particularly when monetary greed threatens to dominate important policy making and laws governing access to and delivery of essential services such as healthcare.

Acknowledgments

I take this opportunity to thank and acknowledge family members, friends, colleagues, and neighbors who helped me write this book. As a child, I learned about the importance of human dignity from my parents, Gradie and Lucinda McClellan, both of whom are now deceased. They taught me that a good way to judge people's character is to observe how they treat you when the only thing they know about you is that you are a human being. As I matured, I recognized that in all probability a person meeting me for the first time would also perceive my race, gender, and approximate age. But as Ralph Ellison's protagonist exhorts in the prologue to *Invisible Man*, those perceptions do not mean the person actually sees me as human or acknowledges our common humanity.

As African Americans who migrated from Charleston, South Carolina, to Pittsburgh, Pennsylvania, my parents were participants in the great migration poignantly described by Isabel Wilkerson in *The Warmth of Other Suns*. Like other members of an oppressed racial minority group in America, they engaged in battles—that sometimes seemed daily—for access to work, business establishments, housing, medical care, and educational opportunities for their three children. My mother was a homemaker who cared for three children. My father worked two jobs, devoting eighty hours of labor, six days a week for over forty years, as a steelworker and the owner of a barbershop. Fortunately, as a result of a lifetime of hard work, a pension, private health insurance, Medicare, and Medicaid, both of my parents were able live their senior years with access to quality healthcare that accorded them respect and dignity.

Chapter 11 of this book addresses payment models for healthcare and presents further descriptions of my parents at a time when they had no choice but to depend on their family and community to assist them in gaining access to healthcare. I believe the experiences of my parents reflect those of many seniors in the United States, and I shudder to think of how different my parents' lives would have been during the last part of the twentieth century if there had not been a national consensus that healthcare for seniors is a civil right, if not a human right.

My perspective on healthcare and human dignity has also been shaped by my professional experiences as a medical malpractice lawyer, representing individuals and families who have suffered injuries as a result of the denial of healthcare or the provision of care that falls below the standard of the medical profession. I have learned a great deal about human dignity from each of my clients. When I began writing this book, one of my former clients who had a child who suffered a serious medical injury allowed my daughter, Cara McClellan, now a public interest lawyer, to interview her about her perspectives and feelings about the healthcare and legal systems. Cara asked questions that I never would have thought to ask. The philosophy and perspective of this former client, expressed in the interview, strengthened my inclination to focus on human dignity in this book.

Allen Eaton, an extraordinarily talented lawyer and a considerate human being whom I met as a young lawyer in Washington, D.C., and worked with on many cases representing severely injured individuals, taught me that one of the most important traits a lawyer can have is the ability to put the well-being of his client above his own and to treat the client with the highest level of respect possible. In his view, a client's lack of financial resources intensified the need to treat the client with respect. I am grateful to Allen for these life lessons. He read several draft chapters of this book and reminded me of cases and stories that provided important examples of people who suffered from avoidable medical care injuries because of their economic, racial, or social status.

Allen and I were both fortunate to try our first major medical malpractice case before Judge William Nealon, chief judge of the Middle District of Pennsylvania at the time. Exercising patience and discipline through a long and arduous trial, Judge Nealon demonstrated how to treat litigants, attorneys, jurors and witnesses with respect, while at the same time demanding that all or the participants comply with the legal rules aimed at promoting a just resolution of the lawsuit. Judge Nealon and I were mutual admirers of the late chief judge William H. Hastie, the first African American appointed as a federal judge, and one of the most distinguished jurists in the country. Judge Nealon knew that I had experienced the privilege of serving as a law clerk for Judge Hastie. When my advocacy at trial crossed the boundary line of civility, Judge Nealon would sometimes subtly, and other times directly, remind me that I was trained by Judge Hastie, who won and decided cases based on incisive analysis and advocacy. Judge Nealon and Judge Hastie took great pain to assure that I appreciated the importance of treating everyone with respect, regardless of their position in the social hierarchy. I owe them a great debt for setting such a high standard for professional conduct.

Harold Logan, a former journalist who went on to undertake a successful career in business, provided key critiques of my early draft chapters. Hal's critical assessment of the stories I relate in this book made me appreciate the need to highlight the impact of power disparities on the dignity of patients. My son Toussaint McClellan, a TV broadcast producer, read many chapters and offered insights on how I could revise the telling of the stories to get to the core of the human issues and minimize the legalize that often obscures a lawyer's discussion of legal cases. My oldest son, Malik McClellan, also reviewed chapters and consistently reminded me that if I wanted this book to appeal to a broad audience I had to review and edit the stories from the perspective of a layperson. In the same vein, I was also fortunate to gain the feedback of a kind and thoughtful neighbor, Katherine Finney, who devoted substantial time to reading the stories. A retired secondary school teacher with a wealth classroom experiences, Kate identified the stories she found most interesting and effective to illustrate and support my arguments regarding the critical nature of human dignity in a healthcare system that tends to be preoccupied by economic concerns. My friend and professional colleague James Wood, an orthopedic surgeon who has keen insights into doctor-patient relationships, read many of the draft chapters and offered candid assessments of circumstances in which I failed to appreciate or acknowledge challenges that healthcare financing policies and institutional structures pose for practicing physicians. Dr. Wood frequently reminded me of the need to "walk a mile in my shoes" before you pass judgment. Aretha Marshall, a highly experienced and talented television network producer provided critical insight as to how to tell the stories in this book in a way that engages and informs the general public about complex legal and medical issues.

Doris Braendel, who edited my earlier book, *Medical Malpractice: Law, Tactics, and Ethics*, reviewed the first drafts of early chapters of this book and gave me a candid assessment that prompted me to reorganize and reconceptualize the book. Having been informed by me that my intended audience was not lawyers but the general public, she admonished me to work harder to convey what I wanted to say to my target audience, pointedly advising me, "You don't have a book yet." Doris persuaded me early in the writing process that I could not just write a book relitigating my cases and expect the general public to find the retelling of the stories as exciting as I found them. I went back to the drawing board and shifted my focus from how I saw the world by more purposely adopting the worldviews of former clients and parties in reported legal cases. I hope I succeeded in that transition. Ann-Marie Anderson, Director of Marketing at Temple University Press, had overseen the marketing of my earlier medical malpractice book and was aware of the interest of Rutgers University Press in health and public policy. I am indebted to her for introducing me to Peter

Mickulas, the Executive Editor of Rutgers University Press. Peter submitted the manuscript to external reviewers and then carefully shepherded the manuscript through the demanding editorial process.

My colleagues at the Beasley School of Law provided observations that compelled me to think about approaches to telling the stories about law and human dignity in a manner that might interest law students and lawyers as well as the general public. David Kairys read early drafts of a few chapters and wisely urged me to stop apologizing for being a lawyer and, instead, to write about the important role that lawyers play in promoting social justice in the field of healthcare. Hosea Harvey encouraged me to tell the stories about race honestly and candidly and pointed me to references that served as excellent examples of how to use stories to teach about race and law. Scott Burris, a leading scholar in the field of public health law, offered insightful and challenging feedback regarding the conceptualization of human dignity using some of the fundamental lessons learned from our responses to epidemics.

Special thanks go to my colleagues Henry Richardson and Donald Harris. Professor Richardson read early chapters and pushed me to think about healthcare policy from a global and human rights perspective. Donald Harris not only provided detailed and critical reviews of the substance and style of storytelling presented in the chapters, but made sure that my work on this book moved forward by sharing the time of his research assistant. Mark Rahdert, an expert on insurance, torts, and constitutional law, offered me many insights relevant to the driving forces of healthcare policy, and I benefited from his review of specific chapters and many discussions we have had on these issues over the years.

A book about law aimed at capturing the attention of the general public required feedback from lawyers willing to take the time to consider effective ways of communicating legal precepts and rules to the general public. I am grateful to attorneys Jerry Bailey, Aaron Freiwald, and Elbert Sampson, who carefully read specific chapters and provided feedback on the writing style, legal themes, and policy discussion. Attorney Theresa Blanco originated and litigated some of the most challenging cases described in this book involving innovative therapy. I am indebted to her both as a lawyer and a writer. The cases she litigated provide illuminating examples of the critical role played by professional ethics in protecting human dignity.

Veronica Schad, while completing her senior year of law school at Temple, supported this project with high-quality research and editing that was well beyond my expectations for a research assistant. Her commitment to the editing was extraordinary, more so since she entered the school year expecting to provide research to Professor Harris on intellectual property issues. During this same academic year, Laurel Little, a Villanova law student with the added experience and education of a registered nurse, provided research assistance, editing, and thoughtful suggestions that reflected the insights of a professional who had provided good healthcare in the trenches.

As I struggled to complete this book, the challenge of keeping current with a rapidly changing field increased. Policy battles and legal reform proposals continued to multiply. In reviewing the references and keeping up with the changes, I was fortunate to have the able assistance of several law students at Temple: Kean Maynard, Henry Longley, and Tiffany Yeung. Henry Longley made exceptional research contributions to the bibliography as well as the text.

The basic organization and structure of this book reflect my efforts to revise stories and present policy discussions in a way that would appeal to a multidisciplinary audience. I am grateful to two scholars who read many of the chapters and shared insights from different disciplinary perspectives. Barry Furrow, a law professor who is a leading writer and scholar in the field of healthcare law, went far beyond the work of a customary reviewer. He took time to read and reread chapters and provided critiques and suggestions particularly with respect to policy issues. Nora Jones, PhD, an anthropologist who directs a bioethics program and teaches courses at Temple Medical School on bioethics, read draft chapters and responded with thoughts and perspectives that encouraged me to rethink how many of the cases and stories were presented so that the stories would highlight the impact of the law and public policy on human relationships.

Most of the stories related in this book reveal disparities in health and healthcare. For nearly a decade Verona Brewton has led a multi-disciplinary coalition of individuals and organizations named Movement Is Life. This coalition engages in research and social activism aimed at reducing health disparities based on gender, race, and poverty. As a member of its steering committee, I have received a remarkable education on the different ways in which socioeconomic and cultural factors influence the health of individuals. I must acknowledge that I relied on the research and ideas of many of my colleagues in Movement is Life, about how orthopedic health affects both the overall health and the sense of dignity of all members of a community. Augustus White, MD, one of the most thoughtful and courageous leaders of Movement is Life, has been a consistent source of ideas and inspiration for my research and writing, and I am especially grateful for the time and feedback he provided in reading the introductory chapters and the chapters exploring orthopedic health and the healthcare of seniors. Dr. White persistently asks the coalition, Isn't it time that we treat healthcare as a human right?

I am also grateful to professors W. Eugene Basanta, and Marsha Ryan, MD, JD, who hosted me in 2010 at the University of Southern Illinois as the Garwin Distinguished Professor of Law and allowed me to teach healthcare law and begin in-depth research on many of the topics explored in this book. I was also privileged to give the annual Grayson lecture during which I introduced my thoughts and research on health disparities caused by racial biases.

The paralegal assistance I received in the last stages of writing this book was superb. I will be forever grateful to Angelica Latorre Aguirre, a legal assistant at the Beasley School of Law, and Patty Williams, a long-term friend and paralegal in Washington, D.C., who undertook the critical research, editing, and cite-checking tasks essential to completing the book. Their contributions reflected not only skill and knowledge, but also the highest level of professionalism.

I am also indebted to Dean Gregory Mandel and Assistant Dean Debbie Feldman of the Beasley School of Law at Temple University. They made sure that the resources of Temple University continued to be available to support the writing, research, and teaching efforts that culminated in the publication of this book.

Finally, my wife, Phoebe Haddon, Rutgers University Chancellor, former law dean of the University of Maryland, Carey School of Law, and earlier a colleague at Temple, offered the sage advice of a quintessential editor, both as to writing style and the substantive ideas presented in the chapters she reviewed. Her patience, intellectual feedback, and editing provided critical support to my research and writing efforts. Most importantly, I could not have continued working on this book for over five years without her encouragement and love.

Notes

Introduction

1. Testimony of Ms. Raisman, one of the victims of the U.S. Olympic doctor, at his state sentencing hearing. Nassar, age fifty-four, had already been sentenced to sixty years in federal prison on a conviction for child pornography. The state court hearing was to determine a sentence for multiple sexual assaults. See Scott Cacciola and Christine Hauser, "One after Another, Athletes Face Larry Nassar and Recount Sexual Abuse," *New York Times*, January 19, 2018, https://mobile.nytimes.com/2018/01/19/sports/larry-nassar-women.html.

2. Samantha Schnurr, "Former USA Gymnastics Doctor Larry Nassar Sentenced to 40 to 175 Years in Prison for Sexual Abuse," *E News*, January 24, 2018, https://www.eonline.com/news/906521/former-usa-gymnastics-doctor-larry-nassar-sentenced-to-40-to-175-years-in-prison-for-sexual-abuse.

3. Cacciola and Hauser, "One after Another, Athletes Face Larry Nassar."

4. Ibid.

5. Ibid.

6. Mitch Smith and Anemona Hartocollis, "Michigan State's $500 Million for Nassar Victims Dwarfs Other Settlements," *New York Times*, May 16, 2018, https://www.nytimes.com/2018/05/16/us/larry-nassar-michigan-state-settlement.html.

7. "USC Reaches $215 Million Settlement with Patients of Campus Gynecologist Accused of Sexual Misconduct," Kaiser Health News, accessed December 22, 2018, https://khn.org/morning-breakout/usc-reaches-215-million-settlement-with-patients-of-campus-gynecologist-accused-of-sexual-misconduct/ (providing the class action, *Lucy Chi v. Southern California et al.*, on behalf of 500 students against campus gynecologist, settled for $250 million).

8. For a comprehensive description and analysis of the historical mistreatment of African Americans by the medical profession in the United States, see Harriet A. Washington, *Medical Apartheid: The Dark History of Medical Experimentation on Black Americans from Colonial Times to the Present* (New York: Anchor Books, 2006).

9. James H. Jones, *Bad Blood: The Tuskegee Syphilis Experiment*, rev. ed. (New York: Free Press, 1993).

10. Paul Weindling, Anna von Villiez, Aleksandra Loewenau, and Nichola Farron, "The Victims of Unethical Human Experiments and Coerced Research under National Socialism," *Endeavour* 40, no. 1 (2016), https://doi.org/10.1016/j.endeavour.2015.10.005.

11. Ibid., 6. See also "The Medical Case of the Subsequent Nuremberg Trials," U.S. Holocaust Memorial Museum, accessed November 5, 2018, https://www.ushmm.org/information/exhibitions/online-exhibitions/special-focus/doctors-trial/.

12. Quoted in Jones, *Bad Blood*, 180.

13. Ibid., 179–180.

14. George Kateb, *Human Dignity* (Cambridge, MA: Belknap Press of Harvard University Press, 2011), 3–4.

1. Healthcare and Law

1. *Health Cost Containment and Efficiencies: NCSL Briefs for State Legislators*, National Conference of State Legislatures, May 2011, www.ncsl.org/documents/health/intro andbriefscc-16.pdf.

2. David Barton Smith, *The Power to Heal: Civil Rights, Medicare, and the Struggle to Transform America's Health Care System* (Nashville, TN: Vanderbilt University Press, 2016).

3. *McGann v. H&H Music Co.*, 946 F.2d 401 (5th Cir. 1991); Barbara Gerbert et al., "Primary Care Physicians and AIDS Attitudinal and Structural Barriers to Care," *JAMA*, 266, no. 20 (November 1991): 2837–2842, https://doi:10.1001/jama.1991.03470200049033; Lacrisha Butler, "State Cites AIDS Discrimination," *The Tennessean*, December 10, 1990, 9.

4. Gregory M. Herek and Eric K. Glunt, "An Epidemic of Stigma: Public Reactions to AIDS," *American Psychologist* 43, no. 11 (November 1988): 886–887, http://dx.doi .org/10.1037/0003-066X.43.11.886.

5. Igor Volsky, "Recalling Ronald Reagan's LGBT Legacy ahead of the GOP Presidential Debate," ThinkProgress, accessed October 24, 2018, https://thinkprogress.org /recalling-ronald-reagans-lgbt-legacy-ahead-of-the-gop-presidential-debate -a687b80d679b/.

6. Albert D. Alessi, "Queerbashing Is an Act of Terrorism," *Gay Community News* (Boston), July 25, 1981, 14 (observing that "the assassination of Harvey Milk and George Moscone in 1978 and the subsequent lenient verdict received by Dan White, who shot Harvey Milk, shocked and angered the gay and lesbian community in that city and across the nation," and that the "reactionary anti-gay forces in San Francisco must be considered in order to grasp the full significance of these crimes"); *People v. White*, 117 Cal. App. 3d 270 (Cal. Ct. App. 1981) (the man accused of murdering Harvey Milk, Defendant, Dan White, was ultimately convicted of voluntary manslaughter, arguing the infamous "Twinkie Defense").

7. David France, *How to Survive a Plague: The Inside Story of How Citizens and Science Tamed AIDS* (New York: Vintage Books, 2016), 6.

8. Arthur Ashe and Arnold Rampersad, *Days of Grace: A Memoir* (New York: Ballantine Books, 1993), 215.

9. Requirements, Investigational New Drug Application, 21 C.F.R. § 312.305 (2018). For a historical account, see Eve Nichols, "Institute of Medicine (US) Roundtable for the Development of Drugs and Vaccines against AIDS: Expanding Access to Investigational Therapies for HIV Infection and AIDS," March 12–13, 1990, Conference Summary (Washington, DC: National Academies Press, 1991), 1, "Historical Perspective," https://www.ncbi.nlm.nih.gov/books/NBK234129/.

10. Americans with Disabilities Act, 42 U.S. §12101 (1990); *Bragdon v. Abbott*, 524 U.S. 624 (1998).

11. *Sharrow v. Bailey*, 910 F.Supp. 187 (M.D. Pa. 1995); *Flowers v. Southern Regional Physician Services Inc.*, 247 F.3d 229 (5th Cir. 2001).

12. Rachel Nall, "The History of HIV and AIDS in the United States," *Healthline*, November 30, 2016, http://www.healthline.com/health/hiv-aids/history#cultural -response5.

13. Lev Facher and Ike Swetliz, "Aetna Faces Class-Action Lawsuit over HIV Disclosures," *Stat News*, August 18, 2017, https://www.statnews.com/2017/08/28/aetna -hiv-lawsuit/.

14. Randy Shilts, *And the Band Played On: Politics, People, and the AIDS Epidemic* (New York: St. Martin's Press, 1987), xxiii.
15. Ibid.
16. France, *How to Survive a Plague*, 511.
17. Tony Barnett and Alan Whiteside, *AIDS in the Twenty-First Century: Disease and Globalization* (New York: Palgrave Macmillan, 2002), 7–8.
18. "What Is the U.S. Opioid Epidemic?," About the Epidemic, U.S. Department of Health and Human Services, last modified September 19, 2018, https://www.hhs.gov/opioids /about-the-epidemic/index.html.
19. See Section 504 of the Rehabilitation Act of 1973, 29 U.S.C. § 794 (applies to individuals and institutions receiving federal funds, and to federal agencies); Americans with Disabilities Act, 42 U.S. § 12101 (1990),(tracks discrimination language in the Rehabilitation Act and prohibits discrimination by any person based on a disability); *Bragdon v. Abbott*, 524 U.S. 624 (1998) (person with HIV is protected by the Americans with Disabilities Act).
20. *Langbehn v. Public Health Trust of Miami-Dade County*, 661 F. Supp.2d 1326, 1331 (S.D. Fla. 2009).
21. Ibid., 1332.
22. Ibid.
23. Ibid., 1339.
24. See Alan Meisel, *A 'Dignitary Tort' as a Bridge between the Idea of Informed Consent and the Law of Informed Consent,* 16 J. L. Med & Ethics 210 (1988) (arguing that the informed consent doctrine should support a claim for harm to dignity, without the necessity of proof of other damage).
25. See *Reed v. ANM Health Care*, 225 P. 3d 1012, 1015 (Wash. App. Div. 1 2008).
26. Ibid., 272–273.

2. Philosophical and Legal Conceptions of Dignity

1. *Lucchesi v. Frederic N. Stimmell, M.D., Ltd.*, 716 P.2d 1013 (Ariz. 1986).
2. Ibid.
3. Ibid., 78.
4. Ibid.
5. Ibid., 78–79, quoting *Watts v. Golden Age Nursing Home*, 127 Ariz. 255, 258 (1980).
6. Michael L. Rustad, *Torts as Public Wrongs*, 38 Pepperdine L. Rev. 433 (2011).
7. Adam Schulman, "Bioethics and the Question of Human Dignity," in *Human Dignity and Bioethics: Essays Commissioned by the President's Council on Bioethics*, March 2008, 3–18, https://permanent.access.gpo.gov/lps105992/human_dignity_and _bioethics.pdf.
8. Ibid.
9. Edmund D. Pellegrino, "The Lived Experience of Human Dignity," in *Human Dignity and Bioethics*, 515.
10. Rebecca Dresser, "Human Dignity and the Seriously Ill Patient," in *Human Dignity and Bioethics*, 511–512.
11. Kateb, *Human Dignity*, 3–4.
12. Myres S. McDougal, Harold D. Lasswell, and Lung-chu Chen, *Human Rights and World Public Order: The Basic Policies of an International Law of Human Dignity* (New Haven, CT: Yale University Press 1980), http://digitalcommons.nyls.edu/fac _books/29.

13. Ibid., 7.

14. Ibid.

15. Ibid., 8.

16. Reverend Jackson's recitation of the poem is included on a 2006 DVD. "I Am Somebody with Jesse Jackson," *Sesame Street: Old School*, vol. 1, *1969–1974*, disc 2, no. 8, produced by Dionne Nosek (Warner Brothers, 2006), DVD.

17. Stax Records sponsored this benefit concert to commemorate the seventh anniversary of the Watts riots that took place in Los Angeles in 1965. The concert was made into a film in 1973 titled *Wattstax* that was nominated for a Golden Globe Award for Best Documentary Film in 1974 (filmed by David L. Wolper's crew and directed by Mel Stuart). Jesse Jackson, "I Am Somebody," Wattstax Music Festival, August 20, 1972, speech, 2:16, https://youtu.be/NTVwT3j_zqY.

18. Ambrose Murunga, "Perspective: Tribute to Rosa Parks, Fallen Icon of Human Dignity," *Daily Nation*, November 7, 2005, https://www.nation.co.ke/lifestyle/1190 -91956-dkewscz/index.html.

19. Kateb, *Human Dignity*, 10.

20. Constitution of South Africa, Brand South Africa, accessed June 11, 2017, https:// www.brandsouthafrica.com/governance/constitution-sa-glance/the-constitution-of -south-africa.

21. Ibid.

22. Ibid.

23. *Pharm. Mfrs. Ass'n of S. Afr. v. President of the Republic of S. Afr.*, Case no. 4183/98, High Court of South Africa (Transvaal Provincial Division).

24. See *Burwell v. Hobby Lobby Stores Inc.*, 134 S. Ct. 2751 (2014) (holding that for-profit corporations cannot be mandated to provide insurance coverage for contraception if it goes against religious beliefs).

25. Leslie Meltzer Henry, *The Jurisprudence of Dignity*, 16 U. Pa. L. Rev. 160 (2011).

26. Ibid., 193.

27. Ibid., 203. But see *Heart of Atlanta Motel, Inc. v. U.S.*, 379 U.S. 241, 250 (1964). The U.S. Supreme Court upholds the power of Congress to prohibit discrimination in interstate travel based on the power of Congress to regulate commerce, rather than on the Fourteenth Amendment's protection of individual liberty and dignity.

28. Henry, "The Jurisprudence of Dignity," 209.

29. Ibid., 217.

30. Ibid., 222.

31. See the Civil Rights Act, 42 U.S.C. § 2000e (1964).

32. *Obergefell v. Hodges*, 135 S. Ct. 2584 (2015).

33. Ibid., 2608.

34. Elizabeth B. Cooper, *The Power of Dignity*, 84 Fordham L. Rev. 3 (2015).

35. Kenneth S. Abraham & G. Edward White, *The Puzzle of the Dignitary Torts*, 104 Cornell L. Rev. 317 (2019).

36. Ibid.

37. *Hulver v. U.S.*, 562 F.2d 1132 (8th Cir. 1977); *Munley v. ISC Financial House, Inc.*, 584 P.2d 1336, 1340 (Okla. 1978); *Fogel v. Forbes, Inc.*, 500 F.Supp 1081 (E.D. Pa. 1980).

38. *Bing v. Thunig*, 143 N.E.2d 3 (Ct. App. N.Y. 1957).

39. *Duttry v. Patterson*, 565 Pa. 130 (2001).

40. Eric Pace, "Spottswood W. Robinson 3d, Civil Rights Lawyer, Dies at 82," *New York Times*, October 13, 1998, https://www.nytimes.com/1998/10/13/us/spottswood-w-robinson-3d-civil-rights-lawyer-dies-at-82.html.

41. *Cruzan by Cruzan v. Director, Missouri Dept. of Health*, 497 U.S. 261 (1990); *In re Quinlan*, 70 N.J. 10 (1976); *Satz v. Perlmutter*, 379 So. 2d 359 (Fla. 1980); *Estate of Leach v. Shapiro*, 469 N.E.2d 1047 (Ohio Ct. App. 1984).

42. *Lucchesi v. Frederic N. Stimmell, M.D., Ltd.*, 716 P.2d 1013 (Ariz. 1986).

3. Emergency Care in America

1. Guido Calabresi has been a professor at Yale Law School since 1959 and was the school's dean from 1985 until 1994. In 1994 he was appointed a federal judge for the U.S. Court of Appeals for the Second Circuit. See "Guido Calabresi," Yale Law School, accessed November 8, 2008, https://law.yale.edu/guido-calabresi.

2. Guido Calabresi and Philip Bobbit, *Tragic Choice: Fels Lectures on Public Policy Analysis* (New York: W. W. Norton, 1978), 39.

3. *Burditt v. U.S. Dept. of Health and Human Services*, 934 F.2d 1362, 1366 (5th Cir. 1991).

4. Ibid., 1367.

5. Ibid.

6. Ibid., 1366.

7. Examination and Treatment for Emergency Medical Conditions and Women in Labor, 42 U.S.C. § 1395dd (2011).

8. *Burditt*, 934 F.2d at 1375.

9. "Hippocratic Oath Ethical Code," *Encyclopaedia Britannica*, accessed November 8, 2018, https://www.britannica.com/topic/Hippocratic-oath.

10. *Guerrero v. Copper Queen Hospital*, 537 P.2d 1329 (Ariz. 1975).

11. Ibid.

12. Ibid.

13. Ibid., 106.

14. See *Evitt v. University Heights Hosp.*, 727 F.Supp. 497 (S.D. Ind. 1989); *Jackson v. East Bay Hosp.*, 246 F.3d 1248 (9th Cir. 2001) (where a hospital refuses care in an emergency situation, liability may be predicated upon such a refusal); *Morgan v. North MS Med. Cent., Inc.*, 403 F.Supp. 2d 115 (S.D. Ala. 2005) (hospitals are liable if they fail to admit a patient in good faith or if they use subterfuge to avert liability); *Saint Joseph Healthcare, Inc. v. Thomas*, 487 S.W.3d 864 (Ky. 2016) (hospital emergency room could be liable for twice discharging an indigent paraplegic patient who presented with serious symptoms); *Moses v. Providence Hosp. and Med. Cent., Inc.*, 561 F.3d 573 (6th Cir. 2009) (finding it unreasonable that a hospital's duty was merely to admit a patient without further treatment).

15. *Thompson v. Sun City Community Hosp., Inc.*, 688 P.2d 605 (Ariz. 1984).

16. Ibid., 600.

17. Ibid., 602.

18. See *Anestis v. U.S.*, 52 F.Supp.3d 854 (E.D. Ky. 2014) (Veterans Administration mental health clinic of hospital owed duty of care to a veteran who had previously been treated at the hospital); *Johnson v. University of Chicago Hosp.*, 982 F.2d 230 (7th Cir. 1992) (a hospital that had voluntarily assumed responsibilities of a resource hospital owed patient certain duties of care).

19. *Thompson v. Sun City Community Hosp., Inc.*, 688 P.2d 605 (Ariz. 1984).

20. Necessary Stabilizing Treatment for Emergency Medical Conditions and Labor, 42 U.S.C. §1395dd(b)(1)(B) (2011).

21. "Documents: Reports by Center for Medicare and Medicaid Services on Patient Dumping Case at University of Maryland Medical Center Midtown," *Baltimore Sun*, March 20, 2018, http://www.baltimoresun.com/health/bal-centers-medicare-medicaid -survey-report-htmlstory.html.

22. Ibid.

23. Ibid. The CMS report states that Patient #1 was treated for a head wound, but refused discharge from the hospital. Pursuant to a request from the nurses, security guards escorted her from the hospital and left her at a bus stop wearing only her hospital gown. The CMS noted multiple "deficiencies" in the actions taken by University of Maryland Medical Center, including a violation of law requiring safe and reasonable discharge from the emergency department.

24. Scott Taylor, "Howard University Guards Appear to Dump Woman in a Wheelchair onto Sidewalk," ABC7/WJLA, May 16, 2017, http://wjla.com/news/local/howard -university-security-guards-appear-to-dump-wheelchair-bound-woman-onto-sidewalk.

25. *Grimes v. Kennedy Krieger Institute, Inc.*, 782 A.2d 807 (Md. 2001).

26. Taylor, "Howard University Guards Appear to Dump Woman in a Wheelchair onto Sidewalk," video, 0:57.

27. U.S. Commission on Civil Rights, *Patient Dumping*, September 2014, https://www .usccr.gov/pubs/docs/2014PATDUMPOSD_9282014-1.pdf.

28. Ibid., 10.

4. Professional Bias, Class Bias, and Power

1. For a summary of the principal cases, see Robert L. Fine, M.D., "From Quinlan to Schiavo: Medical, Ethical, and Legal Issues in Severe Brain Injury," *Baylor University Medical Center Proceedings* 18, no. 4 (October 2005): 303–310, https://www.ncbi .nlm.nih.gov/pmc/articles/PMC1255938/.

2. The story presented in this chapter is based on facts set forth in a reported case. However, I have not attempted to retell, relitigate, or critique the case by presenting a verbatim recitation of facts and arguments. Rather, the salient facts are recited to spotlight legal and ethical issues central to human dignity and power. The names of the parties have been changed.

3. Linda T. Kohn, Janet M. Corrigan, and Molla S. Donaldson, eds., *To Err Is Human: Building a Safer Health System* (Washington, DC: National Sciences Press, 1999).

4. For a discussion of the legal standards and procedures governing medical malpractice claims, see generally Frank M. McClellan, *Medical Malpractice: Law, Tactics, and Ethics* (Philadelphia: Temple University Press, 1994).

5. *Schloendorff v. Society of New York Hospital*, 211 N.Y. 125, 105 N.E. 92, 93 (1914).

6. *Canterbury v. Spence*, 464 F. 2d 772 (D.C. Cir. 1972), *cert. denied* 409 U.S. 1064 (1972).

7. Restatement (Second) of Torts § 46, cmt. d (1965).

8. 1 Summ. Pa. Jur. 2d Torts § 10:54 (2d ed. 2017).

9. Ibid.

10. *Lucchesi v. Frederic N. Stimmell, M.D., Ltd.*, 716 P.2d 1013 (Ariz. 1986).

11. *Lucchesi v. Frederic N. Stimmell, M.D., Ltd.*, 149 Ariz. 76, 716 (P.2d) 1013 (1986).

12. *Taylor v. Baptist Medical Center, Inc.*, 400 So.2d 369 (Ala. 1981).

13. Tomi Akinyemiju, Qingrui Meng, and Neomi Vin-Raviv, "Race/Ethnicity and Socioeconomic Differences in Colorectal Cancer Surgery Outcomes," *BMC Cancer* 16 (September 2016): 715, https://doi.org/10.1186/s12885-016-2738-7.

14. "Project Implicit," accessed November 12, 2018, https://implicit.harvard.edu/implicit/; Shankar Vedantam, *The Hidden Brain: How Our Unconscious Minds Elect Presidents, Control Markets, Wage War, and Save Our Lives* (New York: Spiegel and Grau, 2010).

15. Kathleen Nalty, "Strategies for Confronting Unconscious Bias," *Colorado Lawyer* 45, no. 5 (May 2016) (discussing how conscious and unconscious biases impact people's decisions).

16. Atul Gawande, *Complications: A Surgeon's Notes on an Imperfect Science* (New York: Metropolitan Books, 2002), 24.

17. The case was appealed, with the intermediate appellate court and the Supreme Court reaching different conclusions about the legal validity of the mother's claim that the doctors were responsible for her emotional distress. The intermediate court agreed that the evidence supported the jury's conclusion that the doctors had engaged in outrageous conduct beyond the bounds of decency.

18. Gawande, *Complications*, 24.

19. 3 Summ. Pa. Jur. 2d Torts § 37:86 (2017).

20. *Canterbury*, 464 F.2d 772.

21. Ibid., 778.

22. Ibid., 786.

5. The Love Doctor

1. Isabel Wilkerson, "Charges against Doctor Bring Ire and Questions," *New York Times*, December 11, 1988, https://www.nytimes.com/1988/12/11/us/charges-against-doctor-bring-ire-and-questions.html.

2. Ibid.

3. Ibid.

4. Ibid.

5. Ibid.

6. Ibid.

7. *Browning v. Burt,* 613 N.E.2d 993, 997 (Ohio 1993).

8. France Griggs, "Breaking Tradition," *Chicago Tribune*, August 25, 1991, https://www.chicagotribune.com/news/ct-xpm-1991-08-25-9103030670-story.html.

9. Ibid.

10. Ibid.

11. Ibid.

12. Ibid.

13. Ibid.

14. Ibid.

15. *Moore v. Burt*, 645 N.E.2d 749 (Ohio App. 2 Dist. 1994).

16. *Browning*, 613 N.E.2d at 1000.

17. Ibid.

18. Ibid.

19. Ibid.

20. Ibid.

21. Ibid.

22. Susan Donaldson James, "Ohio Woman Still Scarred by 'Love' Doctor's Sex Surgery," *ABC News*, December 13, 2012, http://abcnews.go.com/Health/ohio-woman-writes-book-love-doctor-mutilated-sex/story?id=17897317.

23. Ibid.

24. Ibid.

25. Ibid.

26. *Browning*, 613 N.E.2d at 996.

27. Ibid., 996–997.

28. Ibid., 997.

29. Ibid.

30. Ibid., 998.

31. Ibid., 996.

32. Ibid., 1002.

33. Ibid.

34. *Darling v. Charleston City Hospital*, 211 N.E. 2d 253 (Ill. 1965); *Johnson v. Misericordia Community Hospital*, 301 N.W. 2d 156 (Wis. 1980); *Whittington v. Episcopal Hospital*, 768 A.2d 1144 (Pa. Super. Ct. 2001). For a discussion of the general rules governing medical malpractice claims, see McClellan, *Medical Malpractice*.

6. Innovative Therapy and Medical Experimentation

1. Admin, "Did Dr. Norwood Go Too Far? (Part One)," *Philadelphia Magazine*, May 15, 2006, http://www.phillymag.com/articles/did-dr-norwood-go-too-far-part-one/.

2. Ibid.

3. U.S. Food and Drug Administration, "Institutional Review Boards Frequently Asked Questions—Information Sheet," https://www.fda.gov/RegulatoryInformation/Guidances/ucm126420.htm#ClinicalInvestigations.

4. Ibid.

5. Deborah S. Fruitman, "Hypoplastic Left Heart Syndrome: Prognosis and Management Options," *Paediatrics and Child Health* 5, no. 4 (2000): 219–225.

6. Despite the public records of some of the cases discussed, to provide grieving parents some privacy, the names of the victims and their families have been changed.

7. Federal Food, Drug, and Cosmetic Act (FD&C Act), 21 U.S.C. §§ 301 et seq., and the Medical Device Amendments (MDA), 21 U.S.C. §§ 360 et seq.

8. Thomas Burton, "NuMED Is Guilty in FDA Case," *Wall Street Journal*, July 31, 2007, http://www.wsj.com/articles/SB118584916741583044.

9. Admin, "Did Dr. Norwood Go Too Far? (Part One)."

10. C. Lee Ventola, "Off-Label Drug Information: Regulation, Distribution, Evaluation, and Related Controversies," *Pharmacy and Therapeutics* 34, no. 8 (2009): 428–440.

11. Anna B. Laakmann, "When Should Physicians Be Liable for Innovation?," 36 *Cardozo Law Review* 913, 923 (2015).

12. Ibid.

13. Nancy A. Nussmeier, "Management of Temperature during and after Cardiac Surgery," *Texas Heart Institute Journal* 32, no. 4 (2005): 472–476; Robert S. Bonser, Domenico Pagano, and Axel Haverich, *Brain Protection in Cardiac Surgery* (London: Springer Verlag, 2011).

14. John W. Moore, "Food and Drug Administration (FDA) Regulation of Pediatric Cardiovascular Devices," *Pediatric Cardiology Today* 2, no. 5 (May 2004): 4–5, http://www.pediatriccardiologytoday.com/index_files/PCT-MAY04-RGB.pdf.

15. Ibid.

16. Laura Ungar, Adam Taylor, and Jennifer Goldblatt, "A. I. duPont Firings Leave Parents, Doctors Wondering What's Next," *Pediatric Cardiology Today* 2, no. 5 (May 2004): 1–3, http://www.pediatriccardiologytoday.com/index_files/PTC-MAY04-RGB.pdf.

17. See *Guinan v. A. I. duPont Hosp. for Children*, 597 F.Supp.2d 517 (E.D. Pa. 2009).

18. For a case adopting and explaining the school of thought defense to a medical malpractice case, see *Jones v. Chidester*, 531 Pa. 31, 610 A.2d 964 (1992). See also B. Sonny Bal, "An Introduction to Medical Malpractice in the United States," *Clinical Orthopedics and Related Research* 467, no. 2 (2009): 399–347; *Standard Civil Jury Charges (Medical Malpractice)*, https://www.15thjdc.org/uploads,MedicalMalpractice CivilCharges.pdf.

19. Marilyn Field and Richard Behrman, eds., *Ethical Conduct of Clinical Research Involving Children* (Washington, DC: National Academies Press, 2004), https://www .ncbi.nlm.nih.gov/books/NBK25549/.

20. Edward L. Raab, "The Parameters of Informed Consent," *Transactions of the American Ophthalmological Society* 102 (December 2004): 225–232.

21. Admin, "Did Dr. Norwood Go Too Far? (Part Two)"; Admin, "Did Dr. Norwood Go Too Far? (Part Two)," *Philadelphia Magazine*, May 15, 2006, https://www.phillymag .com/articles/2006/05/15/did-dr-norwood-go-too-far-part-two/.

22. Trevor Butterworth, "Heartless Regulation May End Up Killing Kids," *Huffington Post*, July 6, 2007, https://www.huffpost.com/entry/heartless-regulation-may_b_55171.

23. Robert Johnson and Adam Cureton, "Kant's Moral Philosophy," in *The Stanford Encyclopedia of Philosophy* (2004; rev. 2016), https://plato.stanford.edu/entries/kant -moral/.

24. Admin, "Did Dr. Norwood Go Too Far? (Part Two)." Read more at https://www.philly mag.com/news/2006/05/15/did-dr-norwood-go-too-far-part-two/#eTsLgd4zf5DJ W1aA.99.

25. Ibid.

26. *Grimes v. Kennedy Kreiger Institute, Inc.*, 782 A.2d 807 (Md. 2001).

27. *Guinan v. A. I. duPont Hosp. for Children*, 597 F.Supp.2d 517 (E.D. Pa. 2009); *Conway v. A. I. duPont Hosp. for Children*, 2007 WL 560502; *Hess v. A. I. duPont Hosp.*, 2009 WL 595602 (in all three cases, Dr. Norwood was named as a defendant).

7. Perspectives on Racism

1. Derrick Bell, *Faces at the Bottom of the Well: The Permanence of Racism* (New York: Basic Books, 1992).

2. Ibid.; Linda Greenhouse, "The End of Racism, and Other Fables," *New York Times*, September 20, 1992, https://timesmachine.nytimes.com/timesmachine/1992/09/20 /180092.html?action=click&contentCollection=Archives&module=LedeAsset& region=ArchiveBody&pgtype=article.

3. Vincent Harding, *There Is a River: The Black Struggle for Freedom in America* (New York: Harvest, 1993).

4. *Brown v. Board of Educ. of Topeka, Kan.*, 347 U.S. 483 (1954) (finding school segregation unconstitutional), 349 U.S. 294 (1955) (remanding cases to trial courts to formulate appropriate remedies for the constitutional violations proved by the evidence in the various cases).

5. Richard Kluger, *Simple Justice: The History of Brown v. Board of Education and Black America's Struggle for Equality* (New York: Alfred A. Knopf, 1976) (a detailed discussion of the legal battle for black equality).

6. Derrick Bell, *The Racism Is Permanent Thesis: Courageous Revelation or Unconscious Denial of Racial Genocide,* 22 CAL. L. REV. 571 (1993).

7. Leroy D. Clark, *A Critique of Professor Derrick A. Bell's Thesis of the Permanence of Racism and His Strategy of Confrontation,* 73 DENV. U. L. REV. 23 (1995) (challenging

Professor Bell's claim that racism is permanent by exploring and interpreting American history and, current as of 1995, American culture); Zeus Leonardo and Angela P. Harris, "Living with Racism in Education and Society: Derrick Bell's Ethical Idealism and Political Pragmatism," *Race Ethnicity and Education* 16, no. 4 (2013): 470–488 (focusing on the tension within Professor Bell's work between its racial realism and its ethical idealism).

8. Compare Derrick Bell's idea that the racism is permanent and Dr. Martin Luther King Jr.'s dream for a "beloved community," which sparked several civil rights leaders to aspire to and believe in the notion; see Charles Marsh, *The Beloved Community: How Faith Shapes Social Justice from the Civil Rights Movement to Today* (New York: Basic Books, 2004) (connecting the idea of "Christian love" to the African American civil rights movement and to how it can power social justice issues); Alec Regimbal, "Envisioning a Beloved Community: Yakima Civil Rights Leader Passionate about Working toward King's Dream," *Yakima Herald*, January 14, 2018, https://www .yakimaherald.com/news/local/envisioning-a-beloved-community-yakima-civil -rights-leader-passionate-about/article_58d4551e-f9c7-11e7-baca-eb79c0cc0fa1.html.

9. William P. Jones, "Freedom for Every Citizen: The Missed Opportunity of the Kerner Report," *The Nation*, April 5, 2018, https://www.thenation.com/article/freedom-for -every-citizen/; Justin Driver, "The Report on Race That Shook America," *The Atlantic*, May 2018, https://www.theatlantic.com/magazine/archive/2018/05/the-report -on-race-that-shook-america/556850/ (discussing how little has changed in the fifty years since the Kerner Commission's *Report of the National Advisory Commission on Civil Disorders* discussed two societies, "one black, one white—separate and unequal," in 1968; Leland Ware, *A Century of Segregation: Race, Class, and Disadvantage* (Lanham, MD: Lexington Books, 2018) (examining the major U.S. Supreme Court decisions and congressional legislation that shaped America's history of school and residential segregation from the twentieth century to the present day).

10. Phoebe A. Haddon, *Has the Roberts Court Plurality's Colorblind Rhetoric Finally Broken Brown's Promise?*, 90 Denv. U. L. Rev. 1251 (2013); Richard Rothstein, *The Color of Law: A Forgotten History of How Our Government Segregated America* (New York: Liveright, 2017).

11. Anna B. Laakman, *When Should Physicians Be Liable for Innovation?*, 36 Cardozo L. Rev. 913 (2015).

12. Michelle Alexander, *The New Jim Crow: Mass Incarceration in the Age of Colorblindness* (New York: New Press, 2012) (discussing the modern caste-like system in the United States resulting from the high population of incarcerated African Americans); Floyd D. Weatherspoon, *The Mass Incarceration of African-American Males: A Return to Institutionalized Slavery, Oppression, and Disenfranchisement of Constitutional Rights*, 13 Tex. Wesleyan L. Rev. 599 (2007).

13. David A. Ansell, *The Death Gap: How Inequality Kills* (Chicago: University of Chicago Press, 2017).

14. Chantal Da Silva, "Two Black Men Arrested at Starbucks for Not Ordering Settle for $2—and a $200,000 Promise," *Newsweek*, May 3, 2018, https://www.newsweek.com /two-black-men-wrongly-arrested-starbucks-settle-2-and-200000-promise-909253 (the symbolic gesture of a two dollar award was accompanied by "a promise from local officials that the city will invest $200,000 to set up a pilot program geared towards supporting young entrepreneurs"); Michael Omi and Howard Winant, *Racial Formation in the United States: From the 1960s to the 1990s*, 2nd ed. (New York: Routledge, 1994).

15. Vedantam, *The Hidden Brain*.

16. Ansell, *The Death Gap*.

17. Ibid.

18. Amanda Taub, "'White Nationalism,' Explained," *New York Times*, November 21, 2016, https://www.nytimes.com/2016/11/22/world/americas/white-nationalism-explained.html (article discussing "white nationalism" and how it affects American politics); Pamela Perry, "White," in *Keywords for American Cultural Studies* (New York University Press, 2014), http://keywords.nyupress.org/american-cultural-studies/essay/white/ (essay discussing the privileges and idealism associated with being "white" that were brought to culture and politics in Caribbean and North American colonies).

19. Dayna Bowen Matthew, *Just Medicine: A Cure for Racial Inequality in American Health Care* (New York: New York University Press, 2015); Ruqaiijah Yearby, *Breaking the Cycle of 'Unequal Treatment' with Health Care Reform: Acknowledging and Addressing the Continuation of Racial Bias*, 44 CONN. L. REV. 1281 (2012).

20. Institute of Medicine (US) Committee on Understanding and Eliminating Racial and Ethnic Disparities in Health Care, *Unequal Treatment: Confronting Racial and Ethnic Disparities in Health Care*, ed. B. D. Smedley, A. Y. Stith, and A. R. Nelson (Washington, DC: National Academies Press, 2003), https://www.ncbi.nlm.nih.gov/books/NBK220358/; Ansell, *The Death Gap*.

21. 79 A.L.R.2d 1028.

22. 88 A.L.R.3d 1008 §2; *Harrison v. U.S.*, 284 F.3d 293 (1st Cir. 2002).

23. *2016 National Healthcare Quality and Disparities Report*, AHRQ Pub. No. 17-0001 (Rockville, MD: Agency for Healthcare Research and Quality, July 2017), http://www.ahrq.gov/research/findings/nhqrdr/nhqdr16/index.html.

24. *Dred Scott v. Sandford*, 60 U.S. 393 (1857).

25. *Toyosaburo Korematsu v. U.S.*, 323 U.S. 214 (1944).

26. Adia Harvey Wingfield, "Color-Blindness Is Counterproductive," *The Atlantic*, September 13, 2015, https://www.theatlantic.com/politics/archive/2015/09/color-blindness-is-ounterproductive/405037/ (article discussing the social unacceptableness of racism and how purported "color-blindness" may actually lead to disadvantages to racial minorities).

27. Vickie Mays, Ninez A. Ponce, Donna L. Washington, and Susan D. Cochran, "Classification of Race and Ethnicity: Implications for Public Health," *Annual Review of Public Health* 24 (2002): 83–100, https://www.ncbi.nlm.nih.gov/pmc/articles/PMC3681827/.

28. "Project Implicit Director Kate Ratliff on Implicit Bias in Gainesville," Project Implicit, August 30, 2017, https://implicit.harvard.edu/implicit/.

29. Vedantam, *The Hidden Brain*.

30. Alessio Avenanti, Angela Sirigu, and Salvatore Aglioti, "Racial Bias Reduces Empathic Sensorimotor Resonance with Other-Race Pain," *Current Biology* 20 (2010): 1018–1022 (finding that "differential pain-specific empathic brain responses to ingroup and outgroup pain are linked to implicit racial bias").

31. Jennifer Gratz, *Discriminating toward Equality: Affirmative Action and the Diversity Charade* (Washington, DC: Heritage Foundation, 2017), http://www.heritage.org/poverty-and-inequality/report/discriminating-toward-equality-affirmative-action-and-the-diversity.

32. Christine Emba, "What Is White Privilege?," *Washington Post*, January 16, 2016, https://www.washingtonpost.com/blogs/post-partisan/wp/2016/01/16/white-privilege-explained/?noredirect=on&utm_term=.274c5b0a8010.

33. Rebecca Skloot, *The Immortal Life of Henrietta Lacks* (New York: Broadway Books, 2011); "Death by Delivery," season 2, episode 2 of *The Naked Truth*, directed by Lyttanya Shannon, featuring Nelufar Hedayat, aired March 8, 2017, on IMDb (an in-depth documentary on the greater rates of maternal death and health complications for black women).

34. *Fisher v. Carrousel Motor Hotel, Inc.*, 424 S.W.2d 627 (Tex. 1967).

35. *Contreras v. Crown Zellerbach*, 88 Wash.2d 735, 736 (1977).

8. Healthcare Disparities as a Lived Experience

1. See Ansell, *The Death Gap*.

2. Colby Itkowitz, "Closure of Two D.C. Maternity Wards Hurts Low-Income Women Most," *Washington Post*, https://www.washingtonpost.com/local/closure-of-two-dc -maternity-wards-hurts-low-income-women-most/2017/10/28/753e4dee-ad06-11e7 -9e58-e6288544af98_story.html?utm_term=.b085c65f1cb2.

3. Ibid.

4. Ibid.

5. Ibid., 7.

6. Ibid., 8.

7. Tim Wise, "How Racism Explains America's Class Divide and Culture of Economic Cruelty," in *Under the Affluence: Shaming the Poor, Praising the Rich and Sacrificing the Future of America* (San Francisco: City Lights, 2015), http://www.timwise .org/2015/04/how-racism-explains-americas-class-divide-and-culture-of-economic -cruelty-an-excerpt-from-under-the-affluence/ (excerpt describing how conscious historical decisions propagated the racial divide); Coleman Hughes, "Black American Culture and the Racial Wealth Gap," *Quillette*, July 19, 2018, https://quillette.com /2018/07/19/black-american-culture-and-the-racial-wealth-gap/ (article discussing that slavery and New Deal policies are the two major historical factors contributing to the racial wealth gap in America).

8. Richard Rothstein, *The Color of Law: A Forgotten History of How Our Government Segregated America* (New York: Liveright, 2017); Isabel Wilkerson, *The Warmth of Other Suns: The Epic Story of America's Great Migration* (New York: Random House, 2010); David Barton Smith, *Health Care Divided: Race and Healing a Nation* (Ann Arbor: University of Michigan Press, 1999); David Barton Smith, *The Power to Heal: Civil Rights, Medicare, and the Struggle to Transform America's Health Care System* (Nashville: Vanderbilt University Press, 2016).

9. Wilkerson, *The Warmth of Other Suns*.

10. Peter Ubel, "Why Poor People Like Hospitals," *Forbes Magazine*, September 13, 2017, https://www.forbes.com/sites/peterubel/2013/09/17/why-poor-people-like -hospitals/#36d9e6d638a7; "Healthcare Access in Rural Communities," Rural Health Information Hub, accessed June 9, 2017, https://www.ruralhealthinfo.org/topics /healthcare-access.

11. "Key Facts about the Uninsured Population," Kaiser Health News, accessed November 29, 2017, https://www.kff.org/uninsured/fact-sheet/key-facts-about -the-uninsured-population/; Beatrix Hoffman, *Healthcare for Some: Rights and Rationing in the United States since 1930* (Chicago: University of Chicago Press, 2012).

12. "Key Facts about the Uninsured Population"; Beth Levin Crimmel, "Health Insurance Coverage and Income Levels for the US Noninstitutionalized Population under Age 64," Medical Expenditure Panel Survey, Statistical Brief #40 (May 2004).

13. Ansel, *The Death Gap*, 125–126.

14. See Global Health Data Exchange, http://ghdx.healthdata.org/us-data for health data for different locations throughout the United States.

15. Derrick Bell, *Faces at the Bottom of the Well: The Permanence of Racism* (New York: Basic Books, 1992).

16. *Whittington v. Episcopal Hospital*, 768 A.2d 1114 (Pa. Super. 2001).

17. Paula S. Rothenberg, *White Privilege: Essential Readings on the Other Side of Racism* (New York: Worth, 2008).

18. Carol Weisse, Paul Sorum, Kafi Sanders, and Beth L. Syat, "Do Gender and Race Affect Decisions about Pain Management?," *Journal of General Internal Medicine* 16, no. 4 (April 2001): 211–217; Shedra Amy Snipes et al., "Is Race Medically Relevant? A Qualitative Study of Physicians' Attitudes about the Role of Race in Treatment Decision-Making," *BMC Health Services Research* 11 (August 5, 2011): 183.

19. "The Troubles at King/Drew," *Los Angeles Times*, August 21, 2015, http://www.latimes.com/nation/la-kingdrewpulitzer-sg-storygallery.html (*Los Angeles Times* website listing each article in the series about King-Drew Hospital that was submitted for Pulitzer Prize consideration). Articles include Tracy Weber, Charles Ornstein, and Mitchell Landsberg, "Deadly Errors and Politics Betray a Hospital's Promise," December 5, 2004; Charles Ornstein, Tracy Weber, and Steve Hymon, "Underfunding Is a Myth, but the Squandering Is Real," December 6, 2014; Charles Ornstein and Tracy Weber, "How Whole Departments Fail a Hospital's Patients," December 8, 2004; Mitchel Landsberg, "Why Supervisors Let Deadly Problems Slide," December 9, 2004; Tracy Weber and Charles Ornstein, "One Doctor's Long Trail of Dangerous Mistakes," December 7, 2004.

20. Sean Alfano, "'Killer King' L.A. Hospital in Peril," *CBS News*, June 22, 2007, https://www.cbsnews.com/news/killer-king-la-hospital-in-peril/.

21. Ibid.

22. Ibid.

23. Victoria Colliver, "How 'Killer King' Became the Hospital of the Future," *Politico*, November 8, 2017, https://www.politico.com/agenda/story/2017/11/08/the-hospital-of-the-future-000572.

24. "Urban Health Institute," Cooper University Health Care, https://www.cooperhealth.org/services/urban-health-institute-1.

25. Ibid.

26. Jeffrey Brenner, "A Revolutionary Approach to Improving Health Care Delivery," Robert Wood Johnson Foundation, February 1, 2014, https://www.rwjf.org/en/library/articles-and-news/2014/02/improving-management-of-health-care-superutilizers.html.

27. Ibid.

9. Catastrophic Injuries

The story and case discussed in this chapter are loosely based on a reported case, but the facts have been changed somewhat and identifying information for the parties involved has been omitted.

1. 42 U.S.C. § 280g-15 (2011) (authorizing the Secretary of Health and Human Services "to award demonstration grants to States for the development . . . of alternatives to current tort litigation for resolving disputes over injuries allegedly caused by health care providers").

2. The National Childhood Vaccine Injury Act of 1986, 42 U.S.C. §§ 300aa-1, et seq., was put into effect to set up a federal vaccine injury compensation program and to establish legal requirements for vaccine providers to follow. The compensation program incorporates a no-fault approach to compensating children's injuries related to vaccinations. Examples of states that have adopted no-fault approaches to medical malpractice are Virginia and Florida. See Va. Code Ann. § 38.2-5000, et seq. (Virginia Birth-Related Neurological Injury Compensation Act); Fla. Stat. Ann. § 766.303 (Florida Birth-Related Neurological Injury Compensation Plan). See also James A. Henderson Jr., "The Virginia Birth-Related Injury Compensation Act: Limited No-Fault Statutes as Solutions to the 'Medical Malpractice Crisis,'" in Institute of Medicine (US) Committee to Study Medical Professional Liability and the Delivery of Obstetrical Care, *Medical Professional Liability and the Delivery of Obstetrical Care*, vol. 2, *An Interdisciplinary Review*, ed. V. P. Rostow and R. J. Bulger (Washington, DC: National Academies Press, 1989), 194–212, https://www.ncbi.nlm.nih.gov/books/NBK218645/ (describing the "no fault" approach).

10. Orthopedic Health Disparities

1. *Loving v. Virginia*, 388 US 1 (1967) (finding that miscegenation statutes in Virginia that were put in place to prevent marriages between persons of different races were unconstitutional, since they violated the equal protection and due process clauses of the Fourteenth Amendment).
2. Augustus White III, with David Chanoff, *Seeing Patients: Unconscious Bias in Health Care* (Cambridge, MA: Harvard University Press, 2011).
3. Ibid., 11.
4. Ibid., 212–213.
5. I credit my colleague Professor Jane Baron for this succinct and pithy statement.
6. Frank M. McClellan, James E. Wood Jr., and Sherin M. Fahmy, *It Takes a Village: Reforming Law to Promote Health Literacy and Reduce Orthopedic Health Disparities*, 8 J. HEALTH & BIOMEDICAL L. 333 (2013). For the original research supporting this statement, see Charles L. Nelson, "Disparities in Orthopedic Surgical Intervention," *JAAOS* 15, suppl. 1 (2007): S13–17.
7. Bonnie Simpson Mason and Vani Sabesan, "Easy and Low-Impact Exercises for People with Osteoarthritis," *Consult* 360 (July 16, 2018), https://www.consultant360.com/blog/hmpprimary/easy-low-impact-exercises-people-osteoarthritis.
8. See *Canterbury v. Spence*, 464 F.2d 772 (D.C. Cir. 1972).
9. McClellan, Wood, and Fahmy, *It Takes a Village*, 372–375.
10. See Jay Katz, *The Silent World of Doctor and Patient* (Baltimore: Johns Hopkins University Press, 1984).
11. Except see *Truman v. Thomas*, 27 Cal. 3d 285 (1980) (introducing the concept of informed refusal).
12. Lynne C. Jones, Yashika Watkins, and Duanny Alva, "Operation Change: A New Paradigm Addressing Behavior Change and Musculoskeletal Health Disparities," *Journal of Racial and Ethnic Health Disparities* 5(6), 1264–1272, doi:10.1007/s40615-018-0473-2 (April 24, 2018): 1–9, https://doi.org/10.1007/s40615-018-0473-2.
13. Jones, Watkins, and Alva, "Operation Change."
14. Ibid.
15. "Project TEACH Classes," Philadelphia FIGHT Community Health Centers, https://fight.org/programs-and-services/project-teach-classes/.

16. Ana Natale-Pereira, Kimberly Enard, Lucinda Nevarez, and Lovell Jones, "The Role of Patient Navigators in Eliminating Health Disparities," *Cancer* 117 (15 Suppl) (2011): 3543–3552, https://www.ncbi.nlm.nih.gov/pmc/articles/PMC4121958/.

17. Jay McDonald, "A Health Navigator Helps with Obamacare and More," Bankrate, June 9, 2014, https://www.bankrate.com/finance/insurance/health-navigators.aspx (article discussing the impact of Obamacare on patient navigators); "Trump Administration Cuts Grants to Help People Get Obama Care," Reuters, July 10, 2018, https://www.reuters.com/article/us-usa-healthcare-obamacare/trump-administration-cuts-grants-to-help-people-get-obamacare-idUSKBN1K102W?il=0 (article discussing that reducing funding for navigators is one of the Trump administration's strategies to kill Obamacare).

18. Jeffrey Brenner, "A Revolutionary Approach to Improving Health Care Delivery," in *Reducing Hospital Readmissions*, Robert Wood Johnson Foundation, February 1, 2014, https://www.rwjf.org/en/library/articles-and-news/2014/02/improving-management-of-health-care-superutilizers.html.

19. Dea C. Lott, *Teaching Holistic Justice: Medical-Legal Partnerships in the Clinical Setting*, 9 IND. HEALTH L. REV. 549 (2012); Elizabeth Tobin Tyler, Ellen Lawton, Kathleen Conroy, Megan Sandel, and Barry Zuckerman, eds., *Poverty, Health and Law: Readings and Cases for Medical-Legal Partnership* (Durham, NC: Carolina Academic Press, 2011).

11. Paying for Healthcare

1. Paul Krugman, "Health Care Realities," *New York Times*, July 30, 2009, https://www.nytimes.com/2009/07/31/opinion/31krugman.html.

2. Olivia Dean, Claire Noel-Miller, and Keith Lind, "Who Relies on Medicare? A Profile of the Medicare Population," factsheet, AARP Public Policy Institute, November 2017, https://www.aarp.org/content/dam/aarp/ppi/2017/11/who-relies-on-medicare-a-profile-of-the-medicare-population.pdf.

3. Rebecca Riffkin, "Americans with Government Health Plans Most Satisfied," *Gallup*, November 6, 2015, https://news.gallup.com/poll/186527/americans-government-health-plans-satisfied.aspx; Commonwealth Fund, "New Study: Elderly Medicare Beneficiaries Most Satisfied with Their Health Insurance; Working-Age Adult[s] with Private Coverage Report More Trouble Accessing Care, Paying Medical Bills," press release, July 18, 2012, https://www.commonwealthfund.org/press-release/2012/new-study-elderly-medicare-beneficiaries-most-satisfied-their-health-insurance?redirect_source=/press-release/2012/new-study-elderly-medicare-beneficiaries-most-satisifed-their-health-insurance.

4. Richard Foster and M. Kent Clemens, "Medicare Financial Status, Budget Impact, and Sustainability—Which Concept Is Which?," *Health Care Financing Review* 30, no. 3 (Spring 2009): 77–90.

5. Ibid.

6. Ibid.

7. Ibid.

8. J. D. Vance, *Hillbilly Elegy: A Memoir of a Family and Culture in Crisis* (New York: Harper, 2016) (memoir critiquing government assistance, claiming that all people need to do is work harder to overcome misfortune); David Lauter, "How Do Americans View Poverty? Many Blue-Collar Whites, Key to Trump, Criticize Poor People as Lazy and Content to Stay on Welfare," *Los Angeles Times*, August 14, 2016), http://www.latimes.com/projects/la-na-pol-poverty-poll/ (article discussing the common

public opinion among blue-collar white Americans that there are "plenty of jobs available for poor people").

9. "Fact Sheet: Distribution of Medicare Beneficiaries by Race/Ethnicity," Kaiser Family Foundation, 2016, https://www.kff.org/medicare/state-indicator/medicare-beneficiaries -by-raceethnicity/?currentTimeframe=0&sortModel=%7B%22colId%22:%22Location %22,%22sort%22:%22asc%22%7D.

10. Kellie Ell, "April Jobs Report Shows Racial Disparities in Unemployment Rates Continue," CNBC, May 4, 2018, https://www.cnbc.com/2018/05/04/aprils-jobs-report -shows-racial-inequalities-in-unemployment-rate.html; Valerie Wilson, "Racial Inequalities in Wages, Income, and Wealth Show That MLK's Work Remains Unfinished," Economic Policy Institute, January 11, 2018, https://www.epi.org/publication/racial -inequalities-in-wages-income-and-wealth-show-that-mlks-work-remains -unfinished/.

11. Tracy Jan, "White Families Have Nearly 10 Times the Net Worth of Black Families. And the Gap Is Growing," *Washington Post*, September 28, 2017, https://www .washingtonpost.com/news/wonk/wp/2017/09/28/black-and-hispanic-families-are -making-more-money-but-they-still-lag-far-behind-whites/?utm_term= .0ea11af4316a; "Labor Force Statistics from the Current Population Survey," U.S. Department of Labor, Bureau of Labor Statistics, July 6, 2018, https://www.bls.gov /web/empsit/cpsee_e16.htm.

12. See *Nat'l Federation of Independent Bus. v. Sebelius*, 567 U.S. 519 (2012) (holding that a mandate imposing a minimum coverage under which people must purchase health insurance was unconstitutional under the Commerce Clause).

13. Rachel Garfield et al., "The Coverage Gap: Uninsured Poor Adults in States That Do Not Expand Medicaid," Kaiser Family Foundation, June 12, 2018, https://www.kff .org/medicaid/issue-brief/the-coverage-gap-uninsured-poor-adults-in-states-that-do -not-expand-medicaid/.

14. Frank M. McClellan, *Is Managed Care Good for What Ails You? Ruminations on Race, Age and Class*, 4 VILL L. REV. 227 (1999).

15. Ibid., 228–229.

16. Atul Gawande, *Being Mortal: Medicine and What Matters in the End* (Dallas: Metropolitan Press, 2014).

17. *Wickline v. State of California*, 239 Cal. Rptr. 810 (Cal. App. 2d Dist. 1986).

18. *Pegram v. Herdrich*, 530 U.S. 211, 221 (2000).

19. Daniel Callahan, *Setting Limits: Medical Goals in an Aging Society* (New York: Simon & Schuster, 1987).

20. Philip A. Perry and Timothy Hotze, "Oregon's Experiment with Prioritizing Public Health Services," *AMA Journal of Ethics* 13, no. 4 (April 2011): 241–247, https:// journalofethics.ama-assn.org/article/oregons-experiment-prioritizing-public-health -care-services/2011-04 (discussing that the main ideas of the Oregon Health Plan were that access to basic healthcare should be universal, society should bear the responsibility of covering healthcare for those who cannot afford it, and the level of care provided should be determined publicly).

21. Mark Shaffer, "The Idealistic HMO: Can Good Care Survive the Market?," accessed May 30, 2019, http://www.hedricksmith.com/site_criticalcondition/program/ideal Summary.htm (discussing how in 1989, Kaiser Permanente created an AIDS-specific program to help patients manage their own care; the organization was created in response to HIV/AIDS patients' protests).

22. Barry R. Furrow, *Access to Health Care and Political Ideology: Wouldn't You Really Rather have a Pony?*, 29 W. New Eng. L. Rev. 405 (2007).

23. Ibid., 410.

24. Annalisa Merelli, "A History of Why the US Is the Only Rich Country without Universal Health Care," *Quartz*, July 18, 2017, https://qz.com/1022831/why-doesnt-the -united-states-have-universal-health-care/.

25. Furrow, "Access to Health Care and Political Ideology," 17.

26. Thomas Kaplan and Robert Pear, "24 Million More among Uninsured under G.O.P. Plan," *New York Times*, March 14, 2017.

27. Ta-Nehisi Coates, *We Were Eight Years in Power: An American Tragedy* (London: One-world Publications, 2017) (providing a penetrating and disturbing description of how the election of the first black president unleashed a backlash of racism); Peter Baker, "A President Who Fans, Rather Than Douses, the Nation's Racial Fires," *New York Times*, January 12, 2018, https://www.nytimes.com/2018/01/12/us/politics /trump-racism.html (discussing many of President Trump's comments that have helped fuel, rather than diminish, racism).

28. See Chris Riotta, "GOP Aims to Kill Obamacare Yet Again after Failing 70 Times," *Newsweek*, July 29, 2017, https://www.newsweek.com/gop-health-care-bill-repeal -and-replace-70-failed-attempts-643832; "Efforts to Repeal the Patient Protection and Affordable Care Act," Wikipedia, accessed May 30, 2019, https://en.wikipedia.org /wiki/Efforts_to_repeal_the_Patient_Protection_and_Affordable_Care_Act (for a good timeline list of repeal efforts).

29. Kyle Dropp and Brendan Nyhan, "One-Third Don't Know Obamacare and Affordable Care Act Are the Same," *New York Times*, February 7, 2017, https://www.nytimes .com/2017/02/07/upshot/one-third-dont-know-obamacare-and-affordable-care-act -are-the-same.html.

30. Robert Reich, "Why Medicare Should Be Available to All," *Newsweek*, July 27, 2015, https://www.newsweek.com/why-medicare-should-be-available-all-357404; Bernie Sanders, "Medicare for All," https://berniesanders.com/medicareforall/.

31. Shefali Luthra, "Once Its Greatest Foes, Doctors Are Embracing Single-Payer," *Kaiser Health News*, August 7, 2018, http://bit.ly/2KuYTaH; Ricardo Alonso-Zaldivar and Laurie Kellman, "62 Percent of U.S. Want Federal Government to Ensure Health Care for All, Poll Says," PBS, July 20, 2017, https://www.pbs.org/newshour/health /62-percent-u-s-want-federal-government-ensure-health-care-poll-says; Kristen Bialik, "More Americans Say Government Should Ensure Health Care Coverage," Pew Research Center, January 13, 2017, http://www.pewresearch.org/fact-tank/2017/01 /13/more-americans-say-government-should-ensure-health-care-coverage/.

12. Healthcare and Human Dignity in a Diverse and Changing World

1. Michael Rodriguez and Robert Garcia, "First, Do No Harm: The US Sexually Transmitted Disease Experiments in Guatemala," *American Journal of Public Health* 103, no. 12 (2013): 2122–2126, https://www.ncbi.nlm.nih.gov/pmc/articles/PMC3828982/.

2. Gina Kolata, "Decades Later, Condemnation for a Skid Row Cancer Study," *New York Times*, October 17, 2013, https://www.nytimes.com/2013/10/18/health/medical-experi ments-conducted-on-bowery-alcoholics-in-1950s.html.

3. Ibid.

4. David Livingston Smith, *Less Than Human: Why We Demean, Enslave, and Exterminate Others* (New York: St. Martin's Press, 2011).

5. Jonathan Metzl, *Dying of Whiteness: How the Politics of Racial Resentment Is Killing America's Heartland* (New York: Basic Books, 2019).

6. Ibid., 4.

7. Anne Fadiman, *The Spirit Catches You and You Fall Down: A Hmong Child, Her American Doctors, and the Collision of Two Cultures* (New York: Farrar, Straus and Giroux, 1997).

8. *Grimes v. Kennedy Krieger Institute, Inc.*, 782 A.2d 807 (2001).

9. Ibid., 853.

10. *In re Quinlan*, 355 A.2d 647 (1976).

11. Kim Brooks, "America Is Blaming Pregnant Women for Their Own Deaths," opinion, *New York Times*, November 16, 2018, https://www.nytimes.com/2018/11/16/opinion/sunday/maternal-mortality-rates.html.

12. *Whittington v. Episcopal Hospital*, 768 A.2d 1144 (Pa. Super. Ct. 2001).

13. Kim Brooks, "America Is Blaming Pregnant Women for Their Own Deaths," *New York Times*, November 16, 2018, https://www.nytimes.com/2018/11/16/opinion/sunday/maternal-mortality-rates.html.

14. Laura Unger, "What States Aren't Doing to Save New Mothers' Lives," *USA Today*, September 19, 2018, https://www.usatoday.com/in-depth/news/investigations/deadly-deliveries/2018/09/19/maternal-death-rate-state-medical-deadly-deliveries/547050002/.

15. *In re AC*, 573 A.2d 1235 (D.C. Ct. App. 1990).

16. I have deliberately chosen not to discuss the myriad ethical, moral, and legal issues arising out of the debates about abortion in this book. I acknowledge the dignity issues involved in healthcare decisions about abortion. However, in my view, those issues will continue to elude a resolution that is accepted by all engaged in the debate. The positions will always reflect the personal moral and religious perspectives that individuals embrace. Unless we are willing to endorse a dictatorship or an abolition of the right to freedom of religion, the protection of a woman's privacy should remain the governing legal standard. In any event, a serious discussion of these issues requires a book devoted to the topic.

17. It remains to be seen to what extent the politics around abortion will affect legal standards protecting a woman's right to choose healthcare when she is pregnant in circumstances similar to those presented in *In re A.C.* If *Roe v. Wade*, 410 U.S. 113 (1973), is overturned, the battle over a pregnant woman's right to make healthcare decisions about her body will shift to the federal and state legislatures. The results of the political conflict will be profound.

18. Vincent Harding and Daisaku Ikeda, *America Will Be! Conversations on Hope, Freedom, and Democracy* (Cambridge, MA: Dialogue Path Press, 2013).

Selected Bibliography

Books and Articles

Angelou, Maya. *The Complete Poetry*. New York: Random House, 2015.

Admin. "Did Dr. Norwood Go Too Far? (Part One)." *Philadelphia Magazine*, May 15, 2006. https://www.phillymag.com/articles/2006/05/15/did-dr-norwood-go-too-far-part -one/.

———. "Did Dr. Norwood Go Too Far? (Part Two)." *Philadelphia Magazine*, May 15, 2006. https://www.phillymag.com/articles/2006/05/15/did-dr-norwood-go-too-far-part -two/.

Akinyemiju, Tomi, Qingrui Meng, and Neomi Vin-Raviv. "Ethnicity and Socio-economic Differences in Colorectal Cancer Surgery Outcomes: Analysis of the Nationwide Inpatient Sample." *BMC Cancer* 16 (September 2016): 715. https://doi.org/10.1186/s12885 -016-2738-7.

Alexander, Michelle. *The New Jim Crow: Mass Incarceration in the Age of Colorblindness*. New York: New Press, 2012.

Alfano, Sean. "'Killer King' L.A. Hospital in Peril." *CBS News*, June 22, 2007. https://www .cbsnews.com/news/killer-king-la-hospital-in-peril/.

Alonso-Zaldivar, Ricardo, and Laurie Kellman. "62 percent of U.S. Want Federal Government to Ensure Health Care for All, Poll Says." https://www.pbs.org/newshour/health /62-percent-u-s-want-federal-government-ensure-health-care-poll-says.

Ansell, David. *The Death Gap: How Inequality Kills*. Chicago: University of Chicago Press, 2017.

Ashe, Arthur, and Arnold Rampersad. *Days of Grace: A Memoir*. New York: Knopf, 1993.

Avenanti, Alessio, Angela Sirigu, and Salvatore M. Aglioti. "Bias Reduces Empathic Sensorimotor Resonance with Other-Race Pain." *Current Biology* 20, no. 11 (2010): 1018–1022.

Baker, Peter. "President Who Fans, Rather Than Douses, the Nation Racial Fire." *New York Times*, January 12, 2018. https://www.nytimes.com/2018/01/12/us/politics/trump -racism.html.

Bal, B. Sonny. "An Introduction to Medical Malpractice in the United States." *Clinical Orthopedics and Related Research* 467, no. 2 (2009): 399–347.

Barnett, Tony, and Alan Whiteside. *AIDS in the Twenty-First Century: Disease and Globalization*. New York: Palgrave Macmillan, 2002.

Behrman, Greg. *The Invisible People: How the U.S. Has Slept through the Global AIDS Epidemic, the Greatest Humanitarian Catastrophe of Our Time*. New York: Free Press, 2004.

Bell, Derrick. *Faces at the Bottom of the Well: The Permanence of Racism*. New York: Basic Books, 1992.

Bialik, Kristen. "More Americans Say Government Should Ensure Health Care Coverage." Pew Research Center, January 13, 2017. http://www.pewresearch.org/fact-tank/2017/01 /13/more-americans-say-government-should-ensure-health-care-coverage/.

Bonser, Robert S., Domenico Pagano, and Axel Haverich, eds. *Brain Protection in Cardiac Surgery*. London: Springer Verlag, 2011.

Brenner, Jeffrey. "A Revolutionary Approach to Improving Health Care Delivery." Robert Wood Johnson Foundation, February 1, 2014. https://www.rwjf.org/en/library/articles -and-news/2014/02/improving-management-of-health-care-superutilizers.html.

Brooks, Kim. "America Is Blaming Pregnant Women for Their Own Deaths." *New York Times*, November 16, 2018, https://www.nytimes.com/2018/11/16/opinion/sunday /maternal-mortality-rates.html.

Burton, Thomas. "NuMED Is Guilty in FDA Case." *Wall Street Journal*, July 31, 2007. http://www.wsj.com/articles/SB118584916741583044.

Butler, Lacrisha. "State Cites AIDS Discrimination." *The Tennessean*, December 10, 1990, 9.

Butterworth, Trevor. "Heartless Regulation May End Up Killing Kids." *HuffPost Life*, July 6, 2007.

Cacciola, Scott, and Christine Hauser. "One after Another, Athletes Face Larry Nassar and Recount Sexual Abuse." *New York Times*, January 19, 2018. https://mobile.nytimes.com /2018/01/19/sports/larry-nassar-women.html.

Calabresi, Guido, and Philip Bobbitt. *Tragic Choices: The Conflicts Society Confronts in the Allocation of Tragically Scarce Resources*. New York: W. W. Norton, 1978.

Callahan, Daniel. *Setting Limits: Medical Goals in an Aging Society*. New York: Simon and Schuster, 1987.

Campbell, Catherine. *"'Letting Them Die': Why HIV/AIDS Prevention Programmes Fail."* Bloomington: Indiana University Press, 2003.

Catte, Elizabeth. *What You Are Getting Wrong about Appalachia*. Cleveland: Belt Publishing, 2018.

Coates, Ta-Nehisi. *We Were Eight Years in Power: An American Tragedy*. New York: Oneworld Publishing, 2017.

Colliver, Victoria. "How 'Killer King' Became the Hospital of the Future." *Politico*, November 8, 2017. https://www.politico.com/agenda/story/2017/11/08/the-hospital -of-the-future-000572.

Commonwealth Fund. "New Study: Elderly Medicare Beneficiaries Most Satisfied with Their Health Insurance; Working-Age Adult[s] with Private Coverage Report More Trouble Accessing Care, Paying Medical Bills." Press release, July 18, 2012. https://www .commonwealthfund.org/press-release/2012/new-study-elderly-medicare -beneficiaries-most-satisfied-their-health-insurance?redirect_source=/press-release /2012/new-study-elderly-medicare-beneficiaries-most-satisifed-their-health -insurance.

Conley, Dalton. *Being Black, Living in the Red: Race, Wealth, and Social Policy in America*. Berkeley: University of California Press, 2009.

Constitution of the Republic of South Africa. Brand South Africa, accessed June 11, 2017. https://www.brandsouthafrica.com/governance/constitution-sa-glance/the -constitution-of-south-africa.

Da Silva, Chantal. "Two Black Men Arrested at Starbucks for Not Ordering Settle for $2— and a $200,000 Promise." *Newsweek*, May 3, 2018. https://www.newsweek.com/two -black-men-wrongly-arrested-starbucks-settle-2-and-200000-promise-909253.

Dean, Olivia, Claire Noel-Miller, and Keith Lind. "Who Relies on Medicare? A Profile of the Medicare Population." Factsheet, AARP Public Policy Institute, November 2017. https://www.aarp.org/content/dam/aarp/ppi/20'17/11/who-relies-on-medicare-a -profile-of-the-medicare-population.pdf.

Dickinson, Emily. "I'm Nobody! Who Are You?" The Literature Network. http://www .online-literature.com/dickinson/448/.

"Documents: Reports by Center for Medicare and Medicaid Services on Patient Dumping Case at University of Maryland Medical Center Midtown." *Baltimore Sun*, March 20, 2018. http://www.baltimoresun.com/health/bal-centers-medicare-medicaid-survey-report-htmlstory.html.

Dresser, Rebecca. "Human Dignity and the Seriously Ill Patient." In *Human Dignity and Bioethics: Essays Commissioned by the President's Council on Bioethics*, 511–512. March 2008. https://permanent.access.gpo.gov/lps105992/human_dignity_and_bioethics.pdf.

Driver, Justin. "The Report on Race That Shook America." *The Atlantic*, May 2018. https://www.theatlantic.com/magazine/archive/2018/05/the-report-on-race-that-shook-america/556850.

Dropp, Kyle, and Brendan Nyahan. "One-Third Don't Know Obamacare and Affordable Care Act Are the Same." *New York Times*, February 7, 2017. https://www.nytimes.com/2017/02/07/upshot/one-third-dont-know-obamacare-and-affordable-care-act-are-the-same.html.

Dusenberry, Maya. Doing Harm: The Truth about How Bad Medicine and Lazy Science Leave Women Dismissed, Misdiagnosed, and Sick. San Francisco: HarperOne, 2018.

Dworkin, Ronald. A Matter of Principle. Cambridge, MA: Harvard University Press, 1985.

"Efforts to repeal the Patient Protection and Affordable Care." Wikipedia, last modified April 1, 2019. https://en.wikipedia.org/wiki/Efforts_to_repeal_the_Patient_Protection_and_Affordable_Care_Act.

Ell, Kellie. "April Jobs Report Shows Disparities in Unemployment Rates Continue." CNBC, May 4, 2018. https://www.cnbc.com/2018/05/04/aprils-jobs-report-shows-racial-inequalities-in-unemployment-rate.html.

Ellison, Ralph. The Invisible Man. 2nd Vintage International ed. New York: Vintage Books, 1995.

Emba, Christine. "What Is White Privilege?" *Washington Post*, January 16, 2016.

Facher, Lev, and Ike Swetliz. "Aetna Faces Class-Action Lawsuit over HIV Disclosures." *Stat News*, August 18, 2017. https://www.statnews.com/2017/08/28/aetna-hiv-lawsuit/.

Kaiser Family Foundation. "State Health Facts: Distribution of Medicare Beneficiaries by Race/Ethnicity, 2017." Accessed June 20, 2019. http://bit.ly/31ObOua.

Fadiman, Anne. *The Spirit Catches You and You Fall Down: A Hmong Child, Her American Doctors, and the Collision of Two Cultures.* New York: Farrar, Straus and Giroux, 1997.

Field, Marilyn, and Richard Behrman, eds., *Ethical Conduct of Clinical Research Involving Children*. Washington, DC: National Academies Press, 2004. https://www.ncbi.nlm.nih.gov/books/NBK25557/.

Fine, Robert L. "From Quinlan to Schiavo: Medical, Ethical, and Legal Issues in Severe Brain Injury." *Baylor University Medical Center Proceedings* 18, no. 4 (October 2005): 303–310. https://www.ncbi.nlm.nih.gov/pmc/articles/PMC1255938/.

Foster, Richard, and M. Kent Clemens. "Medicare Financial Status, Budget Impact, and Sustainability—Which Concept Is Which?" *Health Care Financing Review* 30, no. 3 (Spring 2009): 77–90.

France, David. *How to Survive a Plague: The Inside Story of How Citizens and Science Tamed AIDS*. New York: Vintage Books, 2016.

Fruitman, Deborah S. D. "Hypoplastic Left Heart Syndrome: Prognosis and Management Options." *Paediatrics and Child Health* 5, no. 4 (2000): 219.

Gaines, Ernest. *A Lesson before Dying*. New York: Vintage Books, 1993.

Gawande, Atul. *Being Mortal: Medicine and What Matters in the End*. Dallas: Metropolitan Press, 2014.

———. *Complications: A Surgeon's Notes on an Imperfect Science*. New York: Picador, 2003.

Gerbert, Barbara, B. T. Maguire, T. Bleecker, T. J. Coates, and S. J. McPhee. "Primary Care Physicians and AIDS: Attitudinal and Structural Barriers to Care." *JAMA* 266, no. 20 (November 1991): 2837. https://doi:10.1001/jama.1991.03470200049033.

Global Health Data Exchange. http://ghdx.healthdata.org/us-data.

Gratz, Jennifer. *Discriminating toward Equality: Affirmative Action and the Diversity Charade*. Washington, DC: Heritage Foundation, 2017. http://www.heritage.org/poverty-and-inequality/report/discriminating-toward-equality-affirmative-action-and-the-diversity.

Gray, Fred. Bus Ride to Justice: Changing the System by the System. Montgomery, AL: BlackBelt Press, 1995.

Hall, Mark, et al. Medical Liability and Treatment Relationships. 4th ed. New York: Wolters Kluwer, 2018.

Harding, Vincent. Hope and History: *Why We Must Share the Story of the Movement*. Maryknoll, NY: Orbis Books, 1990.

Harding, Vincent, and Daisaku Ikeda. America Will Be! Conversations on Hope, Freedom, and Democracy. Cambridge, MA: Dialogue Path Press, 2013.

"Healthcare Access in Rural Communities." Rural Health Information Hub, accessed June 9, 2017. https://www.ruralhealthinfo.org/topics/healthcare-access.

Henderson, James A., Jr. "The Virginia Birth-Related Injury Compensation Act: Limited No-Fault Statutes as Solutions to the Medical Malpractice Crisis." In Institute of Medicine (US) Committee to Study Medical Professional Liability and the Delivery of Obstetrical Care, Medical Professional Liability and the Delivery of Obstetrical Care, vol. 2, An Interdisciplinary Review, ed. V. P. Rostow and R. J. Bulger. Washington, DC: National Academies Press, 1989. 194–212.

Herek, Gregory M., and Eric K. Glunt. "An Epidemic of Stigma: Public Reactions to AIDS." *American Psychologist* 43, no. 11 (November 1988): 886–891. http://dx.doi.org/10.1037/0003-066X.43.11.886.

"Hippocratic Oath." *Encyclopaedia Britannica*, accessed November 8, 2018. https://www.britannica.com/topic/Hippocratic-oath.

Hoffman, Beatrix. *Healthcare for Some: Rights and Rationing in the United States since 1930*. Chicago: University of Chicago Press, 2012.

Hornblum, Allen. *Acres of Skin: Human Experiments at Holmesburg Prison*. New York: Routledge, 1998.

Itkowitz, Colby. "Closure of Two D.C. Maternity Wards Hurts Low-Income Women Most." *Washington Post*, October 8, 2017. https://www.washingtonpost.com/local/closure-of-two-dc-maternity-wards-hurts-low-income-women-most/2017/10/28/753e4dee-ad06-11e7-9e58-e6288544af98_story.html?utm_term=.b085c65f1cb2.

Jackson, Jesse. "I Am Somebody." Wattstax Music Festival, August 20, 1972, speech, 2:16. https://youtu.be/NTVwT3j_zqY.

———. "I Am Somebody with Jesse Jackson." Disc 2, no. 8, *Sesame Street: Old School, 1969–1974*, vol. 1. Produced by Dionne Nosek. Burbank, CA: Warner Brothers, 2006. DVD.

Jan, Tracy. "White Families Have Nearly 10 Times the Net Worth of Black Families. And the Gap Is Growing." *Washington Post*, September 28, 2017. https://www.washingtonpost

.com/news/wonk/wp/2017/09/28/black-and-hispanic-families-are-making-more
-money-but-they-still-lag-far-behind-whites/?utm_term=.0ea11af4316a.

Jones, Cleve. *When We Rise: My Life in the Movement.* New York: Hachette, 2016.

Jones, James. *Bad Blood: The Tuskegee Syphilis Experiment.* Rev. ed. New York: Free Press, 1993.

Jones, L. C., Yashika Watkins, and Duanny Alva. "Operation Change: A New Paradigm Addressing Behavior Change and Musculoskeletal Health Disparities." *Journal of Racial and Ethnic Health Disparities* 5, no. 6 (April 2018): 1264–1274.

Jones, William P. "Freedom for Every Citizen: The Missed Opportunity of the Kerner Report." *The Nation*, April 5, 2018. https://www.thenation.com/article/freedom-for
-every-citizen/.

Kalipeni, Ezekiel, Susan Craddock, Joseph R. Oppong, and Jayati Ghosh, eds. *HIV and AIDS in Africa: Beyond Epidemiology.* Australia: Blackwell Publishing, 2004.

Kaplan, Thomas, and Robert Pear. "24 Million More among Uninsured under G.O.P. Plan." *New York Times*, March 14, 2017.

Kateb, George. *Human Dignity.* Cambridge, MA: Belknap Press of Harvard University Press, 2011.

Katz, Jay. *The Silent World of Doctor and Patient.* Baltimore: Johns Hopkins University Press, 1984.

Kerner Commission. *Report of the National Advisory Commission on Civil Disorders.* Washington, DC: Government Printing Office, 1968.

"Key Facts about the Uninsured Population." Kaiser Health News, accessed November 29, 2017, https://www.kff.org/uninsured/fact-sheet/key-facts-about-the-uninsured
-population/.

Kluger, Richard. *Simple Justice: The History of Brown v. Board of Education and Black America's Struggle for Equality.* New York: Alfred A. Knopf, 1976.

Kohn, Linda T., Janet M. Corrigan, and Molla S. Donaldson, eds. *To Err Is Human: Building a Safer Health System.* Washington, DC: National Sciences Press, 1999.

Kolata, Gina. "Decades Later, Condemnation for a Skid Row Cancer Study." *New York Times*, October 17, 2013. https://www.nytimes.com/2013/10/18/health/medical
-experiments-conducted-on-bowery-alcoholics-in-1950s.html.

Krugman, Paul. "Health Care Realities. *New York Times*, July 30, 2009. https://www
.nytimes.com/2009/07/31/opinion/31krugman.html.

"Labor Force Statistics from the Current Population Survey." U.S. Department of Labor, Bureau of Labor Statistics, April 5, 2019. https://www.bls.gov/web/empsit/cpsee_e16
.htm.

Lauter, David. "How Do Americans View Poverty? Many Blue-Collar Whites, Key to Trump, Criticize Poor People as Lazy and Content to Stay on Welfare." *Los Angeles Times*, August 14, 2016. http://www.latimes.com/projects/la-na-pol-poverty-poll/.

Luthra, Shefali. "Once Its Greatest Foes, Doctors Are Embracing Single-Payer." *Kaiser Health News*, August 7, 2018. http://bit.ly/2KuYTaH.

Marks, Stephen P., ed. *Health and Human Rights: Basic International Documents.* Cambridge, MA: Harvard University Press, 2004.

Marsh, Charles. *The Beloved Community: How Faith Shapes Social Justice, from the Civil Rights Movement to Today.* New York: Basic Books, 2004.

Mason, Bonnie Simpson, and Vani Sabesan. "Easy and Low-Impact Exercises for People withOsteoarthritis." *Consult* 360 (July 16, 2018). https://www.consultant360.com/blog
/hmpprimary/easy-low-impact-exercises-people-osteoarthritis.

Matthew, Dayna Bowen. *Just Medicine: A Cure for Racial Inequality in American Health Care*. New York: New York University Press, 2015.

Mays, Vickie, Ninez A. Ponce, Donna L. Washington, and Susan D. Cochran. "Ethnicity: Implications for Public Health." *Annual Review of Public Health* 24 (2002): 83. https://www.ncbi.nlm.nih.gov/pmc/articles/PMC3681827/.

McClellan, Frank, *Medical Malpractice: Law, Tactics, and Ethics*. Philadelphia: Temple University Press, 1994.

McClellan Frank M., Augustus A. White, Ramon A. Jimenez, and Sherin Fahmy. "Do Poor People Sue Doctors More Frequently? Confronting Unconscious Bias and the Role of Cultural Competency." *Clinical Orthopaedic and Related Research* 470, no. 5 (2012):1393–1397. doi:10.1007/s11999-012-2254.

McClellan, Frank M., James E. Wood Jr., and Sherin M. Fahmy. *It Takes a Village: Reforming Law to Promote Health Literacy and Reduce Orthopedic Health Disparities*, 8 J. HEALTH & BIOMEDICAL L. 333 (2013).

McDonald, Jay. A Health Navigator Helps with Obamacare and More." Bankrate, June 9, 2014. https://www.bankrate.com/finance/insurance/health-navigators.aspx.

McDougal, Myres S., Harold D. Lasswell, and Lung-chu Chen. *Human Rights and World Public Order: The Basic Policies of an International Law of Human Dignity*. New Haven, CT: Yale University Press, 1980. http://digitalcommons.nyls.edu/fac_books/29.

Merelli, Annalisa. "A History of Why the US Is the Only Rich Country without Universal Health Care." *Quartz*, July 18, 2017. https://qz.com/1022831/why-doesnt-the-united-states-have-universal-health-care/.

Metzl, Jonathan. *Dying of Whiteness: How the Politics of Racial Resentment Is Killing America's Heartland*. New York: Basic Books, 2019.

Murunga, Ambrose. "Perspective: Tribute to Rosa Parks, Fallen Icon of Human Dignity." *Daily Nation*, November 7, 2005. https://www.nation.co.ke/lifestyle/1190-91956-dkewscz/index.html.

Nall, Rachel. "A History of HIV and AIDS in the United States." *Healthline*, November 30, 2016. http://www.healthline.com/health/hiv-aids/history#cultural-response5.

Nalty, Rebecca. "Strategies for Confronting Unconscious Bias." *Colorado Lawyer* 45, no. 5 (May 2016).

Natale-Pereira, Ana, Kimberly Enard, Lucinda Nevarez, and Lovell Jones. "The Role of Patient Navigators in Eliminating Health Disparities." *Cancer* 117 (15 Suppl) (2011): 3543–3552. https://www.ncbi.nlm.nih.gov/pmc/articles/PMC4121958/.

The Naked Truth. Season 2, episode 2. Directed by Lyttanya Shannon, featuring Nelufar Hedayat. Aired March 8, 2017, on IMDb.

National Conference of State Legislatures. *Health Cost Containment and Efficiencies: NCSL Briefs for State Legislators*. May 2011. www.ncsl.org/documents/health/introandbriefscc-16.pdf.

Nelson, Charles L. "Disparities in Orthopedic Surgical Intervention." *JAAOS* 15, suppl. 1 (2007): S13–17.

Nichols, Eve. "Institute of Medicine (US) Roundtable for the Development of Drugs and Vaccines against AIDS: Expanding Access to Investigational Therapies for HIV Infection and AIDS," March 12–13, 1990, Conference Summary. https://www.ncbi.nlm.nih.gov/books/NBK234129/.

Nussmeier, Nancy A. "Management of Temperature during and after Cardiac Surgery." *Texas Heart Institute Journal* 32, no. 4 (2005): 472–476.

Ofri, Danielle. *What Doctors Feel: How Emotions Affect the Practice of Medicine*. Boston: Beacon Press, 2013.

Omi, Michael, and Howard Winant. *Racial Formation in the United States: From the 1960s to the 1990s.* 2nd ed. New York: Routledge, 1994.

Pace, Eric. "Spottswood W. Robinson 3d, Civil Rights Lawyer, Dies at 82." *New York Times*, October 13, 1998. https://www.nytimes.com/1998/10/13/us/spottswood-w-robinson-3d -civil-rights-lawyer-dies-at-82.html.

Pellegrino, Edmund D. "The Lived Experience of Human Dignity." In *Human Dignity and Bioethics: Essays Commissioned by the President's Council on Bioethics.* March 2008, 515. https://permanent.access.gpo.gov/lps105992/human_dignity_and_bioethics.pdf.

Perry, Pamela. "White." In *Keywords for American Cultural Studies.* New York University Press, 2014. http://keywords.nyupress.org/american-cultural-studies/essay /white/.

Perry, Philip A., and Timothy Hotze. "Oregon's Experiment with Prioritizing Public Health Services." *AMA Journal of Ethics* 13, no. 4 (April 2011): 241–247. https://journalofethics .ama-assn.org/article/oregons-experiment-prioritizing-public-health-care-services /2011-04.

Project Implicit. Accessed November 12, 2018. https://implicit.harvard.edu/implicit/. "Project Implicit Director Kate Ratliff on Implicit Bias in Gainesville." Project Implicit, August 30, 2017. https://implicit.harvard.edu/implicit/.

"Project TEACH Classes." Philadelphia FIGHT Community Health Centers. https://fight .org/programs-and-services/project-teach-classes/.

Rabb, Edward L. "The Parameters of Informed Consent." *Transactions of the American Ophthalmological Society* 102 (December 2004): 225–232.

Randall, Vernellia. *Dying while Black: An In Depth Look at a Crisis in the American Healthcare System.* Dayton, OH: Seven Principles Press, 2006.

Regimbal, Alec. "Envisioning a 'Beloved Community': Yakima Civil Rights Leader Passionate about Working toward King's Dream." *Yakima Herald*, January 14, 2018. https:// www.yakimaherald.com/news/local/envisioning-a-beloved-community-yakima-civil -rights-leader-passionate-about/article_58d4551e-f9c7-11e7-baca-eb79c0cc0fa1.html.

Reich, Robert. "Why Medicare Should Be Available to All." *Newsweek*, July 27, 2015. https://www.newsweek.com/why-medicare-should-be-available-all-357404.

Reid, T. R. *The Healing of America: A Global Quest for Better, Cheaper, and Fairer Health Care.* New York: Penguin Press, 2009.

Riffkin, Rebecca. "Americans with Government Health Plans Most Satisfied." *Gallup*, November 6, 2015. https://news.gallup.com/poll/186527/americans-government-health -plans-satisfied.aspx.

Riotta, Chris. "GOP Aims to Kill Obamacare Yet Again after Failing 70 Times." *Newsweek*, July 29, 2017. https://www.newsweek.com/gop-health-care-bill-repeal-and-replace-70 -failed-attempts-643832.

Roberts, Dorothy. *Killing the Black Body: Race, Reproduction, and the Meaning of Liberty.* New York: Penguin Random House, 1997.

Rodriguez, Michael, and Robert Garcia. "First, Do No Harm: The US Sexually Transmitted Disease Experiments in Guatemala." *American Journal of Public Health* 103, no. 12 (2013): 2122–2126. https://www.ncbi.nlm.nih.gov/pmc/articles/PMC3828982/.

Rothenberg, Paula S. *White Privilege: Essential Readings on the Other Side of Racism.* New York: Worth, 2008.

Rothstein, Robert. *The Color of Law: A Forgotten History of How Our Government Segregated America. New York*: Liveright, 2017.

Schnurr, Samantha, "Former USA Gymnastics Doctor Larry Nassar Sentenced to 40 to 175 Years in Prison for Sexual Abuse. *E News*, January 24, 2018. https://www.eonline

.com/news/906521/former-usa-gymnastics-doctor-larry-nassar-sentenced-to-40-to-175
-years-in-prison-for-sexual-abuse.

Schulman, Adam. "Bioethics and the Question of Human Dignity." In *Human Dignity and Bioethics: Essays Commissioned by the President's Council on Bioethics.* March 2008. https://permanent.access.gpo.gov/lps105992/human_dignity_and_bioethics.pdf.

Shaffer, Mark. "Idealistic HMO: Can Good Care Survive the Market?" Accessed May 30, 2019. http://www.hedricksmith.com/site_criticalcondition/program/idealSummary .htm.

Shilts, Randy. *And the Band Played On: Politics, People, and the AIDS Epidemic.* New York: St. Martin's Press, 1987.

Smedley, B. D., A. Y. Stith, and A. R. Nelson, eds. *Unequal Treatment: Confronting Racial and Ethnic Disparities in Health Care.* Institute of Medicine (US) Committee on Understanding and Eliminating Racial and Ethnic Disparities in Health Care. Washington, DC: National Academies Press, 2003. https://www.ncbi.nlm.nih.gov/books /NBK220358/.

Smith, David Barton. *Health Care Divided: Race and Healing a Nation.* Ann Arbor: University of Michigan Press, 1999.

——. *The Power to Heal: Civil Rights, Medicare, and the Struggle to Transform America's Health Care System.* Nashville, TN: Vanderbilt University Press, 2016.

Smith, David Livingston. *Less Than Human: Why We Demean, Enslave, and Exterminate Others.* New York: St. Martin's Press, 2011.

Smith, Mitch, and Anemona Hartocollis. "Michigan State's $500 Million for Nassar Victims Dwarfs Other Settlements." *New York Times,* May 16, 2018. https://www.nytimes .com/2018/05/16/us/larry-nassar-michigan-state-settlement.html.

Snipes, Shedra Amy, et al. "Is Race Medically Relevant? A Qualitative Study of Physicians' Attitudes about the Role of Race in Treatment Decision-Making." *BMC Health Services Research* 11 (August 5, 2011): 183.

Stevenson, Bryan. *Just Mercy: A Story of Justice and Redemption.* New York: Spiegel and Grau, 2014.

Taub, Amanda. "'White Nationalism, Explained.'" *New York Times,* November 21, 2016. https://www.nytimes.com/2016/11/22/world/americas/white-nationalism-explained .html.

Taylor, Scott. "Howard University Guards Appear to Dump Woman in a Wheelchair onto Sidewalk." ABC7/WJLA, May 16, 2017. http://wjla.com/news/local/howard-university -security-guards-appear-to-dump-wheelchair-bound-woman-onto-sidewalk.

——. "Howard University Guards Appear to Dump Woman in a Wheelchair onto Sidewalk." ABC7/WJLA, May 16, 2017, video, 0:57. http://wjla.com/news/local/howard -university-security-guards-appear-to-dump-wheelchair-bound-woman-onto -sidewalk.

Toebes, Brigitte C. A. *The Right to Health as a Human Right and International Law.* Antwerp: Intersentia/Hart, 1999.

"The Troubles at King/Drew." *Los Angeles Times,* August 21, 2015. http://www.latimes .com/nation/la-kingdrewpulitzer-sg-storygallery.html.

"Trump Administration Cuts Grants to Help People Get Obama Care." *Reuters,* July 10, 2018. https://www.reuters.com/article/us-usa-healthcare-obamacare/trump-administration -cuts-grants-to-help-people-get-obamacare-idUSKBN1K102W?il=0.

Tweedy, Damon. *Black Man in a White Coat: A Doctor's Reflections on Race and Medicine.* London: Picador, 2015.

Tyler, Elizabeth Tobin, Ellen Lawton, Kathleen Conroy, Megan Sandel, and Barry Zuckerman, eds. *Poverty, Health and Law: Readings and Cases for Medical-Legal Partnership.* Durham, NC: Carolina Academic Press, 2011.

Ubel, Peter. "Why Poor People Like Hospitals." *Forbes Magazine,* September 13, 2017. https://www.forbes.com/sites/peterubel/2013/09/17/why-poor-people-like-hospitals/#36d9e6d638a7.

Ungar, Laura. "What States Aren't Doing to Save New Mothers' Lives." *USA Today,* September 19, 2018. https://www.usatoday.com/in-depth/news/investigations/deadly-deliveries/2018/09/19/maternal-death-rate-state-medical-deadly-deliveries/547050002/.

Ungar, Laura, Adam Taylor, and Jennifer Goldblatt. "A. I. duPont Firings Leave Parents, Doctors Wondering What's Next." *Pediatric Cardiology Today* 2, no. 5 (May 2004): 4–5. http://www.pediatriccardiologytoday.com/index_files/PTC-MAY04-RGB.pdf.

"Urban Health Institute." Cooper University Health Care. https://www.cooperhealth.org/services/urban-health-institute-1.

U.S. Commission on Civil Rights. *Patient Dumping.* September 2014. https://www.usccr.gov/pubs/docs/2014PATDUMPOSD_9282014-1.pdf.

Vance, J. D. *Hillbilly Elegy: A Memoir of a Family and Culture in Crisis.* New York: Harper, 2016.

Vedantam, Shankar. *The Hidden Brain: How Our Unconscious Minds Elect Presidents, Control Markets, Wage Wars, and Save Our Lives.* New York: Spiegel and Grau, 2010.

Volsky, Igor. "Recalling Ronald Reagan's LGBT Legacy ahead of the GOP Presidential Debate." ThinkProgress.org. Accessed October 24, 2018. https://thinkprogress.org/recalling-ronald-reagans-lgbt-legacy-ahead-of-the-gop-presidential-debate-a687b80d679b/.

Ware, Leland. *A Century of Segregation: Race, Class, and Disadvantage.* Lanham, MD: Lexington Books, 2018.

Washington, Harriet A. *Medical Apartheid: The Dark History of Medical Experimentation on Black Americans from Colonial Times to the Present.* New York: Anchor Books, 2006.

Weindling, Paul, Anna von Villiez, Aleksandra Loewenau, and Nichola Farron. "The Victims of Unethical Human Experiments and Coerced Research under National Socialism." *Endeavour* 40, no. 1 (March 2016). https://doi.org/10.1016/j.endeavour.2015.10.005.

Weisse, Carol, Paul Sorum, Kafi Sanders, and Beth L. Syat. "Paul Sorum, Kafi Sanders, and Beth L. Syat.005.2015.10.005" *Journal of General Internal Medicine* 16, no. 4 (April 2001): 211 Med.

White, Augustus, III, with David Chanoff. *Seeing Patients: Unconscious Bias in Health Care.* Cambridge, MA: Harvard University Press, 2011.

Wildman, Stephanie M. *Privilege Revealed: How Invisible Preference Undermines America.* New York: New York University Press, 1996.

Wilkerson, Isabel. *The Warmth of Other Suns: The Epic Story of America's Great Migration.* New York: Random House, 2010.

Wingfield, Adia Harvey. "Color-Blindness Is Counterproductive." *The Atlantic,* September 13, 2015. https://www.theatlantic.com/politics/archive/2015/09/color-blindness-is-ounterproductive/405037.

Wilson, Valerie. "Racial Inequalities in Wages, Income, and Wealth Show That MLK's Work Remains Unfinished." Economic Policy Institute, January 11, 2018. https://www

.epi.org/publication/racial-inequalities-in-wages-income-and-wealth-show-that-mlks
-work-remains-unfinished/.

Wise, Tim. "How Racism Explains America's Class Divide and Culture of Economic Cruelty." In *Under the Affluence: Shaming the Poor, Praising the Rich and Sacrificing the Future of America.* San Francisco: City Lights, 2015. http://www.timwise.org/2015/04
/how-racism-explains-americas-class-divide-and-culture-of-economic-cruelty-an
-excerpt-from-under-the-affluence/.

Cases

Anestis v. U.S., 52 F.Supp.3d 854 (E.D. Ky. 2014) (providing that a patient's suicide is not presumptively an intervening cause, especially in a medical malpractice litigation involving mental health care issues).

Bing v. Thunig, 143 N.E.2d 3 (N.Y. 1957) (signalling a departure from the doctrine that accorded hospitals immunity for the negligence of their employees, and providing that the liability of hospitals must be governed by the same principles of law that apply to other employers).

Bragdon v. Abbott, 524 U.S. 624 (1998) (establishing that the human immunodeficiency virus, also known as HIV, is a disability under the ADA).

Browning v. Burt, 613 N.E.2d 993, 997 (Ohio 1993).

Brown v. Board of Educ. of Topeka, Kan., 347 U.S. 483 (1954) (holding unanimously that racial segregation in public schools is unconstitutional and violates the Equal Protection Clause of the Fourteenth Amendment).

Burditt v. U.S. Dept. of Health and Human Services, 934 F.2d 1362 (5th Cir. 1991) (affirming the order to assess a $20,000 civil penalty against a physician based on substantial evidence in the record showing that the physician violated EMTALA).

Burwell v. Hobby Lobby Stores Inc., 134 S. Ct. 2751 (2014) (providing that regulations requiring corporations to provide health insurance coverage for contraception violate the RFRA because such regulation substantially burdens a business owner's right to exercise their religion).

Canterbury v. Spence, 464 F. 2d 772 (D.C. Cir. 1972), *cert. denied*, 409 U.S. 1064 (1972) (providing that a patient's right of self-determination is based on their ability to make informed medical decisions and requires that their physician disclose information that would be material to a reasonable person in the patient's position).

Contreras v. Crown Zellerbach Corp., 565 P.2d 1173 (Wash. 1977) (providing that recovery under the tort of outrage is available for the victim of outrageous conduct and is not limited to third-person situations only).

Cruzan by Cruzan v. Director, Missouri Dept. of Health, 497 U.S. 261 (1990) (holding that state law can prevent close family members from removing life-sustaining treatment if the patient did not provide such instructions while competent).

Dred Scott v. Sandford, 60 U.S. 393 (1857) (holding that Africans and their descendants who were enslaved in the United States "were not intended to be included, under the word 'citizens' in the Constitution, and can therefore claim none of the rights and privileges which that instrument provides for and secures to citizens of the United States. On the contrary, they were at that time considered as a subordinate and inferior class of beings, who had been subjugated by the dominant race, and, whether emancipated or not, yet remained subject to their authority, and had no rights or privileges but such as those who held the power and the Government might choose to grant them").

Duttry v. Patterson, 771 A.2d 1255 (Pa. 2001) (holding that personal information about a physician, including evidence concerning his or her experience, is not relevant under the doctrine of informed consent).

Estate of Leach v. Shapiro, 469 N.E.2d 1047 (Ohio Ct. App. 1984) (providing that the right to privacy belongs to the individual and that it lapses with the death of the person who enjoys it, such that a decedent's heirs cannot recover for an invasion of the decedent's privacy).

Fisher v. Carrousel Motor Hotel, Inc., 424 S.W.2d 627 (Tex. 1967) (holding that the forceful dispossession of an item is sufficient to constitute a willful battery when the taking is offensive).

Flowers v. Southern Regional Physician Services Inc., 247 F.3d 229 (5th Cir. 2001) (holding that the ADA provides a cause of action for disability-based harassment).

Fogel v. Forbes, Inc., 500 F. Supp 1081 (E.D. Pa. 1980) (providing that Pennsylvania courts use the Restatement (Second) of Torts to separate invasion of privacy into four distinct torts).

Grimes v. Kennedy Krieger Institute, Inc., 782 A.2d 807 (Md. 2001) (providing that a non-therapeutic research study involving a minor normally creates a special relationship with duties that if breached may potentially result in a viable negligence action).

Guerrero v. Copper Queen Hospital, 537 P.2d 1329 (Ariz. 1975) (providing that a general hospital may not deny emergency care to any patient without cause as a matter of public policy, and explaining that there is no requirement to specifically allege that the institution in question is a general hospital because its nature may be developed at trial).

Guinan v. A. I. duPont Hosp. for Children, 597 F.Supp. 2d 517 (E.D. Pa. 2009) (holding that the patient's expert did not provide the testimony regarding causation in order to satisfy the standard under the Delaware statute that the court applied).

Harrison v. U.S., 284 F.3d 293 (1st Cir. 2002) (providing that a physician has a duty to disclose when the information would be material to a reasonable person in the paitent's position).

Heart of Atlanta Motel, Inc. v. U.S., 379 U.S. 241 (1964) (holding that Congress has the constitutional power under the Commerce Clause to regulate local activities, such as racially discriminatory commercial practices, that might have a substantial and harmful effect on interstate commerce).

Hulver v. U.S., 562 F.2d 1132 (8th Cir. 1977) (providing that the statute of limitations for a claim of medical malpractice against the United States will be barred unless it is made within two years after the claim accrues).

In re AC, 573 A.2d 1235 (D.C. App. 1990) (holding that the substituted judgment standard should be followed when circumstances require the court to consider the authoriziation of a medical procedure, and explaining that the standard is based on what the patient would want done if they were competent).

In re Quinlan, 355 A.2d 647 (N.J. 1976) (holding that an incompetent patient's life-support system may be withdrawn without civil or criminal liability after the guardian, family, physician, and consulting body agree concurrently that there is no reasonable possibility that the incompetent will return to a sapient state).

Jackson v. East Bay Hosp., 246 F.3d 1248 (9th Cir. 2001) (explaining that a hospital complies with EMTALA screening requirements when it stabilizes emergency medical conditions that are actually detected, even when other conditions are not detected or stabilized as the hospital never refused treatment).

Johnson v. University of Chicago Hosp., 982 F.2d 230 (7th Cir. 1992) (providing that a private hospital may become subject to the usual obligations in tort after volunteering to provide directions to the ambulance being used to transport the patient to an alternate hospital).

Jones v. Chidester, 610 A.2d 964 (Pa. 1922) (holding that physician liability related to a treatment decision where competent medical authority is divided is to be judged according to whether a considerable number of recognized and respected professionals subscribe to the school of thought underpining the treatment used).

Korematsu v. U.S., 323 U.S. 214 (1944) (holding that the exigencies of war and threat to national security permit the compulsory exclusion of a group of people based on their national origin).

Langbehn v. Public Health Trust of Miami-Dade County, 661 F. Supp. 2d 1326 (S.D. Fla. 2009) (holding that Florida law bars claims brought against physicians and social workers that provide emergency medical care to a patient who is in a long-term same-sex partnership when the hospital initially prevented their partner and shared children from visiting and participating in medical decisions fully).

Loving v. Virginia, 388 U.S. 1 (1967) (holding that restrictions on the freedom to marry based on racial classifications are unconstitutional, and explaining that such restrictions violate the Equal Protection Clause and the Due Process Clause).

Lucchesi v. Frederic N. Stimmell, M.D., Ltd., 716 P.2d 1013 (Ariz. 1986) (providing that summary judgment should not be granted when a physician's conduct creates a factual question as to whether their conduct was outrageous and caused severe emotional distress, as those are factual issues that a jury should decide).

McGann v. H&H Music Co., 946 F.2d 401 (5th Cir. 1991) (holding that the reduction of benefits for AIDS under an employee medical plan does not violate ERISA when it is not motivated by a desire to retaliate against an employee or deprive an employee of the benefit).

Moore v. Burt, 645 N.E.2d 749 (Ohio App. 2 Dist. 1994) (holding that where surgeon was an independent contractor hospital had no duty to warn patient about unorthodox and dangerous methods of practicing medicine).

Morgan v. North MS Med. Cent., Inc., 403 F.Supp. 2d 115 (S.D. Ala. 2005) (holding that a Native American band enjoyed a right of self-governance that prohibited the enforcement of state employment discrimination laws against it).

Moses v. Providence Hosp. and Med. Cent., Inc., 561 F.3d 573 (6th Cir. 2009) (providing that EMTALA does not authorize a private right of action against individual physicians).

Munley v. ISC Financial House, Inc., 584 P.2d 1336 (Okla. 1978) (holding that summary judgment should be granted where defendant's conduct is not reasonably regarded as being so extreme and outrageous as to permit recovery based on the claims of invasion of privacy and emotional and mental distress).

Nat'l Federation of Independent Bus. v. Sebelius, 567 U.S. 519 (2012) (holding that the individual mandate provision of the ACA is a valid exercise of federal taxing power and that existing Medicaid funds cannot be withdrawn from a state for failure to comply with the Act).

Obergefell v. Hodges, 135 S. Ct. 2584 (2015) (holding that same-sex couples have a fundamental right to marry guaranteed by the Due Process and Equal Protection Clauses of the Fourteenth Amendment and that there is no lawful basis for a state to refuse to recognize a lawful marriage).

Pegram v. Herdrich, 530 U.S. 211 (2000) (holding that ERISA preempts a state malpractice claim against an HMO because Congress did not intend for ERISA to treat HMOs as fiduciaries within the meaning of the Act).

Pharm. Mfrs. Ass'n of S. Afr. v. President of the Republic of S. Afr., Case no. 4183/98, High Court of South Africa (Transvaal Provincial Division).

Reed v. ANM Health Care, 225 P.3d 1012 (Wash. Ct. App. 2008) (holding that summary judgment should be granted on claims against a nurse based on the common law torts of outrage and negligence infliction of emotional distress when sufficient evidence is presented to create a genuine factual dispute regarding the nurse's motivations for excluding the patient's life partner).

Saint Joseph Healthcare, Inc. v. Thomas, 487 S.W.3d 864 (Ky. 2016) (providing that hospitals are liable for their physicians' EMTALA violations as duties under EMTALA are nondelegable).

Satz v. Perlmutter, 379 So. 2d 359 (Fla. 1980) (providing that the court should take up questions of law on a case by case basis when there is an absence of legislative action in order to resolve challenging issues arising from advances in medical science).

Schloendorff v. Society of New York Hospital, 105 N.E. 92 (N.Y. 1914) (holding that a charitable hospital is immune from liability related to the conduct of its resident physicians where the hospital does not have a master-servant relationship with its physicians).

Sharrow v. Bailey, 910 F. Supp. 187 (M.D. Pa. 1995) (providing that an HIV-positive patient states a claim for discrimination under the ADA when the hospital delays treatment on account of the patient's disability).

Taylor v. Baptist Medical Center, Inc., 400 So.2d 369 (Ala. 1981) (providing that mental anguish may be a recoverable element of damages in an action for breach of contract or obligation).

Thompson v. Sun City Community Hosp., Inc., 688 P.2d 605 (Ariz. 1984) (holding that a private hospital is required to provide emergency care as a matter of public policy and cannot transfer a patient until all medically indicated emergency care is complete).

Watts v. Golden Age Nursing Home, 619 P.2d 1032 (Ariz. 1980) (holding that a surviving spouse cannot collect punitive damages in their own right since punitive damages are personal to the injured victim).

Whittington v. Episcopal Hospital, 768 A.2d 1144 (Pa. Super. Ct. 2001) (providing that corporate negligence is cumulative in nature and that actual or constructive notice is needed to establish it).

Wickline v. State of California, 239 Cal. Rptr. 810 (Cal. App. 2d Dist. 1986) (holding that a patient's healthcare insurer cannot be held liable for the patient's postsurgical complications because the insurer is not a party to medical decisions).

Law Review Articles

Abraham, Kenneth S., & G. Edward White. *The Puzzle of the Dignitary Torts.* 104 CORNELL L. REV. 317 (2019).

Bell, Derrick. *The Racism Is Permanent Thesis: Courageous Revelation or Unconscious Denial of Racial Genocide.* 22 CAL. L. REV. 571 (1993).

Clark, Leroy D. *A Critique of Professor Derrick A. Bell's Thesis of the Permanence of Racism and His Strategy of Confrontation.* 73 DENV. U. L. REV. 23 (1995).

Cooper, Elizabeth B. *The Power of Dignity.* 84 FORDHAM L. REV. 3 (2015).

Furrow, Barry R. *Access to Health Care and Political Ideology: Wouldn't You Really Rather Have a Pony?* 29 W. NEW ENG. L. REV. 405 (2007).

Haddon, Phoebe A. *Has the Roberts Court Plurality's Colorblind Rhetoric Finally Broken Brown's Promise?* 90 DENV. U. L. REV. 1251 (2013).

Henry, Leslie Meltzer. *The Jurisprudence of Dignity.* 16 U. PA. L. REV. 160 (2011).

Laakman, Anna B. *When Should Physicians Be Liable for Innovation?* 36 CARDOZO L. REV. 913 (2015).

McClellan, Frank M. *Is Managed Care Good for What Ails You? Ruminations on Race, Age and Class.* 4 VILL L. REV. 227 (1999).

Meisel, Alan. *A "Dignitary Tort" as a Bridge between the Idea of Informed Consent and the Law of Informed Consent.* 16 J. L. MED. & ETHICS *210* (1988).

Rustad, Michael L. *Torts as Public Wrongs.* 38 PEPPERDINE L. REV. 433 (2011).

Yearby, Ruqaiijah. *Breaking The Cycle of "Unequal Treatment" with Health Care Reform: Acknowledging and Addressing the Continuation of Racial Bias.* 44 CONN. L. REV. 1281 (2012).

Index

About the Author

Frank M. McClellan is a professor of law emeritus at the Beasley School of Law, Temple University, Philadelphia. He is the author of *Medical Malpractice: Law, Tactics, and Ethics* (Temple University Press, 1994) and co-author of *Tort Law: Cases, Perspectives, and Problems* (LexisNexis, 1991–2007).

Available titles in the Critical Issues in Health and Medicine series:

Beatrix Hoffman, Nancy Tomes, Rachel N. Grob, and Mark Schlesinger, eds., *Patients as Policy Actors*

Ruth Horowitz, *Deciding the Public Interest: Medical Licensing and Discipline*

Powel Kazanjian, *Frederick Novy and the Development of Bacteriology in American Medicine*

Rebecca M. Kluchin, *Fit to Be Tied: Sterilization and Reproductive Rights in America, 1950–1980*

Jennifer Lisa Koslow, *Cultivating Health: Los Angeles Women and Public Health Reform*

Susan C. Lawrence, *Privacy and the Past: Research, Law, Archives, Ethics*

Bonnie Lefkowitz, *Community Health Centers: A Movement and the People Who Made It Happen*

Ellen Leopold, *Under the Radar: Cancer and the Cold War*

Barbara L. Ley, *From Pink to Green: Disease Prevention and the Environmental Breast Cancer Movement*

Sonja Mackenzie, *Structural Intimacies: Sexual Stories in the Black AIDS Epidemic*

Frank M. McClellan, *Healthcare and Human Dignity: Law Matters*

Michelle McClellan, *Lady Lushes: Gender, Alcohol, and Medicine in Modern America*

David Mechanic, *The Truth about Health Care: Why Reform Is Not Working in America*

Richard A. Meckel, *Classrooms and Clinics: Urban Schools and the Protection and Promotion of Child Health, 1870–1930*

Alyssa Picard, *Making the American Mouth: Dentists and Public Health in the Twentieth Century*

Heather Munro Prescott, *The Morning After: A History of Emergency Contraception in the United States*

Andrew R. Ruis, *Eating to Learn, Learning to Eat: School Lunches and Nutrition Policy in the United States*

James A. Schafer Jr., *The Business of Private Medical Practice: Doctors, Specialization, and Urban Change in Philadelphia, 1900–1940*

David G. Schuster, *Neurasthenic Nation: America's Search for Health, Happiness, and Comfort, 1869–1920*

Karen Seccombe and Kim A. Hoffman, *Just Don't Get Sick: Access to Health Care in the Aftermath of Welfare Reform*

Leo B. Slater, *War and Disease: Biomedical Research on Malaria in the Twentieth Century*

Dena T. Smith, *Medicine over Mind: Mental Health Practice in the Biomedical Era*

Matthew Smith, *An Alternative History of Hyperactivity: Food Additives and the Feingold Diet*

Paige Hall Smith, Bernice L. Hausman, and Miriam Labbok, *Beyond Health, Beyond Choice: Breastfeeding Constraints and Realities*

Susan L. Smith, *Toxic Exposures: Mustard Gas and the Health Consequences of World War II in the United States*

Rosemary A. Stevens, Charles E. Rosenberg, and Lawton R. Burns, eds., *History and Health Policy in the United States: Putting the Past Back In*

Barbra Mann Wall, *American Catholic Hospitals: A Century of Changing Markets and Missions*

Frances Ward, *The Door of Last Resort: Memoirs of a Nurse Practitioner*

Shannon Withycombe, *Lost: Miscarriage in Nineteenth-Century America*